BROOKINGS-WHARTON

papers
on
URBAN
AFFAIRS

2003

William G. Gale and
Janet Rothenberg Pack
Editors

BROOKINGS INSTITUTION PRESS
Washington, D.C.

Copyright © 2003
THE BROOKINGS INSTITUTION
1775 Massachusetts Avenue, N.W., Washington, DC 20036

ISSN 1528-7084
ISBN 0-8157-1277-4

BROOKINGS-WHARTON

papers
on
URBAN
AFFAIRS
2003

Bruce Sacerdote *Dartmouth College*
David Weimer *University of Wisconsin, Madison*
William Wheaton *Massachusetts Institute of Technology*

Conference Participants

Jan K. Brueckner *University of Illinois*
Stephen Calabrese *University of South Florida*
Victor Calanog *University of Pennsylvania*
Jerry Carlino *Federal Reserve Bank of Philadelphia*
Sam Chandan *University of Pennsylvania*
Xavier de Souza-Briggs *Harvard University*
Anthony Downs *Brookings Institution*
Michael Feuer *National Academy of Sciences*
Jane Hannaway *Urban Institute*
Andrew Haughwout *Federal Reserve Bank of New York*
Pascale Joassart-Marcelli *University of Massachusetts*
Matthew Kahn *Tufts University*
John Kain *University of Texas at Dallas*
Helen F. Ladd *Duke University*
Joyce Ladner *Brookings Institution*
Amy Liu *Brookings Institution*
Janice Madden *University of Pennsylvania*
Robert Margo *Vanderbilt University*
Therese McGuire *Northwestern University*
Rebecca Menes *George Mason University*
Dick Netzer *New York University*
Carol O'Cleireacain *Brookings Institution*
Steven Raphael *University of California, Berkeley*
Lois Dickson Rice *Brookings Institution*
Isabel Sawhill *Brookings Institution*
Amy E. Schwartz *New York University*
Audrey Singer *Brookings Institution*
Leanna Stiefel *New York University*
Michael Stoll *University of California Los Angeles*
Anita Summers *University of Pennsylvania*
Marge Turner *Urban Institute*
Jacob Vigdor *Duke University*
Richard Voith *Econsult Corporation*
Susan Wachter *University of Pennsylvania*
Margy Waller *Brookings Institution*

Preface

The *Brookings-Wharton Papers on Urban Affairs* is devoted to bringing forward-looking research to bear on urban policy issues in an accessible manner. The collaboration between the Wharton School and the Brookings Institution in this endeavor represents an effort to draw on resources and personnel in both academia and the policy community. We hope and expect that the journal itself will be of interest and use to an even wider audience that includes policymakers and their staffs, interested parties in the private sector, journalists, students, and others.

The existence of this journal owes much to the efforts of key people at Brookings and Wharton. At Brookings, President Strobe Talbott is an enthusiastic supporter of this project. Robert Litan, director of the Economic Studies Program, has encouraged the project at every turn. Bruce Katz, director of the Center on Urban and Metropolitan Policy, has been a tireless and vocal supporter of the journal and its goals, and has helped provide financial support.

At Wharton, Peter Linneman and Joseph Gyourko, former director and current director of the Samuel Zell and Robert Lurie Real Estate Center, have supported this undertaking intellectually and financially from its inception. The dean's office has made its contribution by freeing some of Janet Rothenberg Pack's time to organize the conference and edit the volume. The Department of Business and Public Policy has in numerous ways encouraged her participation in this endeavor.

Several people made vital contributions to the publication of this volume and the conference on which it is based. Saundra Honeysett at Brookings organized conference logistics and managed the paper flow with efficiency and good cheer. Amy Liu and Jamaine Tinker provided valuable support at many stages. The authors and discussants deserve special thanks for making extra efforts to draft their arguments in a clear and accessible manner.

Editors' Summary

The *Brookings-Wharton Papers on Urban Affairs* offers cutting-edge research, presented in accessible ways, to help inform the academic research and policy debates on issues unique to urban areas. Broader economic and policy topics that have special applicability to urban settings are also treated. The papers and comments contained in this volume were presented at a conference at the Brookings Institution on October 24 and 25, 2002.

The papers are divided into two groups. This year's symposium focuses on urban education. Brian A. Jacob and Steven D. Levitt report the results of an experiment designed to detect cheating on standardized tests in Chicago Public Schools. Thomas Nechyba examines the impact of school reform in an urban setting by developing a simulation model in which parents choose where to live, decide whether their children attend public or private schools, and vote on tax levels. Thomas J. Kane, Douglas O. Staiger, and Gavin Samms evaluate the effect of school quality, as measured by local school test scores and composite school ratings, on housing values in Mecklenburg County, North Carolina. Brian A. Jacob explores the determinants of improved academic performance in Chicago Public Schools. The volume includes two other research papers on current issues in urban economics. Douglas S. Massey and Mary J. Fischer document expanding economic inequality across and within geographic

We thank Meghan McNally for outstanding assistance in the preparation of this summary.

regions. Bengte Evenson and William C. Wheaton explore local variation in land use regulations among towns in Massachusetts.

Symposium on Urban Education

Education is one of the most important services provided by urban and local governments. But many large urban school districts in the United States serve their students poorly, as indicated by low test scores, high dropout rates, high rates of teacher turnover, and other problems. These deficiencies have led affluent families with children to leave cities for the suburbs or to move their children to private schools. To the extent that such families move, urban tax bases and economic activity are reduced. To the extent that good students move to private schools, the average academic quality of the remaining public school students falls, which can reduce the quality of the education received in the public schools through the influence on peer group effects and expenditure on schools. For all of these reasons, education reform has emerged as a key issue in urban areas.

Catching Cheating Teachers: An Unusual Experiment

One approach to improving urban schools involves greater emphasis on high-stakes testing. Under this plan schools will be held accountable, through a variety of sanctions, for their students' failure to attain certain scores on standardized tests. Supporters claim that testing provides accountability and raises test scores. Critics note that test score gains have been shown to be test specific, and thus progress may be ephemeral. Another concern is that the emphasis on high-stakes testing may increase the temptation for students, teachers, and administrators to cheat on standardized tests.

Jacob and Levitt examine cheating by teachers using a methodology they developed in previous work. Roughly 100,000 Chicago Public School students take the Iowa Test of Basic Skills each spring, with retesting occurring in 117 classrooms three to four weeks later. Jacob and Levitt use a multinomial logit framework with past, current, and retest scores, demographics, and socioeconomic characteristics as explanatory variables to identify suspicious answer strings (a series of answers to consecutive questions). The authors look at cheating in three types of classrooms: those with unusually large test score gains and highly suspicious patterns of answer strings; classrooms with suspicious answer strings but without unusually large test score gains; and classrooms with anonymous allegations of cheating. They compare the retest performance of these classrooms to two control groups that are not suspected of cheating: classrooms with large test score gains but not suspicious answer strings and classrooms that were chosen at random.

The main result is that classrooms that were suspected of cheating—based on the authors' methodology for identifying suspicious answer strings—saw dramatic declines in test results in the retest relative to the original test, while the control classrooms saw little change in test results. Test score declines were more than one grade-equivalent on average in twenty-nine classrooms out of the seventy suspicious classrooms that were retested. After the retest, school administrators in two schools were suspected of complicity in cheating, given that a significant number of classes in their schools were identified as having cheated. Consequently, the teachers and administrators suspected of cheating were subject to further investigation.

Public School Finance and Urban School Policy

Much analysis of the determinants of school quality focuses narrowly on the effects of financial resources on school performance. In contrast, Thomas Nechyba explores how financing alters school quality in a framework that explicitly incorporates the fact that financing changes may alter the characteristics of neighborhoods, private school attendance rates, and political voting outcomes. He develops these insights in a simulation model calibrated to data from the New Jersey suburbs of New York City. By examining the various policies in a single, consistent model, he is able to isolate the interlocking roles of different factors in determining the impact of changes in school finance. Nechyba examines the effects of centralizing school finance, changing state aid formulas, and issuing state-funded vouchers. A major result of the analysis is that the general equilibrium effects of policy changes on school quality—for example, those that arise from households moving or students changing from public to private schools—often dominate the direct effects of resource levels on school performance.

Among the results: centralization raises housing prices, reduces private school attendance, reduces spending per pupil in public schools, and narrows school quality differences across districts as spending is equalized. Funding formulas that provide state aid programs not targeted at poor school districts result in school improvement in wealthy districts and also cause larger inequalities across districts. However, targeted state aid administered only to poor school districts achieves greater increases in school quality for all schools. State-funded vouchers would reduce quality at poor-performing public schools as students choose to attend better public and private schools. Families in wealthier neighborhoods move to areas with more affordable housing and, using their vouchers, send their children to private school. As a result of these two changes, overall average school quality in poor districts increases slightly because the quality of the new private schools is higher than public schools, and there is a negative effect on public schools in the wealthier districts as well as declining public support for public schools.

School Accountability Ratings and Housing Values

Previous research has found a strong connection between student test scores at neighborhood schools and housing values at a point in time, but there is less evidence on how those variables evolve. This issue, however, will become more important over time as the No Child Left Behind Act of 2001 requires states to test all students in grades three through eight and publicly report the results.

Thomas J. Kane, Douglas O. Staiger, and Gavin Samms evaluate the effects on housing values of test scores and composite school ratings. Using data on the sales prices of homes in Mecklenburg County, North Carolina, they find that a school's long-term average test scores affect housing values in the immediate neighborhood, but that year-to-year fluctuations in scores do not. This suggests that homeowners care about school quality but are aware of how "noisy" test scores can be.

The authors also find that test scores may be related to unmeasured housing and neighborhood characteristics. This idea suggests that people tend to buy houses where they do because of their peers. Housing values tend to be higher closer to a neighborhood school, particularly in poor neighborhoods, and respond more strongly to test scores of white students than of black students. The study also shows that, when composite school ratings were introduced, local house prices did not decline in response to state ratings of "low performing" for local schools. This may imply that residents already knew that these schools were low performing.

Accountability: Lessons from Chicago

After instituting high-stakes testing in 1996, the Chicago Public Schools realized a significant increase in test scores. Little is understood, however, about how high-stakes testing affects performance. Supporters of the program claim that testing makes teachers and students work harder and helps schools become more efficient. Critics claim the rules lead to "teaching to the test" and to reallocations of resources away from nontested subjects like physical education, art, music, and social studies.

Brian Jacob examines the effects of the accountability policies instituted by the Chicago Public Schools (CPS) using school budget information for 456 elementary schools in 1995 and 2000. He distinguishes between changes in educational inputs—including student effort, parental involvement, financial resources—and changes in school technology—such as instructional practices and school organization.

He finds that most of the improvement in CPS scores comes from non-financial inputs like student effort and parental involvement rather than technological improvements. Schools made few changes to financial allocations or school organization. For example, low-achieving schools shifted only a small amount of resources away from nontested areas, like art and music, and the changes in spending are not related to changes in student achievement. Most of the increase in spending was to hire more teachers or raise teachers' salaries rather than to create new positions. Educational efforts by students have had a greater effect on student achievement than changes in instructional practices or school organization. The findings will prove relevant as the federal government begins to implement the No Child Left Behind education policy that was enacted in 2001.

Other Research

Besides the papers on education reform, the volume contains two papers and discussants' comments related to other current issues in urban economics. These papers illustrate the broad reach of urban issues and their overlap with the concerns of many other fields in economic research and public policy.

The Geography of Inequality, 1950–2000

Although trends in income inequality have received substantial attention during the past two decades, trends in the geographic distribution of income have been left relatively unexamined. As the affluent and poor live increasingly isolated from one another, the social and economic worlds and interests of the two groups will naturally diverge, with important implications for public finance and the provision of public services.

Using data available from 1950 to 2000, Douglas S. Massey and Mary J. Fischer measure trends in class segregation and income concentration at the regional, state, and metropolitan levels, and on the neighborhood level for sixty metropolitan areas. The authors find that income and class segregation declined during the past half-century as the rich and poor have become more evenly distributed throughout the country. They also show that the degree of spatial separation between affluent and poor families declined on the regional, state, and metropolitan levels. These findings reflect the creation of new affluence in the South and new poverty in the Northeast, Midwest, and West. The concentration of affluence and poverty, however, has increased in neighborhoods, leading to significant class segregation within metropolitan areas.

Income segregation measures the degree of social and class segregation between poor and affluent families. Massey and Fischer find that during the past half-century, rich and poor have become more evenly distributed throughout the country. On the regional level, income segregation is the lowest and declined by more than half between 1950 and 2000. Similarly, income segregation decreased by nearly 40 percent for states and one-third in metropolitan areas. However, census-tract-level segregation in sixty metropolitan areas has increased dramatically between 1970 and 2000, indicating significant growth in class segregation within neighborhoods. The authors also examined income segregation by race and found that in the regions, states, and metropolitan areas, both blacks and whites experienced a comparable decrease in income segregation over the period. The tract-level data tell a different story as income segregation within both races has increased since 1970 and moderated only slightly during the 1990s.

Falling income inequality, declining poverty rates, and class segregation from 1950 to 2000 also produced declines in the geographic concentration of poverty at the regional, state, and metropolitan levels. Overall, the concentration of poverty fell sharply and hit a fifty-year low in 2000. Poverty isolation is greater for African Americans, since far more blacks live in the south and thus are distributed more unevenly than whites. The concentration of poverty in *neighborhoods* of metropolitan areas, in contrast to the decrease in overall concentration, increased by 80 percent between 1970 and 2000. Moreover, the concentration of poverty within neighborhoods for black families exceeded that for white families in each decade from 1970 through 2000.

According to Massey and Fischer, the concentration of affluence in regions, states, and metropolitan areas increased between 1950 and 2000. Since class segregation and income inequality declined, the growth in the concentration of affluence is attributed to the increasing proportion of affluent families. This is also true on the neighborhood level. By 2000, the concentration of affluence in metropolitan neighborhoods was greater than the concentration of poverty. However, the authors find that the concentration of affluence does not differ by race in regions, states, or metropolitan areas. However, the concentration of affluence was greater for whites than blacks within neighborhoods.

Massey and Fischer show that rich and poor families came to inhabit the same regions, states, and metropolitan areas while simultaneously moving into different neighborhoods segregated by class. Class segregation did grow during the 1970s, and the concentration of poverty increased through the 1980s, yet the trends leveled off through the 1990s, indicating that because of the great prosperity in the 1990s, the situation has not deteriorated significantly as indicated by other research. However, the trends have not been reversed. Growing concentrations of poverty and affluence within neighborhoods indicate an increasingly divided society. Rich people are interacting with affluent peers and living in safe communities, and the poor have little social mobility and are living in high-risk, unstable neighborhoods with few prospects for economic development, contradicting the historic commitment to equity in the United States.

Local Variation in Land Use Regulations

The causes and effects of local land use regulation are a long-standing topic of concern, but to date little evidence has been brought to bear on this issue. Bengte Evenson and William C. Wheaton use a unique data set created for the state of Massachusetts to study local land use regulations. They analyzed patterns of residential, commercial, industrial, open, and other land use allocations.

The authors found that current zoning regulations of a town are a strong indicator of future zoning and development. Wealthy towns tend to protect more land and allow for less housing and commercial and industrial development while lower-income towns tend to permit higher-density commercial and industrial development. However, a town's current residential or commercial density is a much better indicator of future density than is income. Evenson and Wheaton also find that towns farther from Boston zone less open land for commercial and industrial uses, protect more open land, and put tighter constraints on density. Overall, the authors' findings support the current theoretical land use literature and conventional wisdom. In the future, these unique and comprehensive land use data for Massachusetts can be used to test land use theory and examine land use patterns more extensively.

DOUGLAS S. MASSEY
University of Pennsylvania

MARY J. FISCHER
University of Pennsylvania

The Geography of Inequality in the United States, 1950–2000

IF INCOME INEQUALITY rises during a period in which rich and poor families become more segregated, only one outcome is possible: affluence and poverty both will become more geographically concentrated.[1] Families that are well-off financially will increasingly live near and interact with other affluent families, and those that lack economic resources will live near and interact mainly with other poor families. Under these circumstances, the social worlds of the rich and poor will increasingly diverge.[2] The poor will tend to inhabit high-risk neighborhoods that significantly lower the odds of socioeconomic success, while the affluent will enjoy a safe and secure world that enhances the possibilities of success on a variety of fronts.[3]

As they grow apart, the material interests of poor and affluent communities will also diverge.[4] Residents of high-income households in affluent communities (with high property values) will have an incentive to tax themselves at low rates to provide good public services, while poor people living in poor communities (with low property values) will have to tax themselves at high rates if they are to receive services that even approach the quality of those offered in more affluent communities. With high values, however, the same revenue can be generated with lower rates. If the affluent and poor communities correspond to separate taxing

---

1. Massey and Fischer (2000).
2. Massey (1996).
3. Brooks-Gunn, Duncan, and Aber (1997); Dietz (2002).
4. Massey (1996).

1

authorities, the former will naturally resist raising taxes to offset the high taxes or subsidize the services of the latter.[5]

Thus, the simultaneous occurrence of rising socioeconomic inequality and growing class segregation portends a society that is divided not only geographically, but also socially and politically as well. Many studies show that income inequality rose substantially over the last quarter of the twentieth century in marked contrast to the previous quarter century. Whereas the median family income grew by 208 percent and the Gini coefficient for inequality fell by 6 percent from 1950 to 1975,[6] between 1977 and 1999 the after-tax income of families in the middle of the distribution rose by just 3 percent while the Gini coefficient increased by 14 percent.[7] In contrast to the stagnation observed in the middle of the income distribution, income within the top fifth rose by 38 percent while that in the top 1 percent rose by 120 percent.[8] This pattern of stagnating incomes at the middle accompanied by slow declines at the bottom and rapid increases at the top was replicated throughout the country, although the degree of polarization appeared to be most extreme in the Northeast and Midwest.[9]

Trends with respect to the geographic segregation of families by income are less well documented. Most attempts to measure income segregation have used tract-level data for specific urban areas. Massey and Eggers found that residential dissimilarity between affluent and poor families increased by 4 percent in the 30 largest metropolitan areas between 1970 and 1980.[10] The largest increases in class segregation were again observed in the Northeast and Midwest. In the ten largest metropolitan areas, the degree of residential dissimilarity between affluent and poor families rose by 6 percent during the 1970s and 8 percent during the 1980s.[11] Using a somewhat different measure (the class sorting index) over a wider set of metropolitan areas, Jargowsky found that class segre-

---

5. Massey (1996).

6. Danziger and Gottschalk (1995); Levy (1998).

7. U.S. Bureau of the Census. 2002. "Historical Tables—Income Inequality." "Table IE-6. Measures of Household Income Inequality: 1967 to 2001." Department of Commerce (www.census.gov/hhes/income/histinc/ie6.html [February 2003]).

8. Phillips (2002).

9. Levy (1998); Bernhardt and others (2000).

10. Massey and Eggers (1993).

11. Massey (1996).

gation rose by 13 percent from 1970 to 1980 and by 10 percent from 1980 to 1990, at least among whites.[12]

Available data thus suggest that both income inequality and class segregation increased during the period from 1970 to 1990, which predicts a growing spatial concentration of both affluence and poverty within neighborhoods of American cities.[13] Using the P* isolation index, Massey and Eggers[14] found that within the 30 largest metropolitan areas the geographic concentration of poverty rose by 20 percent between 1970 and 1980 and the spatial concentration of affluence grew by 13 percent. Between 1980 and 1990 the concentration of poverty rose by another 10 percent and that of affluence by 21 percent in the ten largest metropolitan areas.[15]

These scattered results provide an incomplete picture of the geography of inequality, however. First, prior analyses have measured segregation and concentration only at one geographic level—the census tract—yet other spatial units are also of interest. Second, computations are available only for a limited subset of metropolitan areas. Finally, although data on income inequality are now available through the year 2000, estimates of class segregation, poverty concentration, and the spatial concentration of affluence have not been updated to incorporate new data from the latest census.

This paper seeks to address these issues by undertaking a multilevel analysis of available data from 1950 through 2000. Specifically, we combine data from the Integrated Public Use Microdata Samples (IPUMS) with small area data from the Summary Tape Files (STF) for census years in the latter half of the twentieth century to measure trends in class segregation and income concentration at the regional, state, metropolitan, and tract levels.

Data and Methods

In order to measure segregation by socioeconomic status, we must define a set of class categories based on income. For simplicity we

12. Jargowsky (1996).
13. Massey and Fischer (2000).
14. Massey and Eggers (1993).
15. Massey (1996).

Figure 1. Distribution of U.S. Families by Income Class, 1950-2000

Proportion in class

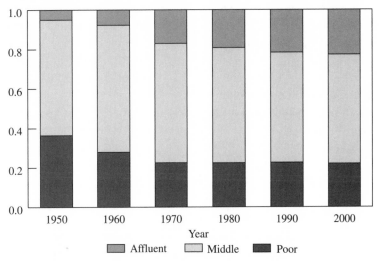

divided the distribution of family income into three broad groups: affluent, middle class, and poor.[16] Poor families are those with incomes below
the official federal poverty threshold for a family of four during the year
prior to the census. In nominal dollars, this threshold stood at $17,029 in
2000, $12,674 in 1990, $7,412 in 1980, $3,743 in 1970, and $2,973 in
1960. Because the 1950 census occurred before the federal government
had defined a poverty standard, we used consumer price indexes to convert the 1959 threshold into 1949 dollars, which yielded a figure of
$2,432 for incomes reported on the 1950 census.

We defined affluent incomes as those exceeding four times the
poverty threshold for a family of four.[17] This operation yielded an affluence threshold of $9,728 in 1950, $11,892 in 1960, $14,972 in 1970,
$29,648 in 1980, $50,696 in 1990, and $68,116 in 2000. Middle class
family incomes were defined as those falling between the thresholds of
poverty and affluence.

Figure 1 shows changes in the distribution of families by income category during the last half of the twentieth century using data taken from

16. Massey and Eggers (1990, 1993).
17. Following Smith (1988) and others: Massey and Eggers (1990); Massey and Fischer (1999).

the IPUMS. In many ways, conditions in 1950 were not far removed from those prevailing in the Great Depression. Indeed, the decade of the 1940s has been viewed as "the great compression," a period of dramatic reduction in wage dispersion.[18] Although massive government spending during World War II restored full employment, the ratio of the top (eightieth percentile) to the bottom (twentieth percentile) of the income distribution fell from 1.45 to 1.05 from 1940 to 1950.[19] As a result, a relatively large share (36 percent) of American households remained mired in poverty while the relative share of affluent families stood at just 5 percent.

From 1950 to 1970, the percentage of families in poverty dropped steadily and rapidly, falling to 28 percent in 1960 and reaching 23 percent in 1970. The relative number of affluent families did not change sharply during the 1950s (shifting from 5 percent in 1950 to 8 percent in 1960) but the affluent proportion grew quite rapidly in the 1960s (going from 8 percent to 17 percent). Over the next decade, declines in the poverty rate bottomed out, and from 1980 through 2000 the proportion of poor families hovered around 22 percent. In contrast, the proportion of affluent families continued to increase after 1970, reaching 23 percent in 2000. In other words, by the end of the century there were more affluent than poor families. As others have noted, the post-1970 economy generally produced a shrinking middle class, an expanding share of affluent families, and a persistent population of poor individuals and households.[20] The reasons for this shift are varied: technological change, the globalization of factor markets, changing tax policies, the aging of the population, and immigration.

Unlike earlier analyses, we sought to measure poverty concentration, income segregation, and the concentration of affluence across multiple geographic levels, using as our model an analysis of racial segregation and isolation in the twentieth century.[21] This method shows that black-white segregation declined from 1900 to 1960 at the regional and state levels and then leveled off. By contrast, racial segregation increased at the neighborhood level from 1900 to 1960, and after 1970 racial segrega-

18. Goldin and Margo (1992).
19. See also Piketty and Saez (2001).
20. Bernhardt and others (2000).
21. Massey and Hajnal (1995).

tion also rose at the municipal level. Here we seek to measure the degree to which affluent and poor families are segregated from one another at the regional, state, metropolitan, and tract levels.

Data on the distribution of families by income across regions, states, metropolitan areas, and counties were obtained from the IPUMS for 1950 through 1990. Although IPUMS data from the 2000 census are not yet available, we were able to perform calculations for that year using file 3A of the newly released STF. The STF were also used to compute measures of tract-level segregation and concentration for the period 1970 to 2000 (computerized tract-level data are not generally available before 1970). Unlike the IPUMS data, however, STF data are not presented at the individual level but are tabulated at the tract or block level. Unfortunately, file 3A of the 1990 STF did not include family income by race, so in that year we were forced to rely on the distribution of household income instead.

Because STF data are tabulated for geographic aggregates, income is reported in terms of categorical distributions that change over time. We collapsed categories to produce three income classes that approximated the thresholds for poverty and affluence defined above, as specific threshold values usually did not match the category cutoffs employed by the census. We used linear interpolation within income categories to estimate the number of families falling above and below the thresholds for affluence and poverty.

The resulting approximation is relatively accurate in defining poverty. In 1970, for example, the theoretical poverty threshold of $3,743 fell very near the category boundary of $3,999. Likewise, in 1980 the threshold of $7,412 was close to the boundary of $7,499. In 1990 and 2000, the distance between threshold and cutoff was somewhat greater but still quite close—in the former year, $12,674 compared to $14,999 and in the latter, $17,029 compared to $19,999. Errors were more likely in defining affluence, especially in 1980 and 2000 when the affluence threshold fell in the middle of a fairly wide range of categories.

Income Segregation at the Macro Level

We measure segregation using the well-known index of dissimilarity, which compares the distribution of two groups across a set of geographic units.[22] Although highly correlated with the Gini index, the dissimilarity measure has become standard in studies of geographic segregation.[23] In this case, we focus on residential dissimilarity between affluent and poor families, thus measuring the degree of social class segregation between families located at the two ends of the income distribution. Because our definitions of poverty and, in particular, affluence are ultimately arbitrary and shift through time, we repeated each calculation by comparing the top fifth of the income distribution with the bottom fifth.

The index of dissimilarity varies between 0 and 1.0 and achieves its minimum when affluent and poor are evenly distributed across geographic units and its maximum when no affluent families share a unit in common with poor families. The index represents the relative number of poor and affluent families that would have to exchange places to achieve an even distribution (expressed as a ratio of the number that would have to move under conditions of maximum segregation).[24]

Overall Trends, 1950–2000

The top panel of table 1 examines trends in class segregation at the macro-geographic level by computing indexes of affluent-poor dissimilarity at the regional, state, and metropolitan levels from 1950 through 2000. As is mathematically required, the degree of segregation increases as one moves from larger to smaller geographic units.[25] At each date, the degree of separation between affluent and poor families is least at the regional level and greatest at the metropolitan level, with state-level segregation falling in between.

In general, we observe declines in class segregation at macro levels of census geography from 1950 through 1980, followed by an increase between 1980 and 1990, and then a return to decline after 1990. At the regional level, affluent-poor dissimilarity decreased from .222 to .097 from 1950 through 1980, rose to .130 in 1990, and then fell back down to .097 in the year 2000. At the state level, the values are roughly parallel, with the dissimilarity index going from .249 to .133 between 1950 and 1980, before rising to .179 in 1990 and falling to .155 in 2000. At the

22. Massey and Denton (1988).
23. Massey, White, and Phua (1996).
24. James and Taeuber (1985); Massey and Denton (1988).
25. Blau (1977); James and Taeuber (1985).

Table 1. Segregation by Family Income, by Region, State, and Metropolitan Area Level as Measured by Indexes of Affluent/Poor Dissimilarity, Selected Years, 1950–2000

Level and race	1950	1960	1970	1980	1990	2000
Affluent versus poor						
Region						
White	0.179	0.190	0.163	0.085	0.123	0.086
Black	0.373	0.418	0.324	0.141	0.182	0.119
Total	0.222	0.236	0.189	0.097	0.130	0.097
State						
White	0.226	0.231	0.211	0.137	0.182	0.161
Black	0.454	0.491	0.390	0.202	0.266	0.197
Total	0.249	0.260	0.222	0.133	0.179	0.155
Metro						
White	0.361	n.a.	0.284	0.230	0.283	0.275
Black	0.582	n.a.	0.414	0.247	0.309	0.257
Total	0.359	n.a.	0.278	0.211	0.253	0.246
Top versus bottom quintile						
Region						
White	0.182	0.188	0.158	0.083	0.128	0.089
Black	0.441	0.431	0.320	0.139	0.187	0.121
Total	0.244	0.240	0.184	0.095	0.134	0.100
State						
White	0.203	0.216	0.203	0.134	0.187	0.166
Black	0.503	0.505	0.384	0.198	0.271	0.201
Total	0.263	0.259	0.216	0.132	0.184	0.159
Metro						
White	0.320	n.a.	0.275	0.226	0.292	0.283
Black	0.564	n.a.	0.406	0.244	0.318	0.262
Total	0.338	n.a.	0.270	0.209	0.262	0.253

n.a. = Not available.

metropolitan level, the 1950 dissimilarity index between affluent and poor families fell from .359 in 1950 to .211 in 1980, then rose to .253 over the next decade and then ended the century at .246. Overall, from 1950 to 2000 net income segregation declined by 56 percent at the regional level, 38 percent at the state level, and 31 percent at the metropolitan level. Over the last half-century, rich and poor have become more evenly distributed throughout the country.

The bottom panel of table 1 repeats the analysis, substituting the top and bottom quintiles of the income distribution for affluent and poor populations defined according to absolute thresholds. Naturally, the numbers change somewhat when quintiles are used to define *rich* and *poor,* as they refer to fixed rather than variable shares of the income distribution. Nonetheless, dissimilarity indexes are generally quite similar in each year no matter which categories are used, and overall trends across years are roughly comparable.

At the regional level, for example, the dissimilarity index between families at the top and the bottom quintiles of the income distribution declined from .244 in 1950 to .134 in 1980 then rose to .134 in 1990 before dropping back to a value of .100 in 2000. Thus, the total decline in the period 1950–2000 was 59 percent In general, the declines were roughly comparable to those obtained using absolute definitions of affluence and poverty—about 59 percent at the regional level, 39 percent at the state level, and 25 percent at the metropolitan.

Trends for Blacks and Whites

No matter how one defines *rich* and *poor,* therefore, the degree to which opposite ends of the income distribution were separated from one another across regional, state, and metropolitan lines declined from 1950 through 1980, rose briefly during the 1980s, and then returned to decline during the 1990s. Table 1 also reports dissimilarity indexes computed separately for blacks and whites to measure the degree of income segregation by race. In general both racial groups exhibit the same pattern of temporal change at the macro level. As in the general population, blacks and whites experienced declining class segregation from 1950 through 1980 followed by a short-term increase in 1990, and then a return to a declining trend between 1990 and 2000. This trend is observed at all macro-geographic levels (region, state, and metropolitan area) and regardless of which definition of *rich* and *poor* is chosen (quintiles or absolute definitions of poverty and affluence).

At each date, however, the degree of observed class segregation is relatively greater among blacks than among whites, with the exception of metropolitan level affluence/poor segregation in 2000. In 1950, for example, the degree of affluent-poor dissimilarity for whites stood at .179 at the regional level, .226 at the state level, and .361 at the metropolitan level. In contrast, the respective figures for blacks were .373, .454, and .582. In other words, the degree of income segregation among blacks was twice that among whites at the regional and the state levels, and 1.61 times greater at the metropolitan level. To a much greater extent than whites, poor blacks in 1950 remained concentrated in certain geographic areas (e.g., states and metropolitan areas of the South) while affluent blacks were located in other geographic regions (states and metropolitan areas of the North and West).

Although both racial groups experienced a downward trend in class segregation over the course of the last half of the twentieth century (except for the upward blip during 1980–1990), the decline was considerably more among blacks than among whites. At mid-century affluent blacks tended to live in qualitatively different geographic areas than poor blacks; by the century's end, however, affluent and poor blacks were much more evenly distributed across regions and levels of class segregation had become more similar to those characteristic of whites (though still higher). For example, affluent-poor segregation for blacks at the regional level declined by 68 percent (from .373 to .119) between 1950 and 2000 and affluent-poor segregation for whites by only 52 percent (from .179 to .086). The magnitude of the black decline in class segregation also increases as one moves down the geographic hierarchy, as does the size of the racial differential. Thus, the drop in class segregation was 47 percent for blacks and 28 percent for whites at the state level, but 56 percent for blacks and 24 percent for whites at the metropolitan level.

In summary, during the last half of the twentieth century, the extent of class segregation among blacks became roughly equal to that among whites, and levels and trends were nearly the same whether one defined *rich* and *poor* in terms of absolute thresholds or quintiles. At the dawn of the twenty-first century, therefore, some 9 to 12 percent of affluent and poor Americans would have to exchange regions to achieve an even distribution by income; 16 percent–20 percent would have to exchange state residences; and 25 percent–28 percent would have to exchange metropolitan residences.

Income Segregation at the Micro Level

A multilevel analysis of racial segregation found that as segregation between blacks and whites fell at the regional and state levels, it grew at the neighborhood level.[26] In other words, as blacks and whites came to inhabit the same geographic units at the macro level, they were increas-

26. Massey and Hajnal (1995).

Table 2. Tract-Level Income Segregation and Concentration of Poverty and Affluence in Sixty Metropolitan Areas, Selected Years, 1970–2000

Index and race	1970	1980	1990	2000
Affluent and poor populations				
(measured by absolute thresholds of income)				
Income segregation				
White	0.261	0.364	0.403	0.351
Black	0.336	0.435	0.521	0.428
Total	0.287	0.398	0.430	0.373
Poverty concentration				
White	0.127	0.138	0.258	0.227
Black	0.160	0.206	0.332	0.282
Total	0.136	0.162	0.279	0.246
Affluence concentration				
White	0.310	0.281	0.361	0.345
Black	0.239	0.200	0.298	0.272
Total	0.308	0.276	0.356	0.338
Top and bottom quintiles				
Segregation				
White	0.254	0.343	0.418	0.360
Black	0.338	0.407	0.537	0.435
Total	0.287	0.371	0.446	0.382
Poverty concentration				
White	0.127	0.202	0.214	0.208
Black	0.161	0.282	0.285	0.261
Total	0.136	0.227	0.235	0.226
Affluence concentration				
White	0.306	0.297	0.304	0.314
Black	0.239	0.215	0.246	0.243
Total	0.307	0.292	0.300	0.307

ingly sorted into different units at the micro level. In a sense, tract-level segregation emerged as a substitute for racial separation at the regional and state levels. Table 2 considers whether a similar macro-macro substitution occurred with respect to class.

The U.S. Census Bureau defines census tracts only for officially designated metropolitan areas. Hence, as the number of metropolitan areas recognized by the bureau has increased over time (from 164 in 1970 to 348 in 2000) the number of census tracts available for analysis has also changed. In order to consider a constant geographic universe over time, we focus on a racial segregation study of 60 metropolitan areas.[27] This

27. Massey and Denton (1987, 1993).

data set includes the 50 largest metropolitan areas plus ten others with sizable Latino populations.

Overall Trends, 1970–2000

As with racial segregation, the downward trend in class segregation observed at the macro level appears to have been substantially offset by a rise in class segregation at the micro level, at least through 1990. Overall, the degree of affluent-poor dissimilarity rose from .287 in 1970 to .430 in 1990 (an increase of 50 percent in just 20 years). During this period, which encompassed the core years of American industrial restructuring, U.S. cities became sharply more class segregated. The index of dissimilarity then fell slightly during the economic boom of the 1990s (dropping to .373 in 2000, a decline of about 13 percent). In the metropolitan areas under scrutiny here, therefore, the net increase in neighborhood-level class dissimilarity between 1970 and 2000 was about 30 percent.

Similar trends are observed when *rich* and *poor* are defined in terms of income quintiles. Between 1970 and 1990 the quintile-based dissimilarity index went from .287 to .446, before dropping to .382 in 2000, yielding a net increase over the entire period of 33 percent. In both series, the sharpest increase in class segregation occurred during the 1970–1980 decade, which spans the watershed period 1973–1975 that marks the transition between rising and falling income inequality.[28] Of the total increase in affluent-poor segregation observed among tracts between 1970 and 1990, 78 percent occurred during the 1970s and 22 percent during the 1980s (see table 2).

Trends for Blacks and Whites

These overall trends in class segregation for the general population parallel similar trends observed among blacks and whites. In both groups, the degree of tract-level segregation between rich and poor increased sharply from 1970 to 1990 and then declined thereafter. At each of these two points in time, however, class segregation among blacks was higher than among whites. During 1970, the affluent-poor dissimilarity index stood at .261 for whites but was 29 percent more at .336 for blacks. By 1990, the black index had risen to .521, compared to

28. Danziger and Gottschalk (1995); Levy (1998).

.403 for whites, but the differential remained the same—at 29 percent. During the 1990s, class segregation fell for both racial groups, reaching values of .428 for blacks and .351 for whites, a differential of 22 percent.

Although both groups shifted toward more class segregation at the tract level between 1970 and 1990 and then moderated between 1990 and 2000, the shifts were such that intergroup differentials generally diminished. By the century's end, the degree of neighborhood segregation between affluent and poor families was more similar for blacks and whites in U.S. metropolitan areas than in 1970; and as in prior analyses, virtually the same levels and trends in class segregation are observed using quintiles instead of absolute thresholds for income classes (see bottom panel of table 2).

Concentration of Poverty at the Macro Level

In the context of well-known shifts in the U.S. income distribution,[29] changes in patterns and levels of class segregation yield specific predictions regarding the geographic concentration of poverty at the macro level. During the period 1950 through 1970, the prediction is unambiguous: falling income inequality, declining poverty rates, and lessening class segregation should have produced sharp declines in the geographic concentration of poverty at the regional, state, and metropolitan levels.

Although class segregation continued to decline through 1980, the downward trend in income inequality reversed after 1970. Then during the 1980s both income inequality and class segregation increased. These trends predict a slowing of the decline in poverty concentration during the 1970s and a reversal during the 1980s. But we would expect the end of rising income inequality in the 1990s and the resumption of declining class segregation to yield another drop in the concentration of poverty across levels.

Overall Trends, 1950–2000

The calculations in table 3 generally confirm these predictions. We measure poverty concentration using the P* isolation index,[30] which cap-

---

29. Levy (1998).
30. Following Massey and Eggers (1998).

Table 3. Concentration of Poverty, by Region, State, and Metropolitan Area Level and by Absolute and Variable Poverty Measures

Level and race	1950	1960	1970	1980	1990	2000
Poverty population (defined by the federal poverty level)						
Region						
White	0.382	0.291	0.231	0.225	0.230	0.158
Black	0.467	0.340	0.248	0.233	0.239	0.230
Total	0.396	0.300	0.234	0.226	0.231	0.223
State						
White	0.387	0.295	0.234	0.227	0.235	0.226
Black	0.495	0.355	0.245	0.236	0.243	0.234
Total	0.404	0.305	0.235	0.228	0.235	0.227
Metro						
White	0.412	n.a.	0.242	0.234	0.245	0.176
Black	0.494	n.a.	0.247	0.238	0.244	0.229
Total	0.425	n.a.	0.243	0.234	0.244	0.234
Poverty population (defined by bottom quintile)						
Region						
White	0.226	0.213	0.207	0.200	0.204	0.203
Black	0.287	0.253	0.223	0.207	0.212	0.210
Total	0.237	0.220	0.210	0.201	0.205	0.203
State						
White	0.229	0.216	0.210	0.202	0.208	0.206
Black	0.317	0.268	0.220	0.211	0.216	0.214
Total	0.245	0.225	0.211	0.203	0.208	0.206
Metro						
White	0.244	n.a.	0.217	0.208	0.217	0.216
Black	0.324	n.a.	0.222	0.213	0.218	0.209
Total	0.258	n.a.	0.218	0.209	0.216	0.213

n.a. = Not available.

tures the proportion of poor families living in the neighborhood of the average poor family.[31] It may be interpreted as the probability of within-unit contact among poor families and it measures the propensity of the poor regularly to encounter and interact with each other. The top panel of the table contains isolation indexes computed for families falling below the federal poverty threshold and the bottom panel contains the same computation for those falling in the bottom quintile of the income distribution.

As can be seen from the top panel, overall poverty concentration fell rather sharply at all three macro-geographic levels between 1950 and 1980. The index of poor isolation fell from .396 to .226 among regions (a

31. Massey and Denton (1988).

decline of 43 percent), from .404 to .235 among states (42 percent), and from .425 to .234 among metropolitan areas (45 percent). Most of the decline occurred between 1950 and 1970, and as predicted the rate of decline slowed between 1970 and 1980. At the regional level, for example, the decline of .162 (.396-.234) observed during the 1950–1970 period was followed by a drop of only .008 (.234 to. 226) during the subsequent decade.

During the 1980s the concentration of poverty increased slightly, rising from .226 to .231 at the regional level, from .228 to .235 at the state level, and from .234 to .244 at the metropolitan level. As expected, however, poverty concentration resumed its decline during the 1990s and generally made up for earlier desegregation gains. By the year 2000, the degree to which poor families were isolated at macro-geographic levels hit a 50-year low, reaching .223 among regions, .227 among states, and .234 among metropolitan areas.

Similar trends prevail when poor families are defined in terms of the bottom quintile rather than the federal poverty threshold, except that the magnitudes of the P* indexes are uniformly lower. For example, using quintiles the isolation index for regions fell from .237 in 1950 to .203 in 2000 (compared to respective figures of .396 and .223 using the poverty threshold); the isolation index for states went from .245 to .206 (compared to .404 and .227); and the index for metropolitan areas went from .258 to .213 (.425 to .234 before). Although the general direction of the trends and period fluctuations are similar, they are less pronounced when quintiles are used instead of the official poverty definition.

The discrepancy results because P* indexes are sensitive to the relative size of the subgroup for which isolation is being considered.[32] At any given level of geographic dissimilarity, a relatively larger subgroup will yield more subgroup isolation. Suppose for example, that the poor are evenly distributed across neighborhoods of two cities, yielding a dissimilarity index of zero in both cases, but that in one city the poor constitute 40 percent of the total city population and in the other just 5 percent. In the former case, the P* isolation index for the poor would be .40 and in the latter .05.

The use of quintiles to measure the poor effectively holds composition constant across years. Year-to-year changes in P* indexes, therefore, only

32. Massey and Denton (1988).

reflect changes in the relative evenness or unevenness in the distribution of the poor across geographic units, not their relative proportion in the population. By contrast, P* indexes defined using the absolute poverty threshold incorporate changes in the relative size of the poverty population as well as shifts in the evenness or unevenness of its distribution.

Thus, the proportion of poor falls from 36 percent in 1950 to 22 percent in 1970 and thereafter remains fairly constant, while the proportion in the bottom quintile is always 20 percent. The much higher concentration of poverty measured in 1950 using the absolute poverty threshold reflects the relatively larger proportion of poor encompassed by using an absolute as opposed to a relative standard. Likewise, the similarity between the two sets of indexes after 1970 reflects the fact that the relative size of the poverty population stabilizes at a level very close to the quintile (about 22 percent).

Trends for Blacks and Whites

Essentially the same patterns and time trends in poverty concentration hold when blacks and whites are considered separately. Since blacks are distributed more unevenly across macro-geographic units than whites (still having more concentration in southern states) and there are relatively more poor among blacks than whites, the degree of poverty isolation is generally greater for African Americans. At the regional level, black poverty concentration dropped from .467 in 1950 to .230 in 2000 while white poverty concentration went from .382 to .158. Despite the different index values, however, the relative magnitude of the decline was similar (59 percent for whites, 51 percent for blacks), and period-specific fluctuations were identical. Both exhibited large declines between 1950 and 1970, stagnation between 1970 and 1980, a slight reversal from 1980 to 1990, and a resumption of the decline after 1990. As with the total population, absolute values of the P* indexes are lower when quintiles are used instead of absolute poverty thresholds; once again, however, the trends are the same.

Concentration of Poverty at the Micro Level

Patterns of inequality and segregation observed at the neighborhood level since 1970 likewise predict a specific trend with respect to poverty concentration. Because income inequality and class segregation both increased between 1970 and 1990 we predicted a sharp increase in geographic concentration of poverty within census tracts; but because income inequality moderated during the 1990s and class segregation fell, we expected a decline in the concentration of poverty during that decade.

Overall Trends, 1970–2000

As the middle rows of the top panel of table 2 show, this prediction is confirmed by the data. Overall, in the 60 metropolitan areas in our data set, the concentration of neighborhood poverty increased by a factor of two between 1970 and 1990, going from .136 to .279. In 1970 the average poor family lived in a census tract with 13.6 percent of the population being poor. Two decades later the percentage had risen to 27.9 percent. As expected, lessening inequality and declining class segregation during the 1990s brought about a reduction of poverty concentration, with the isolation index falling to a value of .246 by 2000, thus wiping out about a quarter of the prior increase. Over the last three decades of the twentieth century, the concentration of poverty within neighborhoods of large metropolitan areas—first noted by Wilson (1987) using 1970s data from Chicago—increased by a net of roughly 80 percent. Because poverty rates were relatively constant around 22 percent after 1970, indexes computed from poverty thresholds and those based on quintiles do not exhibit as great a discrepancy (see table 2).

Trends for Blacks and Whites

Given that blacks are still highly segregated by race at the neighborhood level and that class segregation and poverty rose more sharply for blacks in the 1970s and 1980s, we would expect to observe a greater concentration of poverty among African Americans than among whites. As table 2 shows, this expectation is borne out. The degree to which the black poor were isolated geographically at the neighborhood level rose from .160 in 1970 to .332 in 1990, while the degree of white poverty concentration increased only from .127 to .258. Nonetheless, the relative increase was similar, with poverty concentration roughly doubling for both groups.

By 1990 the average poor black family in our data set inhabited a neighborhood where one-third of the families were poor, compared to a figure of one-quarter for poor whites. As in the general population, the moderating of income inequality and the reduction of class segregation after 1990 brought about a lowering of poverty concentration for both groups, with isolation reaching .282 for blacks and .227 for whites in the year 2000. Once again, similar trends are observed in muted form for both groups when quintiles are substituted for absolute poverty populations.

Concentration of Affluence at the Macro Level

Predicting trends in the concentration of affluence is trickier than anticipating trends in the concentration of poverty, at least before 1970. Prior to this date, falling income inequality and declining macro-level class segregation would augur a lessening in the concentration of affluence at the regional, state, and metropolitan levels; but the steady increase in the relative number of affluent families (see figure 1) creates a greater potential for concentration. During the 1970s, class segregation continued to decline but inequality and the proportion of affluent rose, pushing distributions toward an increase in the concentration of affluence. Meanwhile, during the 1980s segregation, inequality, and the relative number of affluent all rose, pointing unambiguously toward a greater concentration of affluence during that decade. But moderating inequality and declining class segregation, combined with a growing proportion of affluent in the 1990s, introduces more ambiguity about the direction of trends in last decade of the twentieth century.

Overall Trends, 1950–2000

The top panel of table 4 shows P* isolation indexes computed to measure the concentration of affluence at regional, state, and metropolitan levels during the last half of the twentieth century. According to these data, the geographic concentration of affluence increased throughout the period across all levels, at the regional level going from .053 in 1950 to .232 in 2000; at the state level rising from .056 to .239; and increasing from .062 to .257 at the metropolitan level (each representing more than a fourfold increase).

Most of the change was concentrated in the 1950–70 period. For example, of the total .179 increase in the concentration of affluence

Table 4. Concentration of Affluence, by Region, State, and Metropolitan Area Level

Level and race	1950	1960	1970	1980	1990	2000
Affluent population						
Region						
White	0.053	0.082	0.178	0.195	0.223	0.198
Black	0.049	0.080	0.180	0.193	0.222	0.226
Total	0.053	0.082	0.179	0.196	0.223	0.232
State						
White	0.056	0.085	0.184	0.200	0.230	0.237
Black	0.048	0.088	0.194	0.204	0.241	0.241
Total	0.056	0.085	0.185	0.201	0.232	0.239
Metro						
White	0.062	n.a.	0.196	0.211	0.245	0.215
Black	0.060	n.a.	0.216	0.229	0.264	0.268
Total	0.062	n.a.	0.197	0.213	0.248	0.257
Top quintile						
Region						
White	0.213	0.215	0.211	0.203	0.207	0.204
Black	0.203	0.212	0.213	0.201	0.207	0.200
Total	0.213	0.216	0.211	0.204	0.208	0.205
State						
White	0.218	0.221	0.216	0.207	0.214	0.210
Black	0.216	0.227	0.228	0.212	0.225	0.214
Total	0.218	0.221	0.217	0.208	0.217	0.212
Metro						
White	0.234	n.a.	0.229	0.218	0.229	0.226
Black	0.250	n.a.	0.251	0.236	0.249	0.239
Total	0.234	n.a.	0.231	0.220	0.233	0.229

n.a. = Not available.

between 1950 and 2000 at the regional level (rising to .232 from .053), 70 percent occurred before 1970. The corresponding shares at the state and metropolitan levels were 70 percent and 69 percent, respectively. Given that class segregation and income inequality were declining at the macro level between 1950 and 1970, the growing concentration of affluence must be attributed to the increasing proportion of affluent families, a deduction that is confirmed in the bottom panel of table 3, which defines affluence as the top quintile.

When conceptualized in terms of the top 20 percent of the income distribution, the geographic concentration of affluent families appears to be remarkably stable. Instead of rising, the trend in the concentration of affluence is downward over the 50-year period. At the regional level, the isolation of the affluent drops from .213 in 1950 to .205 in 2000, while at the state and metropolitan levels it declined from .218 to .212 and .234 to .229, respectively. Thus, the growing concentration of affluence is largely a result of the proliferation of families earning more than four times the poverty level after 1950.

Trends for Blacks and Whites

Table 4 also shows that, unlike concentrations of poverty, concentrations of affluence do not differ markedly by race. Using the absolute affluence threshold, the white isolation index of .053 at the regional level in 1950 is only slightly more than the black index of .049. Although both indexes rose by 2000, the racial differential had switched direction and only moderately increased, with a value of .198 for whites compared to .226 for blacks. Similar differentials are observed at the state and metropolitan levels. As before, when quintiles are used instead of absolute thresholds, these trends largely disappear.

Concentration of Affluence at the Micro Level

Moving down the geographic hierarchy to the tract level, trends in class segregation and inequality observed after 1970 are consistent in predicting an increasing concentration of affluence at the neighborhood level, particularly before 1990. Up to that date, rising income inequality, a growing share of affluent, and increasing class segregation are expected to yield sharp increases in the concentration of affluence. Moderating inequality and declining class segregation among census tracts after 1990, however, suggests a lessening of this tendency during the last decade of the century.

Overall Trends, 1970–2000

The third set of rows in the top panel of table 2 contains P* isolation indexes measuring the concentration of affluence within census tracts of the 60 metropolitan areas in our data set. As can be seen, the spatial concentration of affluence fell during the 1970s, rose sharply during the 1980s, and then fell somewhat by 2000. From 1980 to 1990, the overall concentration of affluence within neighborhoods increased from .276 to

.356, a 29 percent increase. Although the affluent isolation index fell back to .338 in 2000 (reducing the post-1980 increase to 22 percent), this still left the average affluent family in a neighborhood where a third of families were affluent. During the final three decades of the twentieth century, the poor increasingly came to inhabit poor neighborhoods and the affluent increasingly came to live in affluent neighborhoods. In general, the concentration of affluence (.338 in 2000) was higher than the concentration of poverty (.246).

Once again the foregoing trends disappear when quintiles are used instead of absolute thresholds; the concentration of affluence remained basically constant around .300. The increasing concentration observed using the absolute criterion stems from the fact that, under this definition, the relative number of affluent families climbs from 5 percent in 1950 to 22 percent. Nonetheless, both measures yield essentially the same outcome in the year 2000: affluent families inhabit neighborhoods that are roughly one third affluent and the poor inhabit neighborhoods that are one quarter poor.

Trends for Blacks and Whites

Although blacks experienced a higher concentration of poverty than whites, they evinced a lower concentration of affluence. Compared with their white counterparts, affluent blacks experience less favorable neighborhood circumstances. In 1970, for example, the average affluent black family lived in a neighborhood that was 23.9 percent affluent, compared to a figure of 31.0 percent for the average affluent white family. Over the succeeding decades, trends for each group generally paralleled those observed in the overall population, declining through the 1970s, increasing in the 1980s, and falling only slightly during the 1990s. As of 2000, the neighborhood isolation index for affluent whites stood at .345 and that for blacks at .272, roughly the same proportionate differential as occurred in 1970. Using percentiles instead of absolute affluence thresholds eliminates most of the time trend but yields essentially the same index values in 2000 (.243 for blacks and .314 for whites).

Trends in Specific Metropolitan Areas

As a final exercise, we considered trends in class segregation and the concentration of affluence and poverty at the tract level within four spe-

Table 5. Census Tract–Level Income Segregation and Concentrations of Poverty and Affluence, Four Metropolitan Areas

Index, metro area, and race	1970	1980	1990	2000
Atlanta				
Segregation				
White	0.385	0.476	0.408	0.411
Black	0.535	0.532	0.545	0.530
Total	0.528	0.571	0.482	0.469
Poverty concentration				
White	0.132	0.128	0.196	0.166
Black	0.340	0.380	0.407	0.321
Total	0.235	0.259	0.287	0.234
Affluence concentration				
White	0.392	0.338	0.435	0.429
Black	0.194	0.141	0.279	0.284
Total	0.387	0.323	0.417	0.404
Chicago				
Segregation				
White	0.387	0.473	0.423	0.408
Black	0.497	0.512	0.507	0.480
Total	0.483	0.582	0.493	0.471
Poverty concentration				
White	0.100	0.128	0.209	0.181
Black	0.267	0.361	0.482	0.391
Total	0.164	0.249	0.320	0.262
Affluence concentration				
White	0.415	0.360	0.436	0.429
Black	0.227	0.190	0.252	0.251
Total	0.416	0.342	0.413	0.405

continued on next page

cific metropolitan areas: Atlanta in the South, Chicago in the Midwest, Los Angeles in the West, and New York in the Northeast. In the interest of conserving space, data for populations of affluent and poor are defined only according to absolute thresholds. Separate data trends are, however, reported for blacks and whites.

Atlanta

In the prior discussion, the data show that, in general, class segregation rose at the neighborhood level from 1970 to 1990 and then fell somewhat up through the year 2000. Moreover, class segregation was generally higher among blacks than among whites. Although class segre-

Table 5. Census Tract–Level Income Segregation and Concentrations of Poverty and Affluence, Four Metropolitan Areas (continued)

Index, metro area, and race	1970	1980	1990	2000
Los Angeles				
Segregation				
White	0.435	0.519	0.410	0.444
Black	0.506	0.554	0.489	0.513
Total	0.477	0.557	0.445	0.475
Poverty concentration				
White	0.145	0.160	0.231	0.265
Black	0.282	0.292	0.362	0.371
Total	0.177	0.200	0.274	0.308
Affluence Concentration				
White	0.398	0.384	0.460	0.402
Black	0.205	0.220	0.313	0.262
Total	0.398	0.368	0.432	0.368
New York				
Segregation				
White	0.338	0.410	0.345	0.380
Black	0.395	0.483	0.396	0.386
Total	0.379	0.466	0.371	0.391
Poverty concentration				
White	0.168	0.190	0.273	0.285
Black	0.213	0.285	0.366	0.371
Total	0.184	0.230	0.315	0.324
Affluence concentration				
White	0.326	0.293	0.398	0.364
Black	0.215	0.167	0.272	0.227
Total	0.324	0.282	0.372	0.332

gation in Atlanta followed national patterns of being higher for blacks than for whites, the magnitude of the indexes and their patterns of change over time differed. Compared to national patterns, the dissimilarity between affluent and poor families was higher, peaking at .572 instead of .430, and the peak year was 1980 rather than 1990, when the index had already fallen back to .482 (it dropped further, reaching .469 in 2000). Blacks' income segregation followed national trends and peaked in 1990. As of 2000, affluent-poor dissimilarity was .530 among blacks and .411 among whites.

Overall trends in the concentration of poverty and affluence followed national patterns and peaked in 1990. In Atlanta, the poor isolation index rose from .235 in 1970 to .287 in 1990, and then went to .234 in 2000.

Over the same period, the affluent isolation index rose from .387 to .417 before falling back to .404. Following the trend in metropolitan areas generally, the concentration of poverty in Atlanta was higher among blacks than among whites (.321 versus .166 in 2000), but lower than the concentration of affluence among whites (.284 versus .429 in 2000). In general, Atlanta evinced rather high levels of class segregation and greater racial differentials in the neighborhood concentration of affluence and poverty than the nation as a whole.

Chicago

As in Atlanta, indexes of class segregation peaked in Chicago during 1980 and were similar in value for whites and the total population. Compared with Atlanta, however, class segregation was much lower among Chicago's blacks. For example, the affluent-poor dissimilarity index for blacks peaked at .512 and fell to .480 in Chicago, while the corresponding values for Atlanta were .545 and .530. The concentration of poverty was greater in Chicago than in Atlanta, however, especially for blacks, peaking at .320 in 1990 (with index values of .482 for blacks and .209 for whites) before falling back to .262 in 2000 (.391 for blacks and .181 for whites).

Levels and trends in the concentration of affluence were quite similar in the two metropolitan areas. In both areas, the concentration of affluence stood around .405 in 2000, with an index of .429 for whites. At the neighborhood level, however, the concentration of affluence was .284 for blacks in Atlanta, but only .251 for blacks in Chicago. Neither metropolitan area exhibited strong trends over time with respect to the spatial concentration of affluence.

Los Angeles

Although Chicago was strongly affected by immigration during the 1990s, no metropolitan area was so transformed by immigration as was Los Angeles, which absorbed about one million immigrants per decade during the 1980s and 1990s.[33] The largest portion of this immigration consisted of Latin Americans, implying that a growing share of those labeled *white* in this analysis were actually Latinos born abroad. This

---

33. Waldinger and Bozorgmehr (1996); Bobo and others (2000).

massive immigration makes trends and patterns somewhat difficult to interpret for Los Angeles. Class segregation, in particular, displays no clear trend, rising during the 1970s, falling during the 1980s, and rising again during the 1990s. As of 2000 the affluent-poor dissimilarity index was .475 overall, .513 for blacks and .444 for whites.

Less ambiguous were trends in the concentration of poverty, which rose steadily over the decades, influenced no doubt by the constant arrival of new cohorts of poor Latino immigrants. Overall, the spatial concentration of poverty rose from .177 in 1970 to .308 in 2000. Among whites, the increase was from .145 to .265, among blacks, from .282 to .371. In contrast to the poverty data, the concentration of affluence was characterized by a jagged up-down pattern of decline during the 1970s, an increase during the 1980s, and a decline once again in the 1990s. At century's end, the concentration of white affluence stood at .402, that for blacks, .262, and for the population as a whole .368.

New York

Next to Los Angeles, New York was the second most important destination for immigrants during the 1980s and 1990s.[34] As in the case of Los Angeles, few clear trends emerged in class segregation. Overall, affluent-poor dissimilarity rose during the 1970s, dipped during the 1980s, and rose again during the 1990s. The same up-down pattern held for whites, but class segregation among blacks increased from 1970 to 1980 and then declined through 2000. Trends in the concentration of poverty were less ambiguous. In the general population the poverty isolation index rose steadily from .184 in 1970 to .324 in 2000. Among whites, it increased from .168 to .285; among blacks, from .213 to .371. In general, then, the degree of poverty concentration increased by approximately 75 percent during the last three decades of the century. In contrast, the concentration of affluence displayed a jagged pattern similar to that observed in Los Angeles—declining in the 1970s, rising in the 1980s, and declining once again in the 1990s. As of 2000, the concentration of affluence was .227 for blacks, .364 for whites, and .332 in the population as a whole.

34. Waldinger (1996); Foner (2000).

Conclusions

This analysis considered changes at multiple geographic levels in inequality by measuring trends in class segregation, poverty concentration, and the concentration of affluence from 1950 through 2000. We used census data from the IPUMS and the STF to compute affluent-poor dissimilarity indexes to measure class segregation and P* isolation indexes to measure the concentration of affluence and poverty at the regional, state, metropolitan, and tract levels.

As of the year 2000, the degree of dissimilarity between affluent and poor families was quite low at the regional level (index value of .097) and state level (.155), and higher at the metropolitan level (.246). At all three macro-geographic levels, the indexes have shown a trend of substantial decline during the last half of the twentieth century. From 1950 to 2000, we found spatial separation between affluent and poor families declined by 56 percent at the regional level, 38 percent at the state level, and 31 percent at the metropolitan level. Declines in class segregation at macro-geographic levels reflect the creation of new affluence in the South and new poverty in the Northeast, Midwest, and West. These macro-level trends no doubt occurred both as a result of class-selective patterns of internal and international migration as well as shifts in the distribution of income within regions.

As observed earlier by others with respect to racial segregation,[35] declines in class segregation at the macro level were offset by increases in segregation at the micro level. Overall, affluent-poor dissimilarity increased from .287 in 1970 to .373 in 2000, an increase of 30 percent (table 2). Among whites, class segregation shifted from .261 to .351 (an increase of 34 percent), while it rose only from .336 to .428 (an increase of 27 percent) among blacks. As rich and poor families came to inhabit the same regions, states, and metropolitan areas, therefore, they simultaneously moved into different neighborhoods. Over the latter half of the twentieth century, income segregation at the micro level came to substitute for class segregation at the macro level.

The geographic concentration of poverty is determined by an interaction between trends in class segregation and trends in the distribution of income. Increases in concentration are generally observed during periods

35. Massey and Hajnal (1995).

of rising class segregation and rising inequality; declines occur during periods of falling segregation and declining inequality. Thus, poverty concentration fell sharply at the regional, state, and metropolitan levels between 1950 and 1970 and then bottomed out or remained stable thereafter (table 3). The P* poverty isolation indexes in 2000 were: .223 at the regional level, compared to .396 in 1950; .227 at the state level, compared to .404; and .234 at the metropolitan level, compared to .425. The concentration of poverty at macro-geographic levels generally was greater for blacks than for whites, with interracial differentials in the year 2000 of 46 percent at the regional level, just 4 percent at the state level, and 30 percent at the metropolitan level.

By contrast, the macro-geographic concentration of affluence increased markedly over the past 50 years (table 4). At the regional, state, and metropolitan levels it rose by a factor of around five, with P* isolation indexes rising from around .05 in 1950 to a range of .23–.26 in the year 2000. The rate of increase was highest in the 1960s, with modest but nonetheless steady increases before and after. Although the concentration of black and white affluence was roughly the same in 1950, by the year 2000 it was 14 percent higher for blacks at the regional level, 2 percent higher at the state level, and 25 percent higher at the metropolitan level.

At the micro level of the census tract, the concentration of both poverty and affluence generally rose between 1970 and 1990 and then moderated thereafter (table 2). The concentration of poverty peaked at .279 in 1990 before falling to .246 in 2000, while the concentration of affluence peaked at .356 before dropping to .338. At the neighborhood level, poverty was more concentrated among blacks than whites (with a black isolation index of .282 in the year 2000 compared to .227 for whites). By contrast, affluence was more concentrated among whites than blacks, whites having an index of .345 and blacks, .272.

We performed an alternative set of calculations using the top and bottom quintiles of the income distribution to define *affluent* and *poor* populations rather than absolute thresholds based on the federal poverty level for a family of four. This shift in definitions had little effect on levels or trends of class segregation measured either at the micro or macro level. Because P* indexes are sensitive to the relative number of affluent and poor, fixing these groups at 20 percent of the population eliminated most of the apparent shifts in the geographic concentration of affluence and poverty. Most of the changes in concentration thus reflect the expansion or contraction of the poor and affluent populations, which is eliminated when quintiles are used. Nonetheless, the size of affluent-poor dissimilarity indexes and isolation indexes computed for both poverty and affluence are much the same in the year 2000 whether relative or absolute thresholds are used.

In general, dissimilarity indexes below .30 may be interpreted as *low*, those in the range of .30 to .60 may be labeled *moderate,* and those above .60 are typically viewed as *high*.[36] According to this standard, blacks and whites continue to be highly segregated in most metropolitan areas.[37] The predominance of race over class in determining geographic location is indicated by the fact that under no circumstances do we observe high levels of segregation based on income, and even segregation in the moderate range is unusual. At the regional, state, and metropolitan levels, affluent-poor dissimilarities are all low. Only at the tract level does the degree of class segregation edge into the moderate range.

Under these circumstances, the post-1973 pattern of rising inequality characterized by stagnation at the bottom of the income distribution and rapid increases at the top has produced relatively low concentrations of poverty at the regional, state, and metropolitan levels since 1970 but rising concentrations of affluence across the same geographic units. The concentration of affluence has been especially pronounced at the tract level, with isolation indexes hovering around the boundary of the moderate range.

The foregoing analysis offers both good and bad news to those who seek more equality in American society. On the one hand, the increase in class segregation observed during the 1970s and the remarkable increase in the concentration of neighborhood poverty characteristic of the 1980s do not seem to have continued through the 1990s. If growing up and living in high-poverty neighborhoods undermines the prospects for social mobility and economic advancement, as indicated by a growing body of research, then at least the situation has not deteriorated further since the dislocations of the 1970s and 1980s. On the other hand, neither have they substantially reversed. U.S. urban cities continue to be characterized by the persistent concentration of poverty at historically high levels, especially among African Americans.

36. Kantrowitz (1973).
37. Iceland, Weinberg, and Steinmetz (2002).

More ominous are trends in the concentration of affluence. Since 1950, affluent people increasingly have come to inhabit states and metropolitan areas characterized by concentrated affluence, and since 1970 they increasingly have come to reside in affluent tracts as well. The growing concentration of affluence can be expected to reinforce the advantages already enjoyed by high-income families by virtue of their superior purchasing power—access to first-rate services within safe, secure, and resource-rich environments. To the extent that the affluent are increasingly concentrated in affluent areas while the poor remain stuck in poor areas, moreover, their material and political interests will diverge. Although class segregation and the spatial concentration of poverty may no longer be increasing, their persistence at historically high levels, when juxtaposed with the growing concentration of affluence at all geographic levels, portends a divided society that runs counter to the egalitarian ideology of the United States and its historical commitment to equality.

Comments

William T. Dickens: Massey and Fischer cite a number of compelling reasons for concern with the geographic concentration of poverty. I find the evidence from the Moving to Opportunity experiments most convincing, but I also take seriously their concern that increasing geographic separation between the rich and the poor could lead to political-economic problems.

Since this is mainly a paper about measurement, I will comment on two potential concerns about the measurements it presents. First, a surprising result of the Massey and Fischer paper is how little concentration of poverty there is. Complete geographic equality could be obtained by moving less than 30 percent of the poor while undoing racial segregation would require moving 60 percent of blacks or more. However, since the authors use census survey data on income it is possible that these results are an artifact of the variability of reported annual incomes. Census survey data are contaminated with substantial reporting error, and people's annual income may frequently deviate from their long-term earnings potential. Indeed, neighborhood may be a better reflection of earnings potential than reported income. Consequently, there may appear to be many poor in rich neighborhoods who are not really poor, and people who appear relatively well off in poor neighborhoods that simply had an unusually good year. The exercise I describe below suggests that the concentration measures reported here might be somewhat understated. Dissimilarity indexes I compute for permanent income are generally 20 to 30 percent higher than those reported in the paper for observed annual income—still small relative to measures of racial segregation.

My second concern is with the meaning of the dissimilarity index. If I am told that unemployment among black male teenagers has risen two and a half percentage points over the last year, I have a good idea of what their lost income will be. From existing research I know a range for the possible effects of that unemployment on their lifetime earnings. I can put the problem in perspective and have an idea of how important it might be relative to other problems. Although I can see how the dissimilarity indexes that Massey and Fischer report are qualitatively related to their social concerns, I have no sense of their quantitative significance. I work out a few examples that show that the relationships between the dissimilarity index and the outcomes that concern us are extremely sensitive to the specifics of the index being computed and to assumptions about how concentration of poverty affects social outcomes. This suggests that dissimilarity indexes do not tell us much about the potential extent of problems caused by geographic isolation of the poor.

Permanent Income vs. Survey Income

Poverty is not a permanent state for most people who experience it. The majority of people who report being poor in survey data one year do not report being poor the next year. While blacks tend to experience more sustained poverty, only 40 percent of those impoverished in one year do not escape poverty during at least one of the next two years (Stevens 1999). Family incomes in survey data vary considerably from one year to the next, and this raises the possibility that dissimilarity measures created using survey data on income could be biased downward. Random fluctuations in income from one year to the next (for example due to spells of unemployment) may make truly well-off people appear poor. Conversely, a poor person who receives a windfall could appear well off. Further, an important part of the year-to-year variation in survey income is due to reporting and recording error. This error is not random, but tends to be negatively correlated with actual income—poor people tend to shade their income up while rich people report having less money than they actually do (Bound and Krueger 1991). This is, potentially, a serious problem for the dissimilarity indexes reported in this paper.

To evaluate the importance of these problems I constructed and evaluated the following model. I assumed a continuum of families ordered by their permanent incomes living in a continuum of equal-sized neighborhoods ordered by an index of neighborhood quality. I assumed that both permanent income and neighborhood quality were log-normally distributed and that the underlying normal distributions had a correlation of c_{HP} with each other. I also assumed that the log of observed income was equal to the log of permanent income plus the log of the index of transient income plus an error (all of which are normally distributed).

With this model and some estimates of the variance and covariance of permanent income and observed income from the literature, I was able to compute the dissimilarity index for permanent income that corresponds to any dissimilarity index for observed annual income. The first step was to compute the correlation between observed income and the index of housing quality implied by the dissimilarity indexes presented in the Massey-Fischer paper. For example, in the case of the dissimilarity index for the concentration of poverty this was done by finding the value of c_{HO}, which solves:

$$
d = .5 \int_0^1 \left| \frac{\int_{-\infty}^{\Phi^{-1}(f_p)} b\left[x, \Phi^{-1}(n), c_{HO}\right] dx}{f_p} - \frac{\int_{\Phi^{-1}(f_p)}^{\infty} b\left[x, \Phi^{-1}(n), c_{HO}\right] dx}{1 - f_p} \right| dn,
$$

where d is the reported dissimilarity index, f_p is the fraction of the population that is considered impoverished, Φ^{-1} (Phi) is the inverse cumulative standard normal distribution function, and $b(x,y,c)$ is the bivariate standard normal density function with correlation c_{HO}. The integrals were evaluated using numerical methods. Next, the value of c_{HP} implied by this value of c_{HO} was computed.[38] Finally, the computed value of c_{HP} was

---

38. Under the assumptions stated above and the additional assumptions that the only components of the housing index and observed income that are correlated are the errors in observed income and permanent income, the correlation of the housing index and permanent income can be written as

$$
c_{HP} = \frac{c_{HO}}{c_{PO}} = \frac{c_{HO}\sqrt{Var(P)Var(O)}}{Var(P) + Cov(P,E)},
$$

where $Var(P)$ is the variance of the log of permanent income, $Var(O)$ is the variance of the log of observed income, and $Cov(P,E)$ is the covariance of the log of permanent income and the reporting error in the log of observed income. Gottschalk and Moffit (1994, Table 1, p. 223) calculate that in PSID data the variance of the log of observed income is .432 and that 34 percent of the variance of annual income is transient. However, their analysis does not consider measurement error. Using Bound and Krueger's (1991) results that the substituted in the equation above and the value of the dissimilarity index for permanent income was computed.

Following this procedure I computed the dissimilarity index for permanent income implied by each of the dissimilarity indexes reported in the paper. Nearly all the computed values were 15 to 30 percent larger than the reported results. Although these results are certainly dependent on the assumptions I made in constructing the model, I experimented with several other specifications before arriving at the one described here and all produced very similar results. While I am fairly confident of the robustness of these results, it might still be interesting to compute dissimilarity indexes for variables such as education or per person housing costs, which are sometimes used as proxies for permanent income.

One important qualification of the results reported above is that they are specific to the values of the dissimilarity indexes reported in this paper. For example, a reported dissimilarity index of .65 for the concentration of poverty, computed using observed income and assuming that 20 percent of the population is considered impoverished, would imply a dissimilarity index for permanent income of one.

Are these differences between the dissimilarity indexes for reported and permanent income significant? Without knowing how dissimilarity indexes translate into the social effects of segregation, it is impossible to answer that question.

What Are the Implications of Different Degrees of Economic Segregation?

There is one sense in which the dissimilarity index has a highly intuitive link to the social problems that motivate interest in geographic concentration—it tells us what fraction of the population would have to be moved to remedy whatever problems segregation is causing. The dissim-

---

variance of reporting error in log income in the CPS is about .03, and that the true variance of income is approximately equal to the variance of reported income, it is possible to compute that the covariance of permanent income and the error is -.015. Allowing for a correlation between E and P the variance of the log of permanent income can be found as the value of $Var(P)$, which solves:

$$.34 = \frac{\left(\dfrac{1+Cov(P,E)}{Var(P}\right)^2 Var(P)}{Var(O)}.$$

ilarity index is completely uninformative, however, as to the costs of economic segregation or the value of ameliorating it. It is unlikely that an index of costs of segregation would have a constant relationship to the dissimilarity index.

There are two categories of reasons why we are concerned with geographic concentration of poverty. First, there are distributional concerns. The research Massey and Fischer cite suggest that there are disamenities associated with living among the poor and that if poverty is concentrated these disamenities will be disproportionately experienced by the poor.[39] Suppose that the disamenities decline linearly with the average income in a neighborhood. If this is the case, total social welfare cannot be improved by changing where people live, but the burden can be shifted.

What are the implications of the dissimilarity index for how uneven the burden is? That depends on which dissimilarity index you compute. It makes an enormous difference whether one is computing the index for concentration of poverty, the concentration of the wealthy, or the segregation of the two. For example, in the model described above, if the dissimilarity index for segregation of the rich and poor (defined as the upper and lower quintile) is .5, the average poor person is living in a neighborhood where the average income is about .8 of the overall average income. If the dissimilarity index were computed for the lower 10 percent of the income distribution versus all others, however, then an index of .5 would mean that the average income in the neighborhood inhabited by the average poor person would be only half of the overall average income. If one were concerned about the effects on the poor of living in poor neighborhoods, one would do better reporting average income in the average neighborhood of a poor person rather than a dissimilarity index.

In addition to concerns about distribution, if the effects of average income or other neighborhood characteristics are nonlinear, then segregation of the poor can have efficiency implications. Several theories of the problems caused by economic segregation have this property. For

---

39. One might be concerned that this is double counting in that neighborhood disamenities should be fully capitalized in land values and therefore reflected in the price of housing. Thus, in comparing rich and poor people the cost of these disamenities is fully reflected in the differences in their incomes. However, zoning regulations, which prevent the construction of certain types of housing in certain neighborhoods, and public housing programs may distort this relationship, making it appropriate to consider both income and neighborhood disamenities in thinking about the extent of inequality.

example, O'Reagan and Dickens have developed models in which unemployed people can find jobs through social contacts with employed people.[40] Assuming that many social contacts are made in one's neighborhood, geographic isolation of the unemployed leads to less efficiency in the matching process in the labor market. One can imagine a number of other processes where matching of poor and not poor might have efficiency consequences (for example, if education about advantageous behavior takes place through neighborhood social contacts or if people who know a poor person make better informed decisions about social insurance programs).

It is easy to append a simple Poisson matching model to the economic segregation model described above. Poor people are randomly assigned to one or more other people in their neighborhood. For each non-poor person to whom a poor person is assigned at least one poor person receives some value (for example each non-poor person has information on one available job and the first poor person to ask about it gets it). Parameters of the model determine how many non-poor each poor person can search and how many poor people each non-poor person can help. Value creation is maximized when the poor are spread across all neighborhoods in proportion to their population and declines to zero as the poor become completely isolated. How does relative efficiency vary with the dissimilarity index?

As might be expected from the example just discussed, it matters first which index is being computed. It also matters what the parameters of the matching model are. For some values of the parameters, concentrated poverty has almost no effect until it reaches extreme values (dissimilarity indexes of .8 or greater). For others, significant losses of efficiency take place in the range of values observed in this paper. What this suggests is that without more knowledge about the nature of the social processes that concern us, it is impossible to know whether the levels and changes in dissimilarity indexes for economic segregation reported in this paper are cause for concern or not. This is an important area for future research.

---

40. O'Reagan (1990); Dickens (1999).

Frank Levy: In this interesting paper, the authors have given us an overview of an important research program—initial findings that help to change our thinking while leaving many questions unanswered.

The authors' main finding is that our, or at least my, casual picture of the evolving geography of income is too gloomy. This standard picture is summarized in the paper's first pages. In the picture, a combination of rising income inequality and rising spatial separation between income classes has created a situation such that rich and poor have increasingly limited contact with one another. Both the lack of daily contact and the separation into separate jurisdictions leads to increasing disparity in access to social capital, public goods and services, and other resources that may further perpetuate inequality.

This picture is similar in spirit to Robert Reich's popular writing on "the secession of the successful" and the academic work of Paul Jargowsky.[41] It also overlaps with theories of the rising political power of conservative, suburban voters, an idea discussed in books, including Tom and Mary Edsall's *Chain Reaction*, and many others that assumed this picture of growing geographic stratification was correct.[42]

For this reason the aggregate numbers provided by Massey and Fischer come as a mildly pleasant surprise. They show that segregation between affluent and poor households at the census tract level has not increased in the last twenty years while segregation at the metropolitan level is appreciably lower now than it was in the 1970s. Similarly, the concentration of poverty and of affluence across counties has been stable over time. Similar results apply at other jurisdictional levels. Given the rise in overall income inequality (regardless of geography) over the last twenty years, these results are surprising.

The exceptions to this relatively good news occur at the census tract level within metropolitan areas where the geographic concentration of affluent families has increased fairly sharply over the last twenty years. In addition, the concentration of black poverty has remained fairly stable even as the concentration of white poverty has declined.

The first criterion of a useful paper is to tell us something we did not know. By that standard, this paper is already useful. My main suggestions for future research involve expanding the explanation of the factors

41. Reich (1992).
42. Edsall and Edsall (1992).

that lie behind the numbers—explanations we need in order to know what we should make of these findings.

In some sense this problem stems from the paper's strength: its long historical sweep from 1950 and 2000. Over this period, however, many things have changed. Two examples are the South moving from essentially a separate country to something much closer to national parity and poverty (by the official definition) changing from a largely rural problem to much more of an urban problem.

When the authors talk about converging state patterns, they properly mention the migration of blacks to the North and note how geographical segregation replaced the southern pattern of legal segregation and geographical proximity. What the reader needs is much more of these details behind the numbers, that is, the switch from the rural renaissance of the early 1970s to the bicoastal economy of the 1980s and 1990s, the death and subsequent rebirth of some large cities, and the decline of residential segregation in at least some suburban areas.

These details are needed because the paper's statistics as presented raise two potential problems of interpretation.

First, many of the findings might be caused by several different mechanisms, and the specific mechanism matters to our interpretation. Second, over the period under study, some of the paper's concepts change meaning. Here, too, the specifics will shape our interpretation. I will give examples of both kinds of issues.

With respect to multiple processes, consider the finding of growing concentration of poverty in a census tract. This concentration might mean that gentrification elsewhere in the city is forcing a constant number of poor people to crowd into a small number of neighborhoods. Alternatively, the same concentration figure might mean that segregation had forced the poor and the working class together and the subsequent decline of segregation allowed the working-class families to move elsewhere, leaving the remaining poor in neighborhoods with more concentrated poverty. It is my understanding that something like this happened in the District of Columbia's Anacostia district when housing segregation declined in neighboring Prince George's County in Maryland, which allowed many middle- and working-class blacks to leave the District. Depending on which process is working, we will interpret the statistics differently.

An example of the changing meaning of terms over time involves poverty and who is poor. Between 1959 and the mid-1990s, the proportion of poor who were over age sixty-five declined from one in seven to one in eleven. Conversely, the proportion in families headed by a nonelderly female rose from 16 percent to almost 40 percent. Similarly the growing number of affluent in the paper contains a sharply rising proportion of two-earner couples—families where, for example, it often occurs that nobody is at home during the day When these and other changes are considered, it is possible that a constant index of segregation between affluent and poor over two or three decades in fact masks important changes in daily life.

Similarly, the length of the period under study is sufficient to include the significant increase in the proportion of people living in the Southwest and West, potentially under different kinds of governmental arrangements such as county school districts versus town school districts. That would affect the distribution of public goods. Again, one of the points raised by Reich and other authors is the increased trend of the affluent to purchase privately what used to be considered public goods. Private schools are the most obvious example, but there are others, such as neighborhood security patrols. This trend means that the benefits to the poor of living in a jurisdiction with the affluent may not be as large today as they were twenty or thirty years ago.

My point is not to argue that the authors' story is wrong, but to remind the reader that the authors' statistics do not constitute a complete story, that is, a complete set of implications like the implications offered as one possibility in the paper's beginning. Most people, depending on where they grew up, have a particular frame of reference about these issues: a particular picture of city versus suburb, a particular picture of poverty. In the absence of explanation to the contrary, the paper's statistics tend to be interpreted in that frame of reference, even though any particular interpretation may be wrong.

For this reason, the authors' subsequent work of explaining the meaning of the interesting statistics they present here is eagerly awaited.

References

Bernhardt, Annette, Martina Morris, Mark S. Handcock, and Marc A. Scott. 2001. *Divergent Paths: Economic Mobility in the New American Labor Market.* Russell Sage Foundation.

Blau, Peter M. 1977. *Inequality and Heterogeneity: A Primitive Theory of Social Structure.* Academic Press.

Bobo, Lawrence D., Melvin L. Oliver, James H. Johnson, and Abel Valenzuela Jr. 2000. *Prismatic Metropolis.* Russell Sage Foundation.

Bound, John, and Alan B. Krueger. 1991. "The Extent of Measurement Error in Longitudinal Data: Do Two Wrongs Make a Right?" *Journal of Labor Economics* 9(10): 1–24.

Brooks-Gunn, Jeanne, Greg J. Duncan, and J. Lawrence Aber. 1997. *Neighborhood Poverty.* Russell Sage Foundation.

Danziger, Sheldon, and Peter Gottschalk. 1995. *America Unequal.* Harvard University Press and Russell Sage Foundation.

Dickens, William T. 1999. "Rebuilding Urban Labor Markets." In *Urban Problems and Community Development,* edited by Ronald F. Ferguson and William T. Dickens, 381–435. Brookings.

Dietz, Robert D. 2002. "The Estimation of Neighborhood Effects in the Social Sciences: An Interdisciplinary Approach." *Social Science Research* 31: 539–75.

Edsall, Thomas Byrne, with Mary D. Edsall.1992. *Chain Reaction: The Impact of Race, Rights and Taxes on American Politics.* W. W. Norton.

Foner, Nancy. 2000. *From Ellis Island to JFK: New York's Two Great Waves of Immigration.* Russell Sage Foundation.

Goldin, Claudia, and Robert A. Margo. "The Great Compression: The U.S. Wage Structure at Mid-Century." *Quarterly Journal of Economics* 62: 1–34.

Gottschalk, Peter, and Robert Moffitt. 1994. "The Growth of Earnings Instability in the U.S. Labor Market." *Brookings Papers on Economic Activity* 2: 217–54.

Iceland, John, Daniel H. Weinberg, and Erika Steinmetz. 2002. *Racial and Ethnic Residential Segregation in the United States: 1980–2000.* U.S. Bureau of the Census.

James, David R., and Karl E. Taeuber. 1985. "Measures of Segregation." In *Sociological Methodology 1985,* edited by Nancy Tuma, 1–32. Jossey-Bass.

Jargowsky, Paul A. 1996. "Take the Money and Run: Economic Segregation in U.S. Metropolitan Areas." *American Sociological Review* 61: 984–99.

Kantrowitz, Nathan. 1973. *Ethnic and Racial Segregation in the New York Metropolis.* Praeger.

Levy, Frank. 1998. *The New Dollars and Dreams: American Incomes and Economic Change.* Russell Sage Foundation.

Massey, Douglas S. 1996. "The Age of Extremes: Concentrated Affluence and Poverty in the 21st Century." *Demography* 33: 395–412.

Massey, Douglas S., and Nancy A. Denton. 1987. "Trends in the Residential Segregation of Blacks, Hispanics, and Asians." *American Sociological Review* 52:802–25.

————. 1988. "The Dimensions of Residential Segregation." *Social Forces* 67: 281–315.

————. 1993. *American Apartheid: Segregation and the Making of the Underclass.* Harvard University Press.

Massey, Douglas S., and Mitchell L. Eggers. 1990. "The Ecology of Inequality: Minorities and the Concentration of Poverty, 1970–1980." *American Journal of Sociology* 95: 1153–89.

————. 1993. "The Spatial Concentration of Affluence and Poverty during the 1970s." *Urban Affairs Quarterly* 29: 299–315.

Massey, Douglas S., and Mary J. Fischer. 2000. "How Segregation Concentrates Poverty." *Ethnic and Racial Studies* 23: 670–91.

Massey, Douglas S., and Zoltan Hajnal. 1995. "The Changing Geographic Structure of Black-White Segregation in the United States." *Social Science Quarterly* 76: 527–42.

Massey, Douglas S., Michael J. White, and Voon-Chin Phua. 1996. "The Dimensions of Segregation Revisited." *Sociological Methods and Research* 25: 172–206

O'Regan, Katherine M. 1990. "Social Networks and Low Wage Labor Markets." University of California, Berkeley, Department of Economics.

Phillips, Kevin. 2002. *Wealth and Democracy: A Political History of the American Rich.* Broadway Books.

Piketty, Thomas, and Emmanuel Saez. 2001. "Income Inequality in the United States, 1913–1998." Working Paper W8467. National Bureau of Economic Research, Cambridge, Mass.

Reich, Robert B. 1992. *The Work of Nations.* Vintage.

Smith, James P. 1988. "Poverty and the Family." In *Divided Opportunities: Minorities, Poverty, and Social Policy,* edited by Gary D. Sandefur and Marta Tienda, 141–72. Plenum Press.

Stevens, Ann Huff. 1999. "Climbing Out of Poverty, Falling Back In: Measuring the Persistence of Poverty over Multiple Spells." *The Journal of Human Resources* 34(3): 557–88.

Waldinger, Roger. 1996. *Still the Promised City? African-Americans and New Immigrants in Postindustrial New York.* Harvard University Press.

Waldinger, Roger, and Mehdi Bozorgmehr. 1996. *Ethnic Los Angeles.* Russell Sage Foundation.

Wilson, William Julius. 1987. *The Truly Disadvantaged: The Inner City, the Underclass, and Public Policy.* University of Chicago Press.

BRIAN A. JACOB

Getting Inside Accountability: Lessons from Chicago

THE PASSAGE OF No Child Left Behind (NCLB) in 2001 ensures that school accountability will dominate the educational landscape in this country for the foreseeable future.[1] NCLB requires states to test all children in grades three to eight in reading and mathematics in each year and report the percentage of students meeting state-defined proficiency levels in each school. Results must be broken down by poverty, race, ethnicity, disability, and limited English proficiency. Schools will be required to raise the proportion of students meeting these targets each year according to a schedule that ensures that all students are proficient by 2014. If schools fail to make "adequate yearly progress," they may be subject to increasingly severe interventions, culminating with the closure or reconstitution of the school. Although it is more comprehensive in scope, the federal legislation resembles policies adopted by a number of states and school districts in recent years.

While there is a growing body of research on how accountability policies influence student achievement, dropout rates, and other outcomes, there is little evidence on the *mechanisms* through which accountability policies operate. Proponents contend that high-stakes testing will lead teachers and students to work harder, increase parental involvement, and

I am grateful to Peter Ballard, Johanna Koh, and Todd Rosenkranz for assistance in obtaining and interpreting the Chicago Public Schools budget data and to David Lynch and Jason Freeman for research assistance. I would also like to thank Paul Courant, Julie Berry Cullen, Robin Tepper Jacob, Lars Lefgren, Jens Ludwig, and Janet Rothenberg Pack for helpful suggestions. All remaining errors are my own.

1. P. L. 107-110.

force schools to become more efficient by, for example, instituting new instructional strategies or reorganizing the school day.[2] Critics respond that it will merely lead schools to shift attention away from nontested subjects and cause teachers to focus excessively on narrowly tailored test preparation strategies.[3]

Understanding the mechanisms through which accountability policies work is important for several reasons. For one thing, it can help us to interpret the impact of these reforms and assess the extent of any unintended consequences. Suppose we see science performance decline after the introduction of math and reading standards. Some observers have suggested that this event might simply be owed to the diminished stature of the science exam. If this decline is accompanied by a decrease in the number of science teachers employed by a school system, however, we might be less willing to accept such benign views.[4] Second, knowledge of the mechanisms will help us better understand the potential and limitations of this reform strategy. If the reform works primarily through increasing student effort or parent involvement, for example, without changing the technology of schooling, we might expect student performance to plateau after initial increases. Third, knowledge of the policy mechanisms may shed light on the education production function. If, for example, we see that low-achieving schools that showed considerable improvement in student performance under accountability spent less money on teacher aides and more on professional development, we might take this result as evidence suggesting the efficacy of teacher training.[5]

In this paper, I examine the recent reforms in the Chicago Public Schools (CPS) in an effort to learn more about the mechanisms underlying test-based accountability policies. Chicago provides an excellent case study. It was one of the first large, urban school districts to institute high-stakes testing. There is evidence that the program led to substantial increases in math and reading achievement, particularly among low-

2. Rotherham (2002); James Traub, "The Test Mess," *New York Times*, April 7, 2002.
3 . Elmore (2002); Traub, "The Test Mess."
4. Note that if the explicit intention of the policy were to give greater priority to subjects other than science, this might not be a concern.
5. As I discuss in greater detail, it is still difficult to draw causal interpretations from this evidence. Moreover, even if one were convinced of a causal relationship, it is important to keep in mind that the provision of training under a high-stakes scenario may well be a different "treatment" than the provision of training without accompanying consequences.

performing students and schools.[6] Finally, there has been a considerable amount of high-quality research on the Chicago policy, largely because of a unique collaboration between district officials and a university-based research organization, the Consortium on Chicago School Research (CCSR).

To help make sense of the myriad ways in which individuals and schools may have responded to the reforms, I present a simple model of education production that distinguishes between changes in educational inputs (for example, student effort, financial resources) and changes in the technology of schooling (for example, instructional practices, school organization). In the context of this framework, I discuss a variety of potential mechanisms, drawn from theory and existing research, that might have led to achievement gains under accountability. After reviewing the existing evidence on the Chicago reforms, I turn to school budget data to shed more light on the mechanisms behind accountability in Chicago.

This analysis suggests that the improvements in Chicago were driven by changes in nonfinancial inputs such as student effort, parental involvement, and shifts in content emphasis within a subject, rather than fundamental changes in the technology of schooling as measured by things such as instructional techniques, professional development, or the allocation of resources within schools. The one exception involves the introduction of large, supplemental support programs outside of the typical school structure—most notably the Summer Bridge program and the Lighthouse After-School Program—which may have contributed, at least in part, to the achievement gains. These findings suggest that accountability regimes such as NCLB may not alone be sufficient to change the way in which education is delivered in most schools.

Accountability in Chicago

In 1995, the Illinois legislature passed a major school reform that turned over substantial administrative control of the Chicago public school system to the mayor of the city of Chicago and granted the district the power to sanction low-achieving and nonimproving schools. In the

6. Thompson (1999).

following year, the Chicago Public Schools (CPS) became one of the first large, urban districts in the country to introduce a comprehensive accountability system. The first step in Chicago's accountability effort was to end the practice of "social promotion," whereby students are advanced to the next grade regardless of achievement level. Under the new policy, students in the third, sixth, and eighth grades were required to meet minimum standards in reading and mathematics on the Iowa Test of Basic Skills (ITBS) in order to step up to the next grade. Students who did not meet the standard were required to attend a six-week summer school program, after which they retook the exams. Those who passed were able to move on to the next grade. Students who again failed to meet the standard were required to repeat the grade, with the exception of 15-year-olds who attended newly created "transition" centers. (Note that many students in special education and bilingual programs were exempt from these requirements.) In the fall of 1997, roughly 20 percent of Chicago's third graders and 10 to 15 percent of sixth and eighth graders were held back.[7]

Meanwhile, Chicago instituted an "academic probation" program designed to hold teachers and schools accountable for student achievement. Schools in which fewer than 15 percent of students scored at or above national norms on the ITBS reading exam were placed on probation. If they did not exhibit sufficient improvement, these schools could be reconstituted, which involved the dismissal or reassignment of teachers and school administrators. In the 1996–97 school year, seventy-one elementary schools were placed on academic probation. Chicago recently reconstituted several of these schools, but as early as 1997 teachers and administrators in probation schools reported being extremely worried about their job security, and staff in other schools reported a strong desire to avoid probation.[8]

In earlier work, I have shown that the introduction of the accountability policy led to substantial increases in math and reading achievement in Chicago.[9] Even after controlling for a rich set of observable student characteristics, including prior achievement scores, and pre-existing performance trends in the district, student achievement on the high-stakes ITBS jumped substantially in 1997. The gains averaged 0.20–0.40 standard

7. Roderick and others (1999).
8. Jacob and Lefgren (forthcoming a); Tepper, Stone, and Roderick (forthcoming).
9. Jacob (2002).

deviations and were largest for older students and students in low-achieving schools. Student performance in Chicago increased substantially in comparison to achievement levels in other large, urban school districts in Illinois and the Midwest such as Gary, Indianapolis, St. Louis, and Cleveland.

At the same time, I find evidence that the ITBS gains may not generalize to other outcome measures. Student performance on the state-administered Illinois Goals Assessment Program (IGAP) increased steadily over this period but did not experience a similar break in trend after the introduction of the accountability program. These results are consistent with other studies of test score inflation and high-stakes testing.[10] It is not clear what was responsible for the differing trends, which highlights the importance of understanding what might have been driving the dramatic ITBS gains in Chicago.

The Mechanisms of Accountability

Given the myriad ways in which individuals and schools may respond to high-stakes testing, it is useful to provide some type of conceptual framework within which to understand educational achievement.

Conceptual Framework

The education production literature in economics provides one approach for a conceptual framework. In this view, student achievement (generally measured by standardized test scores) referred to as S is considered a function of various educational inputs (I), as represented by an equation such as the following:

$$S = F(I). \tag{1}$$

This very simple framework suggests that achievement can be influenced by two factors: educational inputs, I, or educational technology reflected by the function $F(.)$. Inputs might include things such as student effort, parental involvement, time devoted to a particular subject, or financial resources as reflected, for example, by lower class size. The technology,

10. Klein and others (2000); Koretz and Barron (1998).

Table 1. Possible Mediators of Achievement Gains under Accountability

Input factors	Technology factors
Student effort	Changes in pedagogy
Teacher effort	Test preparation
Parent involvement	Instructional practices
Financial resources	School organization
Core (for example, reduced class	Alternative allocation of resources
size, newer textbooks)	Principal's management skill or methods
Supplemental (for example,	Professional development
summer or after-school programs)	
Curriculum/instructional time	
Shift within subject	
Shift across subjects	

however, captures the process by which the inputs are utilized to produce student learning. In this case, the technology might include things such as instructional techniques or school organization. While the exercise of classifying various things as inputs or technology is subject to some imprecision (for example, one might reasonably argue that a particular instructional program should be an input), this framework provides a useful starting point.[11]

Table 1 lists a set of possible candidates for explaining the achievement gains in Chicago, classified as changes in inputs or in technology. Inputs are perhaps the most obvious mechanisms. Advocates of accountability programs explicitly cite increased student effort and parental involvement as one of the intended consequences of the reform. Further, many accountability policies provide additional financial resources to struggling schools and students. A less obvious input is instructional time, which I classify as a curricular change since it involves changes in *what* is taught. For example, school personnel may shift instructional time toward tested material, a change that could occur within or across subjects. Spending more time on math than on social studies represents a shift across subjects, for example, whereas devoting more time to algebra than geometry represents a shift within subjects. From the perspective of

11. Many of the ideas underlying the conceptual framework and potential mechanisms outlined here were developed in collaboration with colleagues at the Consortium on Chicago School Research, particularly Melissa Roderick and Anthony Bryk. For earlier discussions of some of these ideas, see Roderick and others (1999) and Roderick, Jacob, and Bryk (forthcoming).

isolating the mechanisms of accountability, the existence and magnitude of such shifts is a positive question, although such changes clearly raise important normative questions as well insofar as they involve trade-offs in what students learn.

Many advocates also hope that accountability will change the technology of schooling. The idea is that accountability will make schools more "efficient," forcing teachers to find "new ways" to teach and compelling principals to reorganize school operations to focus on student learning. These changes may be harder to observe than changes in inputs. However, they might be reflected in how material is taught (that is, the pedagogy of schools) or how school resources (including staff) are allocated. For example, teachers may incorporate more hands-on activities in mathematics or increase the use of group reading activities in an effort to increase student achievement. Principals may try to allocate funds more efficiently by setting aside more money for teacher aides and less money for art and music teachers. In practice, changes in educational technology are likely to be accomplished through various professional development initiatives, which we may be able to observe even if we cannot observe the daily behavior of teachers.

Existing Evidence

In this section, I review several studies on how the accountability policy influenced the attitudes and behaviors of students, parents, teachers, and administrators, seeking to learn what they can tell us about the mechanisms underlying accountability. Before doing so, an important caveat is in order. The search for mediating factors here (or in any policy evaluation) is essentially a speculative process that is best at disconfirming rather than proving certain hypotheses.[12] Various factors changed simultaneously under accountability and, more problematically, these changes were likely correlated with a host of unobservable characteristics of students and teachers that may influence achievement directly. Hence, the problems of selection and causal inference in this case are identical to those in any observational study that focuses only on final outcomes.

---

12. For example, if we determine that one factor, say student effort, did *not* change under the accountability policy, we can conclude that this could *not* have been a mechanism. However, if we determine that student effort did increase, we can only say that effort *may* have been one of the factors.

The chapter on cheating by teachers in this volume suggests that before asking what factors *led* to the achievement gains, one might ask whether the improvement was real. Brian A. Jacob and Steven D. Levitt document that the prevalence of teachers' cheating increased substantially following the introduction of high-stakes testing in Chicago, but the absolute magnitude was still sufficiently small that it could only explain a small fraction of the observed performance gains.[13] Outright cheating, however, is not the only way that teachers and administrators can manipulate student achievement. Jacob shows that special education placements and preemptive grade retention increased following the introduction of the accountability policy.[14] But this type of strategic behavior on the part of school staff is again not sufficient to explain the large observed test score gains.

One of the distinct advantages of studying accountability in Chicago is that there has been considerable research on the reforms. Much of the research described in the following pages relies on detailed surveys of students, teachers, and principals that have been administered (roughly) biannually since 1994 by the Consortium on Chicago School Research. In conjunction with these surveys, researchers at the Consortium conducted a series of interviews with students, teachers, parents, and principals over a two-year period from 1999 through 2000.

Most notably, this research documents that a number of important educational inputs increased under accountability. Robin Tepper, Susan Stone, and Melissa Roderick (hereafter TSR) found evidence that student effort and engagement in school increased substantially following the introduction of the accountability policy.[15] In 1999 surveys, roughly 70 percent of teachers and principals agreed or strongly agreed that the threat of retention motivated students to work harder in school. Teachers explained that the policy provided a clear goal for students to work toward and established another way for teachers to help motivate students. Melissa Roderick and Mimi Engel reported that many low-achieving students indicated spending more time on homework and concentrating more in class following the introduction of the policy.[16] TSR

---

13. Jacob and Levitt (forthcoming).
14. Jacob (2002).
15. Tepper, Stone, and Roderick (forthcoming).
16. Roderick and Engel (2001).

also examined trends in academic engagement, as measured by student survey responses to questions asking them, for example, whether they look forward to class and whether they find the topics studied interesting and challenging. Interestingly, they found that such self-reported engagement increased for low-achieving eighth grade students from 1994 to 2001 but decreased slightly among higher-achieving students.

TSR relate the changes in student effort to increases in parental and teacher support. They found that almost 90 percent of principals and 75 percent of teachers surveyed in 1999 agreed or strongly agreed that the policy had made parents more concerned about their child's progress. This was confirmed by results from student surveys. The researchers created a measure of parental support by combining student responses to a variety of items, including questions about how often they discussed school activities or events with adults at home and how often their parents help them with homework, check to see if assignments are completed, or praise them for doing well in school. They found that both sixth and eighth graders reported significantly higher levels of parental support in 2001 compared with 1994, with low-achieving students showing the largest gains.

Student-reported measures of teacher support—measured by a series of survey questions that ask students, among other things, the extent to which their teacher notices if they are having trouble learning or is willing to give them extra help—also increased over this period. In 1994, the lowest-achieving students reported less academic and personal support from teachers compared with higher-achieving peers. From 1994 to 2001, student reports of support increased for all students, but particularly for low-achieving students and students in low-achieving schools, so that by 2001 low- and high-achieving students reported equal degrees of support.

Another input that increased under accountability was supplemental academic support. In an effort to help at-risk students meet the new standards, the district instituted a six-week summer program referred to as Summer Bridge for students who failed to meet promotional criteria in the spring and an after-school program during the school year called Lighthouse. Although there has never been a formal evaluation of the Lighthouse program on student outcomes, TSR found that teachers and principals frequently cited the after-school program as a key resource in assisting low-achieving students. Consistent with this finding, the proportion of students who reported attending an after-school program regularly increased substantially from 1994 to 2001, with the largest increases among students classified as moderate risk.

Jacob and Lefgren examine the effect of summer school and grade retention on student achievement using a regression-discontinuity design that allows them to overcome the selection issues inherent in evaluating remedial education programs.[17] By comparing the learning trajectories of students who scored just below the promotional cutoff (and therefore had to attend summer school) with those who scored just above the cutoff (and thus did not attend summer school), they can infer the causal impact of the programs. They found that summer school led to modest increases in academic achievement among third graders that faded somewhat after the first year but were still significant two years later. In contrast, they found little if any effect for sixth graders.[18]

Finally, there is some evidence that teachers aligned the content of math and reading classes to more closely match the topics and skills tested on the standardized exam, although the magnitudes of these curricular changes appear quite small. For example, the TSR found that eighth grade teachers increased the pacing of their math classes following the introduction of the accountability program—that is, these Chicago teachers spent less time reviewing elementary concepts and more time covering advanced material than they had in the past. These teachers, for example, increased the time spent on grade-level material from 38 percent in 1994 to 44 percent in 2001. Although the changes captured by teacher surveys are extremely small, they may reflect more substantial changes. For example, in interviews teachers described spending more time on nonfiction reading passages and math estimation problems because they are emphasized on the high-stakes test. Approximately 40 percent of teachers and principals surveyed in 1999 agreed that they were spending less time on social studies and science than they used to as a result of the promotion policy.

17. Jacob and Lefgren (forthcoming b).
18. This study did not examine the effects on eighth grade students because many students do not take the standardized exams in high school. However, Roderick, Jacob, and Bryk (forthcoming) found large achievement gains from June to August for eighth grade students attending summer school, even after controlling for regression to the mean, which suggests that the effects for these students may have been substantial.

Although there is considerable evidence that inputs increased in Chicago, there is little evidence that educational technology changed. Using a combination of interview and survey data, TSR found that teachers did not make any substantial changes in classroom organization, general instructional approach, or specific teaching methods, with the exception of a substantial increase in test preparation. The trends in test preparation are clear but somewhat difficult to evaluate. Roughly one-third of teachers reported spending more than 20 hours per year in 1994 compared with close to 50 percent in 2001, with the greatest increases in low-achieving schools and in grades subject to the promotion policy. Because teacher responses are censored (with the top category being "more than twenty hours"), however, it is difficult to determine the true extent of test preparation activities. Based on teacher interviews, TSR conclude that many teachers in low-achieving schools spend considerably more than twenty hours per year, but that the majority of test preparation time is generally focused in the month before testing. In addition, TSR note that test preparation encompasses a wide range of activities, from reviewing test-taking strategies (for example, the process of elimination) to taking practice exams, which makes it difficult to get a sense of exactly what practices are taking place.

Research on the school probation policy provides additional insight into possible changes in pedagogy during this time. Beginning in 1997, schools in which fewer than 15 percent of students scored at or above national norms in reading were placed on academic probation.[19] To improve student achievement in these schools, the CPS provided probation schools additional resources to buy staff development services from an external organization of their choice. In 1998–99, probation schools were working with seventeen different external partners, including universities, nonprofit organizations, and independent consultants.[20] Jacob and Lefgren and Mark A. Smylie and others document that teachers in low-achieving schools experienced an increase in the number of profes-

19. Linda Lenz, "Winning Ugly," *Chicago Tribune*, October 26, 1997, p 1.
20. During the first year a school was on probation, the Chicago Public Schools (CPS) paid 100 percent of the costs of the external partner (up to $90,000). In the second year, the reimbursement dropped to 50 percent. After two years, the board paid one-third of the cost of external partners. Besides these direct resources, the CPS provided probation schools with technical assistance and monitored the progress of the school. Jacob and Lefgren (forthcoming a).

sional development activities between 1994 and 1999. Jacob and Lefgren use a regression-discontinuity design to examine the impact of these teacher training resources, comparing student achievement gains in schools where just under 15 percent of students met norms (thus placing the school on probation) with gains in schools where slightly more than 15 percent of students met norms (thus allowing the school to avoid probation).[21] They find that teacher training had no impact on student achievement. A report by Kara Finnigan, Jennifer O'Day, and David Wakelyn provides some explanation of these findings, noting a number of implementation difficulties in the external partner program.[22]

Summary

This evidence suggests that the accountability policy substantially increased key inputs but did not influence what might be described as the technology of schooling. Student effort increased over this period, as did teacher support and parental involvement. The district instituted two large, supplemental support programs—Summer Bridge and Lighthouse—which teachers viewed as extremely important. However, with the exception of higher test preparation, there was little change in instructional practice. There was some increase in professional development, though it does not seem to have had a substantial effect on student achievement.

This research leaves open several important questions. The first involves the financial resources available to schools. The apparent importance of supplemental programs such as Summer Bridge and Lighthouse raises the question of whether resources increased in other, core instructional areas. If, for example, the system reduced class sizes or hired more qualified teachers, or allocated additional money for classroom aides, these factors might explain the achievement gains.

The second issue concerns the shifting of resources *across* program areas. Teacher interviews suggest that schools may have been shifting resources into math and reading and away from other academic areas. Consistent with these reports, Jacob found that improvement in science and social studies slowed relative to math and reading under the accountability policy.[23] Similarly, observers have worried that schools may shift

21. Jacob and Lefgren (forthcoming a); Smylie and others (2002).
22. Finnigan, O'Day, and Wakelyn (2001).
23. Jacob (2002).

resources away from nonacademic areas such as art and music in response to high-stakes testing. Yet, in the prior literature, there has been no conclusive evidence that this took place or, perhaps more important, about the magnitude of any resource transfers.

The third issue involves school organization. Even if the total financial resources available to principals did not change, if schools instituted changes in the technology of schooling, we might expect to see evidence of such changes in how schools spend their money. Although the exact nature of the reallocation will, of course, depend on the type of changes instituted, we would certainly expect schools to shift spending toward instructional purposes.

Changes in Resource Allocation in Chicago

While interviews and surveys shed light on what changed in Chicago under the accountability regime, school budgets—which reflect the educational plans and priorities of teachers and administrators—may provide additional insight. In this section, I present some new analysis of budget data that addresses several unanswered questions on the effects of accountability.

An analysis of Chicago Public School budgets allows us to answer two important questions about changes in educational inputs. First, was there an increase in financial resources available to Chicago elementary schools for regular school activities as opposed to supplemental support services? Second, did schools shift resources away from nonacademic areas such as art, music, foreign language, and library?

Budget data also provide some insight into whether the accountability policy led to changes in the educational technology, particularly factors relating to school organization. First, one might expect schools to respond to the achievement-oriented policy by spending more money on instruction and less on school operation or maintenance. At this most fundamental level, we would expect the proportion of spending on teachers, aides, principals, textbooks, and instructional supplies to increase relative to spending on custodial staff, lunchroom personnel, equipment, and expenses related to operations and maintenance.

Second, schools might change the mix of instructional personnel in the school. For example, schools may decide to hire additional teachers to reduce class size. Other schools may choose to focus on teacher aides in the hope that they can provide more individualized attention to students. Or schools may allocate funds for assistant principals or other supervisory staff who act as "mentor teachers" helping to observe, train and coach their peers. Indeed, the use of "literacy coaches" is common in several reform strategies such as the Early Childhood Literacy Program.

Background on School Finance in Chicago

By the time the new CEO of Schools, Paul Vallas, rolled out his accountability plan in 1996, Chicago schools were in many ways well suited to respond to the reform. Eight years earlier, the Illinois legislature had passed the Chicago School Reform Act of 1988 (P.A. 85-1418), which substantially changed the governance and financing of public schools in Chicago.[24] The legislation created a system of school-based decisionmaking that placed considerable authority in locally elected school councils. Composed of the principal, teachers, and locally elected community members, these councils were charged with hiring and evaluating the principal, creating a school improvement plan, and determining the annual budget.

At the same time, the legislation reformed the way in which State Chapter I funds for low-income students were distributed. Before then, Chicago had used Chapter I to fund a variety of positions at the central office and to fill gaps in the general budget, often for programs or personnel not directly serving the impoverished schools for which the funds were intended. The Chapter I provisions of the legislation, which were phased in over a few years in the early 1990s, mandated that the board of education allocate 95 percent of the funds directly to schools, strictly on the basis of the number of students in the school receiving free or reduced price lunch.[25] Thus, unlike their counterparts in other districts,

---

24. See Hess (1991, 1995) and Bryk and others (1998) for a detailed discussion of the factors leading to the reform and the particular provisions of the legislation.

25. Rosenkranz (1994) found that the reallocation of State Chapter I money shifted positions from the central office to the schools, with the percent of staff budgeted directly to schools increasing from 88.5 percent in 1988 to 93.1 percent in 1993. He found that elementary schools spent much of this new Chapter I money on classroom teachers (42.3 percent of Chapter I funds in elementary schools were used to fund teaching positions in 1993) but also used some of it to fund nonteaching positions. Schools increased the number of teacher positions funded by Chapter I by 88 percent, aide positions by 37 percent,

educators in Chicago in the mid-1990s had considerable control over the educational process in their schools and the power to allocate funds to support their educational priorities.

Data and Sample

The main source of data in this study consists of line-item school-level budgets for the Chicago Public Schools. Each year's budget file contains roughly 160,000 budgeted line item expenditures, and each line item consists of more than twenty pieces of information that describe the nature of the expenditure, allowing one to categorize spending in a variety of ways. All dollar values are converted to year 2000 dollars.[26] To provide contextual information, I merge school-level demographic and achievement data into the budget data. School demographic information includes information such as enrollment, racial composition (percent black, white, Hispanic, Asian, and Native American); percent receiving free or reduced price lunch; percent limited English proficient; average daily attendance rates; and average mobility rate. Student achievement data come from the Iowa Test of Basic Skills (ITBS), a standardized, multiple-choice achievement exam that has been used to determine student promotion and school probation in Chicago.

The sample for this analysis includes public elementary schools in Chicago in 1994–95 and 1999–2000. The first year captures expenditure patterns before the introduction of the accountability policy. This provides a particularly good baseline measure since the changes brought about by the 1988 reforms had been phased in, but the 1995 reforms had not passed, ensuring that spending patterns do not reflect any anticipatory effects. The 2000 budget, however, should reflect any responses on the part of the schools. I limit the analysis to elementary schools because they were the focus of the accountability reforms. I exclude schools that predominantly serve special needs students since they were largely unaffected by the accountability regime. Finally, for the sake of consistency, I

and administrators' positions by 240 percent (though administrators' positions only composed 4.5 percent of total Chapter I positions in 1993). In 1999–2000, the average elementary school in Chicago received $491,000 in Chapter I funds.

26. Expenditures are adjusted using data from the CPI for Urban Wage Earners and Clerical Workers in the Chicago-Gary-Kenosha metropolitan statistical area for January 1995 and January 2000. These data can be found at the Bureau of Labor Statistics website (http://data.bls.gov/cgi-bin/surveymost?cw).

keep only those schools that were operating in both years. The primary result of this decision is that I do not include several new schools, including some charter schools, which opened after 1995.

The final sample contains 456 elementary schools. Table 2 shows the descriptive statistics for these schools in 1995. As in many urban areas, elementary schools in Chicago have a large proportion of poor and minority students and score quite low on standardized achievement exams. The average elementary school in Chicago in 1995 enrolled roughly 793 students, 83 percent of whom received free or reduced price lunch. Approximately 54 percent of elementary students in the district were black and another 31 percent were Hispanic. In the average elementary school, only 31 and 27 percent of students scored at or above national norms in math and reading respectively.

Several features of the budget data are worth noting. First, certain expenditures that occur in schools are actually budgeted to the central office. For example, resources devoted to school nurses and speech pathologists are not budgeted to individual schools, although such personnel are assigned exclusively to schools. Similarly, funds for the Lighthouse program were budgeted to the central office. For this reason, the expenditure figures shown in this paper do not reflect the total spending in a particular school. Second, the budget data differ somewhat from final expenditures, as circumstances change during the school year, although these changes are generally minor. Finally, the way in which benefits are budgeted at the school level makes it impossible to attribute these expenditures to a particular position, so that in the analysis I exclude benefits when calculating the proportion of spending in various categories. To the extent that benefits are proportional to regular salaries, this should not bias the results.

I divide expenditures into the following categories. First, I separately consider personnel and nonpersonnel expenditures. Within personnel, I consider six separate types of employees: teachers; teacher aides; principals, assistant principals, and other supervisory staff; secretaries and other clerical staff; operations or maintenance staff (for example, primarily lunchroom and custodial staff); and student support personnel, which consists primarily of social welfare staff (for example, psychologists, social workers, guidance counselors, child welfare and special education advocates), security staff (for example, school security guards and truancy officers), and community-based staff (for example, community

Table 2. Summary Statistics

	1995		2000	
	Mean	*Std. dev.*	*Mean*	*Std. dev.*
Demographics				
Black (%)	54.3	42.9	53.0	43.7
Hispanic (%)	31.4	35.0	33.8	36.8
Limited English proficient (LEP) (%)	16.8	19.0	15.7	17.6
Fraction in special education	0.097	0.049	0.108	0.046
Free or reduced price lunch (%)	82.8	18.7	86.7	16.9
Mobility rate (%)	31.6	16.4	26.5	12.4
Size	793	309	858	370
Student achievement				
ITBS reading (national percentile score)	34.3	10.2	41.4	9.8
Students scoring above national norms in reading (%)	26.7	15.3	36.6	15.9
ITBS math (national percentile score)	36.2	11.6	47.4	11.0
Students scoring above national norms in math (%)	31.0	16.1	46.4	16.2
Resource allocation				
Total expenditures ($ per pupil)	5,383	963	4,794	850
Student-teacher ratio	17.7	2.6	18.4	2.4
Average teacher salary (excluding benefits)	42,888	2,162	46,509	2,148
Fraction of budget spent on instruction	0.712	0.048	0.769	0.048
Expenditures on art, music, and foreign language ($ per pupil)	126	101	105	93
Expenditures on library programs ($ per pupil)	93	37	90	42
Ratio of supervisors to teachers	0.056	0.024	0.054	0.022
Ratio of aides to teachers	0.228	0.104	0.217	0.097
Ratio of counselors to teachers	0.056	0.024	0.038	0.044

Note: Weighted by school enrollment; $N = 456$. All expenditures in year 2000 dollars.

liaisons, parent representatives). I divide nonpersonnel expenditures into five categories: textbooks and supplies, equipment (for example, computers, fax machines, copiers), contracts for professional and technical services (for example, staff development, tutoring), operations (for example, food, transportation, heating fuel), and miscellaneous. For the purpose of this analysis, I define instructional expenditures to include salaries for teachers, aides, and supervisory staff (for example, principals, assistant principals) and spending on textbooks and other instructional supplies.

Noninstructional expenditures therefore include salaries for all clerical, operations, and maintenance staff along with spending on equipment, contracted services, operations, and miscellaneous items.

Results

The studies just described document the importance of the summer and after-school programs instituted under the accountability policy. The district also increased spending in several other areas during this period, creating high school transition centers and other alternative schools, funding charter schools and high school restructuring efforts, expanding prekindergarten programs, and undertaking a large capital investment program. However, the bottom panel of table 2 shows that there was not a substantial increase in resources devoted to regular elementary schools for their academic-year operations. Total per pupil expenditures decreased by roughly 11 percent, and pupil-teacher ratios increased slightly. Teacher salaries increased roughly 7 percent, primarily because of two new contracts that teachers received during this period.[27]

Although total resources for elementary schools increased only slightly, it is possible that school officials shifted money out of noncore areas in order to increase funding devoted to math and reading, the high-stakes subjects under Chicago's accountability. Ideally, one might wish to examine each academic and nonacademic subject or program area separately. Unfortunately, the budget data do not allow one to separately identify spending in many core academic subjects (for example, math versus reading versus science versus social studies) since a single elementary teacher is often responsible for teaching all of these subjects to his or her students.

Table 3 examines expenditure patterns in four areas for which it is possible to clearly identify expenditures: art, music, foreign language, and library. The top panel shows the average level of per pupil expenditures in each area in 1995. In column 1, we see that the average school spent roughly $49 per pupil on art and $58 on music. Given the average

---

27. District officials indicate that average teacher age or education level has not increased significantly in recent years, suggesting that the observed salary increases are because of cost-of-living adjustments and standard raises awarded to teachers in recent contracts. (Communication with Joanna Koh, Chicago Public Schools, Office of Management and Budget, January 14, 2002.)

Table 3. Expenditures in Noncore Subjects

Subject	All schools	Bottom quartile	Second quartile	Third quartile	Top quartile	Test of equality across quartiles (p value)
			Spending level in 1995 for schools with 1995 achievement level in the			
Art	48.9	60.3	44.7	43.3	47.5	0.019
Music	57.7	58.1	50.8	65.3	57.5	0.077
Foreign language	19.4	10.0	10.7	12.3	49.5	0.079
Library	93.1	94.4	87.8	95.6	95.7	0.223
			Change in spending from 1995 to 2000 for schools with 1995 achievement level in the			
Art	−4.2**	−10.8**	−3.2	−0.4	−2.3	0.327
Music	−8.3***	−14.2***	−6.7**	−7.8***	−4.4*	0.215
Foreign language	−6.3***	−6.9***	−5.9***	−7.2**	−4.9**	0.919
Library	−2.2	−1.0	−1.7	−3.1	−3.2	0.972

Note: All figures are weighted by school enrollment. All expenditures in year 2000 dollars, expressed as per pupil expenditures. Changes in the bottom panel are expressed in raw dollar units.
*Significant at 10 percent level.
**Significant at 5 percent level.

enrollment size of roughly 800 students, this figure suggests that the average Chicago elementary school only spent $85,600 per year on these programs in 1995. Schools spent substantially less on foreign language, but nearly as much on library programs. Columns 2 to 5 show expenditures broken down by the 1995 achievement levels, where the quartiles represent a school's rank within the district in that year based on average math and reading scores for all grades in the school. We see that low-achieving schools spend somewhat more on art and music combined, while high-achieving schools spend considerably more on foreign language. There is no difference in library spending across achievement groups.

The bottom panel shows how per pupil expenditures in these areas changed from 1995 to 2000. Column 1 shows that on average spending in art and music declined by roughly 12 percent, spending on foreign language declined by 32 percent, and spending on library programs remained roughly the same. However, insofar as the accountability policy imposed the largest incentives on schools with low achievement levels in 1995, we would expect schools in the bottom quartiles to be most likely to cut spending in these noncore areas. And, in fact, we see that schools in the bottom quartile in 1995 decreased art and music spending by roughly 21 percent compared with top quartile schools that decreased spending by only 7.8 percent. Similarly, schools in the bottom three quartiles cut their spending on foreign language by more than half, whereas top quartile schools made only small cuts in this area. Although the size of the relative decreases is striking, it is important to keep in mind that the absolute magnitude of this change is still small—that is, the declines in art and music spending among bottom quartile schools amount to roughly $20,000 for a school of 800 students, less than one-half of a full-time employee's salary (without benefits) given the average teacher salary.

We now turn to school organization, examining whether the budget data can provide any indication of changes in educational technology. Table 4 examines how instructional spending in Chicago elementary schools changed under accountability. The top panel shows that in 1995 the average school spent roughly $3,082 per pupil on instruction, which constituted roughly 71 percent of the total operating budget. The ratio of instructional staff (that is, all teachers, aides, and supervisory staff) to students was roughly 37 staff per 500 students, which translates to a

Table 4. Changes in Instructional Spending

		Levels in 1995 for schools with 1995 achievement level in the				
	All schools	Bottom quartile	Second quartile	Third quartile	Top quartile	Test of equality across quartiles (p value)
Instructional spending ($ per pupil)	3,081.7	3,280.6	3,062.4	3,030.7	2,938.9	0.000
Budget fraction on instruction	0.712	0.716	0.721	0.716	0.691	0.004
Inst. staff: student ratio (x 500)	37.1	40.3	37.2	36.6	34.1	0.000

		Change from 1995 to 2000 for schools with 1995 achievement level in the				
	All schools	Bottom quartile	Second quartile	Third quartile	Top quartile	Test of equality across quartiles (p value)
Instructional spending ($ per pupil)	127.5**	90.5	85.0*	163.6**	184.3**	0.093
Budget fraction on instruction	0.055**	0.040**	0.048**	0.055**	0.080**	0.000
Inst. staff: student ratio (x 500)	−1.57**	−2.23**	−2.27**	−1.00**	−0.58**	0.006

Note: All figures are weighted by school enrollment. Expenditures in year 2000 dollars. Figures shown in the bottom panel are absolute changes as opposed to percent changes.
*Significant at 10 percent level.
**Significant at 5 percent level.

pupil:staff ratio of approximately 13.5. In columns 2 to 5, we see low-achieving schools enjoyed higher expenditures per pupil than high-achieving schools. This is because of the higher proportion of low-income and special education students in such schools, which entitle the schools to additional state and federal funding.[28]

The bottom panel shows expenditure changes by 1995 achievement quartile. We see that schools on average spent a greater fraction of their budget on instruction in 2000. This is particularly true for top quartile schools, which increased the share of their budgets devoted to instruction by 8 percentage points (or roughly 12 percent). At the same time, however, ratios of instructional staff to students *decreased* by 1.57 on average. Since the vast majority of instructional spending is devoted to salaries, this means that the additional instructional spending was because of salary increases for teachers, aides, and supervisory staff (based on the author's calculation). The difference across schools is still interesting. It seems that higher-achieving schools reallocated spending to maintain roughly the same ratios of staff to students. Low-achieving schools, however, realized declines of more than 2 staff per 500 students. One reason for this difference may lie in the fact that low-achieving schools already had relatively high staff levels in 1995, largely because of the additional teachers and aides purchased with categorical funding from state and federal sources. Given an average enrollment of roughly 800 students, these changes in instruction spending seem quite small.

Table 5 examines the mix of staff in an attempt to determine whether there have been any changes in school organization under accountability. For this purpose, I create three measures to capture staff allocation: the ratio of aides to teachers, the ratio of counselors to teachers, and the ratio of supervisors to teachers. Aides generally work with small groups of students or assist teachers in carrying out lessons. Counselors include social workers, guidance counselors, psychologists, and other staff whose job it is to deal with the social, emotional, and family difficulties that many children bring to school. Supervisors include principals, assistant principals, mentor teachers, and others whose job it is to supervise, mentor, or train teachers. The top panel indicates that in 1995 the average elementary school employed slightly less than one aide for every four teachers, and slightly more than one supervisor for every twenty teachers

---

28. Communication with Joanna Koh, January 14, 2002.

Table 5. Changes in Staff Allocation

| | All schools | Spending level in 1995 for schools with 1995 achievement level in the | | | | Test of equality across quartiles (p value) |
		Bottom quartile	Second quartile	Third quartile	Top quartile	
Ratio of aides to teachers	0.228	0.268	0.243	0.234	0.156	0.000
Ratio of supervisors to teachers	0.056	0.054	0.053	0.058	0.059	0.097
Ratio of counselors to teachers	0.056	0.051	0.054	0.062	0.058	0.461

| | All schools | Change in spending from 1995 to 2000 for schools with 1995 achievement level in the | | | | Test of equality across quartiles (p value) |
		Bottom quartile	Second quartile	Third quartile	Top quartile	
Ratio of aides to teachers	−0.009*	−0.026**	−0.014*	−0.007	0.016**	0.000
Ratio of supervisors to teachers	−0.001*	0.003	0.000	−0.005**	−0.003**	0.030
Ratio of counselors to teachers	−0.019**	−0.016**	−0.016**	−0.019**	−0.022**	0.710

Note: All figures are weighted by school enrollment. Figures shown in the bottom panel are absolute changes as opposed to percent changes.
*Significant at 10 percent level.
**Significant at 5 percent level.

and one counselor for every twenty teachers. Low-achieving schools employed more aides per teacher than higher-achieving schools, with a particularly noticeable difference among top quartile schools. In contrast, high-achieving schools employed more supervisors per teacher than other schools. There is no statistically significant difference in the ratio of counselors to teachers across achievement groups.

The bottom panel indicates that on average schools decreased the number of aides, supervisors, and counselors relative to teachers from 1995 to 2000, although the changes are generally small in magnitude and only significant at the 10 percent level. Low-achieving schools decreased the ratio of aides to teachers significantly more than high-achieving schools. Conversely, these low-achieving schools increased (or decreased less) the ratio of supervisors to teachers in comparison to higher- achieving schools. There were no statistically significant differences across achievement groups for changes in the ratio of counselors to teachers.

Having examined how staff allocation and expenditures in various areas changed under accountability, it is natural to explore whether any of these changes were correlated with student achievement. In doing so, however, it is important to keep in mind the difficulty in drawing causal inferences given the fact that expenditures and budget allocations were not randomly assigned to schools before or after the introduction of the accountability policy. The following results should therefore be taken as suggestive evidence rather than definitive proof.

To investigate the correlation between resource allocation and achievement, table 6 compares the spending changes in schools that made larger than average gains over this period with the changes in schools that had smaller than average gains over this period.[29] Although the results shown in table 3 indicate that low-achieving schools did reduce spending in supplemental areas such as art and music by large percentages, table 6 suggests that there was no significant association between such expenditure changes and changes in student achievement. For example, bottom quartile schools that made large achievement gains decreased spending on art and music by roughly $26 per pupil compared

29. Note that large and small gains are defined across all schools in the sample. Since on average low-achieving schools made larger gains than high-achieving schools under accountability, there are more schools in the large gain category for the bottom two quartiles.

Table 6. Changes in Resource Allocation, by 1995–2000 Achievement Gains

	Schools in the bottom quartile of achievement in 1995		Schools in the second quartile of achievement in 1995	
	Small gains (N=36)	Large gains (N=77)	Small gains (N=61)	Large gains (N=53)
Art ($ per pupil)	–13.5	–9.6	–5.9	–0.1
Music ($ per pupil)	–9.8	–16.2	–9.5	–3.5
Foreign language ($ per pupil)	–7.7	–6.6	–5.4	–6.4
Library ($ per pupil)	–1.5	–0.8	–4.6	1.6
Instructional spending ($ per pupil)	–23.0	142.7	37.6	138.9
Budget fraction on instruction	0.042	0.040	0.045	0.053
Instructional staff: student ratio (x 500)	–3.27	–1.76	–2.72	–1.76
Ratio of aides to teachers	–0.045	–0.017	–0.012	–0.016
Ratio of supervisors to teachers	–0.001	0.004	0.000	0.000
Ratio of counselors to teachers	–0.021	–0.014	–0.011**	–0.026

Note: Expenditures in year 2000 dollars. Figures shown are absolute changes as opposed to percent changes. Tests of statistical significance refer to differences between small and large gain groups within 1995 quartile group.
**Significant at 5 percent level.

with a decrease of $23 per pupil in bottom quartile schools that made smaller achievement gains. (This may not be surprising given the small absolute magnitude of spending changes associated with art and music programs.) For instructional spending, it appears that schools that made above average gains increased instructional spending more than their peers that made lower than average gains, although these differences are not significant at conventional levels. Finally, the comparisons of staff allocations in the bottom three rows indicate that there may be some positive association between higher supervisor- or aide-to-teacher ratios and achievement in bottom quartile schools, although these differences again do not reach statistical significance.

Table 7 presents ordinary least squares estimates of the relationship between student achievement and expenditure patterns that consider the resource variables together and controls for a variety of observable characteristics that may confound the resource-achievement relationship. The unit of observation is the school x year. The dependent variable is the

Table 7. Estimates of the Relationship between Resource Allocation and Student Achievement[a]

	Dependent variable: ITBS math achievement (national percentile score)			
Independent variables	*All schools*	*Bottom quartile*	*Second quartile*	*Top half*
Total expenditures ($100 per pupil)	–0.022	–0.003	–0.055	–0.004
	(0.037)	(0.075)	(0.077)	(0.049)
Fraction spent on instruction	13.88	27.83	30.11	5.19
	(4.70)	(11.03)	(9.99)	(6.00)
Art, music, and foreign language	–0.264	–0.138	0.892	–0.627
spending ($100 per pupil)	(0.354)	(0.706)	(0.862)	(0.476)
Library spending ($100 per pupil)	0.519	0.129	0.936	0.773
	(0.461)	(0.902)	(0.858)	(0.560)
Ratio of supervisors to teachers	–2.35	49.34	1.19	–30.35
	(9.48)	(20.80)	(19.74)	(9.92)
Ratio of aides to teachers	–3.76	–4.53	–4.58	1.86
	(2.84)	(5.36)	(6.40)	(3.37)
Ratio of counselors to teachers	–9.83	–5.74	–18.52	–3.98
	(6.15)	(9.88)	(12.41)	(9.61)
Controls for demographics	Yes	Yes	Yes	Yes
Controls for prior-year achievement	Yes	Yes	Yes	Yes
School fixed effects	Yes	Yes	Yes	Yes
Number of observations	911	226	227	458
Adjusted R^2	0.95	0.82	0.83	0.95

Note: Weighted by school enrollment. Robust standard errors included in parentheses.
a. Ordinary least squares.

school average level on the ITBS mathematics exam as measured by a national percentile score. The results for math are presented since math performance is believed to be more responsive to school factors than reading performance.[30] The key independent variables are the expendi-

30. In the study, the pattern of results is comparable for reading (tables available from the author upon request). The claim that math achievement is more sensitive to educational interventions than reading achievement is based on several strands of research. One strand involves education production function studies, where researchers have found that fixed effects for classrooms or schools explain a greater proportion of variation for math outcomes than for reading outcomes. See Murnane (1975) for one of the first discussions of this finding and Rivkin and others (2001) for recent evidence from Texas. Other evidence comes from the fact that math scores on the National Assessment of Educational Progress (NAEP) have tended to increase more than reading scores since the early 1980s. NCES (2000, pp. ix–xviii). Finally, some evidence comes from the rigorous experimental or quasi-experimental evaluations of specific education interventions, many (though not all) of which find larger effects of the intervention on math than reading achievement. A recent example is an evaluation of special education programs. Hanushek and others (2002).

ture measures discussed above, including total per pupil expenditures, budget share devoted to instruction, per pupil expenditures on art, music, foreign language, and library programs, and the ratios of supervisors, aides, and counselors to teachers. All models include school fixed effects as well as controls for school demographics and last year's achievement score.[31] The combination of fixed school effects and a one-year lagged achievement control means that the coefficients on the expenditure variables reflect how changes in expenditures (from 1995 to 2000) are correlated with changes in school productivity, where productivity is measured by one-year achievement gains.[32] The inclusion of school fixed effects and time-varying demographic and achievement covariates is intended to account for unobservable characteristics that may be correlated with expenditure patterns and student achievement.

Column 1 shows the results for all schools. Both total expenditures and the fraction spent on instruction are positively related to student achievement, although the magnitude of the effects is quite small. For example, these estimates suggest that a one-standard-deviation increase in per pupil expenditures or the share of the budget devoted to instructional purposes both only lead to a slightly less than 1 percentile point increase in mathematics achievement. Spending on art, music, foreign language, and library programs is not related to student achievement. The ratio of counselors to teachers appears to be negatively related to student achievement, although the estimate is only significant at the 10 percent level.

In the previous analyses, we saw that low-achieving schools responded to the accountability policy differently than other schools. Moreover, we might believe that the different student populations in low-achieving schools respond differently to resources or school organization. Hence, columns 2 to 4 present results separately for schools with different initial achievement levels. The first two rows show that the results for total expenditures and instructional budget share remain roughly the same. Spending on noncore areas still has no significant impact on student achievement.

31. Demographic control variables include percent black, percent Hispanic, percent limited English proficient (LEP), percent free/reduced price lunch, percent in special education programs, mobility rate, and binary indicators for small (enrollment < 400) and large (enrollment > 800) schools.

32. This may be thought of as a difference-in-difference estimate: $(Y_{2000} - Y_{1999}) - (Y_{1995} - Y_{1994})$.

The most interesting results concern the effects of staff allocation. In bottom-quartile schools, the ratio of supervisors to teachers has a positive effect on student achievement. According to the coefficient estimates, a one-standard-deviation increase in the ratio of supervisors to teachers results in a 1.09 percentile point increase in average math achievement.[33] Interestingly, this effect does not exist in second-quartile schools and appears to reverse in higher-achieving schools. That is, in schools among the top half of the achievement distribution in Chicago, increases in the ratio of supervisors to teachers is associated with slight decreases in student achievement. The ratio of aides to teachers continues to have no significant effect on achievement. Finally, we see that the negative relationship between counselors and achievement came from second-quartile schools.

The finding that the ratio of supervisors to teachers may have an impact on student achievement is intriguing although, as we just saw, the effect is small given that the ratio itself is very small. In low-achieving schools, this relationship seems positive—more supervisors are related to higher achievement. This might be because of the importance of monitoring and coaching for teachers in these schools, a disproportionate share of whom tend to be less experienced. However, supervisors appear to have a slight negative effect on achievement in higher-achieving schools. This might be because the teachers in these schools are more experienced or have greater skills and do not benefit from such supervision, so that additional administrators simply take money away from other valuable areas.

Discussion

The preceding results suggest schools made few major changes in resource allocation or school organization under accountability. Although financial resources for supplemental programs such as Lighthouse and Summer Bridge increased dramatically, little if any comparable increases occurred in resources for regular, school-time programs. There is evidence that low-achieving schools shifted resources away from nontested areas such as art and music. The relative (percent) shifts

---

33. This is based on the standard deviation of the ratio for bottom quartile schools in 1995, which is roughly 0.022.

in these areas were substantial, although the absolute magnitude of such resource reallocation was small and does not seem to be correlated to changes in student achievement. The slight increase in instructional spending under the accountability policy appears to have been because of increases in salaries rather than a reallocation of funds to support additional positions. There were only slight changes in staff reallocation— schools employed slightly fewer aides and supervisors relative to teachers following the introduction of the accountability policy. Interestingly, the schools most likely to be impacted by the accountability policy— schools in the bottom quartile of the achievement distribution in 1995— exhibited the largest declines in aides relative to teachers and the smallest declines in supervisors relative to teachers, compared with higher-achieving schools.

There are three possible explanations for the fact that the expenditure patterns and staff allocation seemed to change so little in Chicago elementary schools over this period. The first is a lack of discretion. This may be related to the "stickiness" in budget allocations. If, for example, a school employs a certain proportion of teachers to aides, it may be socially or politically difficult for a principal to release several aides in order to hire an additional teacher. A related explanation involves the "lumpiness" of expenditures. Schools that receive a relatively small amount of categorical funding may find it more difficult to change spending patterns because hiring an additional teacher, for example, would constitute a large share of the total available resources. It is possible that because of the small degree of discretionary funding, combined with the stickiness and lumpiness of expenditures described above, principals have little flexibility to institute needed or desired changes. The second is a lack of imagination. It is theoretically possible for principals to use much of the roughly $500,000 in categorical funds each year to hire college students to provide one-on-one tutoring for at-risk children. Even at $15 an hour, this would be sufficient to provide nearly six hours a week of individual attention for 25 percent of students in the school. Yet it is hard to imagine a school ever embarking on such a nontraditional path. The third explanation is that educators have sufficient discretion and imagination to implement change but believe that the necessary changes involve curricular and pedagogical decisions at the classroom level, or other reforms that may not show up in this type of aggregate expenditure analysis.

Conclusions

This paper examines recent reforms in the Chicago Public Schools in an effort to learn more about the mechanisms underlying test-based accountability policies. An economic framework of educational production suggests that increases in student achievement may be driven by changes in educational inputs (for example, student effort, financial resources) or changes in the technology of schooling (for example, instructional practices, school organization). Evidence from surveys and interviews suggests that the Chicago policy led to a substantial increase in certain educational inputs—namely, student effort, teacher and parent support, and supplemental after-school and summer programs for at-risk students—but did not substantially change the educational technology in schools, as measured by instructional practices and school organization. An examination of budget data from Chicago elementary schools confirms this finding, providing little evidence of substantial changes in resource allocation or school organization under accountability.

Of course, it is important not to underestimate the value of the educational inputs that were enhanced during this period in Chicago. The greater levels of student effort, teacher support, and parental involvement have undoubtedly improved the academic lives of many students, and there is evidence that the summer and after-school programs instituted in Chicago have had some positive impact on student learning. However, insofar as classroom instruction and school organization are critical components of student learning that fall short in many districts, these findings highlight an important limitation of test-based accountability.

The Chicago experience provides an important lesson for those now struggling to implement NCLB. It appears to be much easier to change inputs than technology. Insofar as increasing certain inputs and emphasizing test preparation is the most efficient way to raise standardized test scores, we should not be surprised that test-based accountability fosters these changes alone. If policymakers want teachers and administrators to make fundamental changes in the operation of schools, they must provide explicit incentives (and sufficient resources) to this end.

Comments

Paul N. Courant: This paper is an example of valuable work in which the results are generally negative, a genre that is vital to any scientific discipline and too often underrewarded.

Finding, as Brian A. Jacob does in earlier work cited in his paper, that the institution of accountability for test scores in the Chicago public schools led to marked improvement in performance on the math portion of the Iowa Test of Basic Skills leads him to ask a really interesting question: how was this improvement in outcomes produced? Having found a clear link between increasing the stakes associated with measurable outcomes and the attainment of those outcomes, Jacob seeks to exploit the natural experiment to uncover the production function for elementary education in an urban school district. As anyone who has looked at the literature on inputs and outputs in schools knows, this is an enormously ambitious project, and it is not surprising that even a good natural experiment conducted in a data-rich environment still leaves us uncertain about the nature of the production function(s) in schools.

Unfortunately, the only measures of technology available for this study are expenditure categories in school budgets. Thus the investigation seeks to find relationships between increases or decreases in ratios of supervisory to instructional personnel (for example) and improvements in scores on standardized tests. In Jacob's paper, these kinds of changes in input mix are interpreted as changes in the technology of production, rather than as mere changes in input levels. I am not so sure, although in any case finding reliable effects between categories of expenditure and measurable outcomes would be of great value for our understanding in general and for policy.

The discussion of equation 1 early in the paper seems to me to make too much and too little of the difference between changes in input levels and changes in technology. I think that Jacob makes too much of the difference because I would argue that all of the measures that he uses are really input measures. The data in the empirical work are expenditure data on various categories of expenditures in the schools; when we see the expenditures on supervisors increase a little and expenditures on aides decrease a little, I think we are looking at changes in inputs. Jacob wants to distinguish between the mix of expenditures and another kind of input, namely, how hard people work. He cites a paper by Robin Tepper, Susan Stone, and Melissa Roderick (hereafter TSR) that shows that students and teachers worked harder—put in more hours at school and at home in response to high-stakes testing—and also focused their work on improving scores on the high-stakes test.[34] This kind of input change is importantly different from expenditures on supervisors, aides, math teachers, and art teachers, but both kinds of change could be subsumed easily into a more general production function, one that depended on a set of inputs measured by quality-indexed time spent by relevant types of labor (including students and parents), as well as equipment, capital, and the usual set of things that go into production functions.

Jacob may have made too little of the distinction between inputs and technology in that he does not make any use of the formal structure of production functions to illuminate the distinction. Writing down a production function that allows for distinctions among types of inputs, and using the production function to provide at least an analytic typology, if not a full-blown theoretical model, could help us to interpret the analysis of the data. There might well be a stable technology (not that any economist seems to know it, but perhaps good school administrators are able to act as if they know it) according to which the behavior of supervisors, aides, math teachers, and music and art teachers in a given building is translated into measurable outputs. High-stakes testing would change the objective function (bigger weight on Iowa Test of Basic Skills scores, smaller weight on the quality of artwork in the halls, hence changes in

34. Tepper, Stone, and Roderick (forthcoming).

the measurement of marginal value products, hence changes in the optimal input mix.

The motivation of teachers, students, and parents might shift the parameters of such a production function. Writing down a general production function could allow us to see some relationship between the econometric exercise in this paper and the less formal measures that TSR used to find increases in effort and engagement by teachers, students, and parents. If the important mechanisms that cause high-stakes testing to work are found in behaviors of teachers, parents, and students that seem unrelated to conventional economic input measures, then we should be exploring the mechanisms, whether psychological, social, or economic, that cause those mechanisms to operate. In other words, I agree with Jacob that there is something different about the "softer" motivational changes examined by TSR and changes in the expenditure mix, but I am not sure how best to think about the difference. A richer theoretical discussion could aid in the exploration.

Besides changes of the kind discussed by TSR and the changes in expenditures that Jacob examines, we are told in the paper of two programs—an afternoon program called the Lighthouse program and the Summer Bridge program for students who were doing poorly—that were instituted at approximately the same time as high-stakes testing. These programs might be interpreted as changes in the educational technology being applied in the Chicago Public Schools, and they might interact with the more conventional school-specific technologies that are proxied by expenditure data. This paper is certainly incomplete without a formal evaluation of the effects of Lighthouse and Summer Bridge on test scores.

Toward the end of the paper, Jacob provides three reasons why the allocation of expenditure categories did not change as much as they might have in response to high-stakes testing, tracing the lack of response to a combination of failures of imagination and lack of flexibility by school administrators. Suppose instead that the school administrators had already run Jacob's regressions and found that the effects of changes in the expenditure mix were generally weak. That in itself would be good reason for them not to have changed the mix very much.

What I find most striking in this paper are the results from Jacob's earlier work that high-stakes testing affected test scores markedly—and the results from TSR—basically that everyone worked harder and became more engaged. These two sets of results suggest that high-stakes testing matters and that it affects resource allocation. The results in this paper suggest that at least in the relatively short term, the important changes in resource allocation are not well captured by the expenditure categories under the control of individual school buildings. This negative result is still a useful and valuable one. This was exactly the right next paper to write given the earlier results that Jacob cites. The next interesting step would be to marry the TSR results with the analysis of expenditure categories to see where changes in expenditure and changes in engagement by the relevant actors have the strongest synergy.

Jens Ludwig: Why do so many of our urban public schools perform so poorly? Accountability reforms implicitly assume that the problem stems in part from a divergence between the public's priorities and those held by some or all participants in the public school enterprise. A very different view focuses on more structural problems relating to, for example, the extra costs and other challenges associated with educating disadvantaged students. Sorting out the relative importance of each perspective is crucially important for efforts to improve urban public schools, which in turn carries important implications for the long-term health of cities.

The interesting paper in this volume is part of an important series of studies by Brian A. Jacob and his colleagues about accountability reform in Chicago and helps shed light on the problems and potential remedies for big-city school systems. In an earlier study, Jacob demonstrates—convincingly, in my view—that Chicago's reform contributed to substantial improvements on the Iowa Tests of Basic Skills reading and math tests that were used as part of the new accountability system but did not result in student gains on the state's Illinois Goals Assessment Program standardized tests.[35] Given the divergent test-score trends, one lingering—and crucial—question is whether the changes in ITBS results reflect real improvements in student learning.

Jacob's review of other Chicago studies, together with his original analysis of uniquely detailed school-budget data, suggests a series of changes that are at least consistent with real improvements in student learning. In Jacob's view, stated here, his research "suggests that the improvements in Chicago were driven by changes in nonfinancial inputs

35. Jacob (2002).

such as student effort, parental involvement, and shifts in content empha-sis within subject, rather than fundamental changes in the technology of schooling as measured by things such as instructional techniques, profes-sional development, or the allocation of resources within schools. . . . These findings suggest that accountability regimes . . . may not be suffi-cient to change the way in which education is delivered in most schools." Jacob's results do not strike me as necessarily inconsistent with school responses that "change the way in which education is delivered." Taken together these findings seem like good news (or at least not bad news) for those who care about improving our nation's most challenged schools, even if important questions about accountability reforms remain.

Accountability in Chicago

Urban public school systems may perform poorly for many reasons, including lack of effort by students and their parents; lack of effort by school personnel; misdirected effort by school personnel; lack of talent or skills on the part of school personnel; or funding and other externally imposed constraints. Education reforms may improve measured student outcomes by addressing one of these fundamental problems or by induc-ing more cheating by teachers. Brian A. Jacob's work with Steve Levitt suggests that teachers' cheating increased as a result of the reform but cannot explain away the entire observed gain in test scores.[36]

Additional funding also does not seem to account for the outcomes of Chicago's accountability reform. Jacob's table 2 shows that core spend-ing in public elementary schools is essentially flat over this period. Although spending on supplemental academic supports increased, that appears to have had at best modest effects on student outcomes.[37] Chicago's experience suggests that accountability reform can improve measured student outcomes even without an influx of major additional resources. If the changes in ITBS scores do in fact reflect real student learning, then this is good news. Even if accountability reform would be even more effective with more spending, in a resource-constrained world it is useful to have revenue-neutral policy levers at our disposal.

What does seem to have changed substantially in Chicago is the effort that students and parents devote to schooling. As economist John Bishop

36. Jacob and Levitt (forthcoming); and in this volume.
37. Jacob and Lefgren (forthcoming a, b).

argues, many students have little incentive to try very hard in school given that most colleges have unselective admissions processes and that employers typically pay little attention to students' high school records. In response, Bishop suggests that schools should provide their own extrinsic incentives to students to motivate academic effort.[38] Although the jury is still out about the long-term effects of Chicago's reforms on outcomes such as dropout rates, the initial evidence on test score patterns and student and parental effort seems encouraging. And while improvements in student effort do not prove that increased ITBS scores reflect student learning, evidence of harder-working students does not argue against this possibility.

School Responses

Jacob's analysis of Chicago Public Schools budget data, together with previous studies, suggests that lack of or misdirected effort by schools also played some role in the city's problems, and that the accountability reform at least partially addresses this issue.

Chicago's accountability system in some ways induced exactly the response that was intended: teachers in the public schools seem to have devoted more time to covering concepts measured by the accountability system's tests (such as more time on advanced rather than remedial math concepts). Principals also seem to have allocated a bit less money to art, music, and foreign language instruction, and allotted more money to libraries. While some people will be concerned about these shifts in priorities, they are perfectly consistent with the public's priorities as expressed through the accountability reform. As many observers have argued, "teaching to the test" and otherwise reorienting curricula toward what is covered by accountability assessments is not undesirable if these assessments comprehensively and accurately capture what voters and their political representatives think should be learned in school. If Chicago voters believe that the skills captured by the ITBS tests (more advanced math concepts) are more important than those measured by the statewide IGAP tests (less advanced concepts), then changes that improve ITBS but not IGAP scores will be deemed a success by local residents.

---

38. Bishop (1999); Bishop and Mane (2001).

Another way that schools responded to Chicago's accountability reform is by increasing the budget share devoted to instructional spending. The schools seem to have done this by laying off teachers' aides and counselors and devoting the savings (and more) to raising teachers' salaries. The best available evidence suggests that higher salaries for teachers have at least a modest impact on the ability of public schools to attract and retain teachers and improve student outcomes.[39] In contrast, teachers' aides seem to have little or no effect on student outcomes.[40] The direct effect of these budget reallocations on test scores seems fairly modest, at least in the short term. Some back-of-the-envelope calculations that combine the observed changes in spending patterns across Chicago's schools (Jacob's tables 2 through 5) with the implied effects of these changes (table 7) suggest that budget reallocations may explain something on the order of one-tenth of the increases in test scores in Chicago following the accountability reform. Even if the size of this resource shift and the resulting changes in student outcomes are modest, replacing aides with higher salaries for teachers seems like a step in the right direction.

More interesting is whether the budget reallocations signal more fundamental changes in the way that schools do business. These staff reallocations represent an efficiency-enhancing shift by principals, which may or may not be accompanied by other efficiency-enhancing changes in the ways that schools and teachers operate. Measuring changes in educational technology would require detailed observational data on classroom and school practices and cannot be detected by the budget data analyzed here. But there is nothing in the budget data that rules such changes out.

Lessons

Accountability reforms are intended at least in part to realign the incentives facing students, teachers, and principals with the priorities outlined by the public. Chicago's accountability reform shows signs of having accomplished that goal. Scores increased on the ITBS tests that the reform used to measure student learning. Whether the flat trend in the state-sponsored IGAP tests during this period is a cause for concern

39. Hanushek, Kain, and Rivkin (1999, 2001); Loeb and Page (2000).
40. Krueger (1999).

depends in part on the quality of these tests, what these tests capture, and what Chicago-area voters value.

Everyone involved with the public schools seems to have responded at least to some degree in a way that is consistent with real improvements in student learning. Students, parents, and teachers seem to be more engaged with the schooling process, teachers seem to have shifted their attention toward the skills that are emphasized by the accountability system, and principals have shifted resources toward core instructional spending. These changes may come at some cost to other skills or subject areas that are now de-emphasized, but whatever one's own feelings about these trade-offs, they seem consistent with what the public has asked for. Whether there have also been more fundamental changes in the way that teachers teach is not clear, but that cannot be ruled out.

Proponents of accountability reform—and anyone who cares about improving the educational outcomes of low-income urban students—should on the whole probably be heartened by these findings. We would like to learn more about what happened in classrooms in Chicago following the accountability policy, which might shed light on why scores improved on the city's but not the state's testing system. But even if such reforms are not, as Jacob notes, a magic cure for all of a school system's ailments, policymakers have had such limited success in improving big-city schools that we should welcome anything that provides even hints of some leverage over the problem.

References

Bishop, John H. 1999. "Nerd Harassment, Incentives, School Priorities and Learning." In *Earning and Learning: How Schools Matter*, edited by Susan Mayer and Paul Peterson, 231–80. Brookings.

Bishop, John H., and Ferran Mane. 2001. "The Impacts of Minimum Competency Exam Graduation Requirements on High School Graduation, College Attendance and Early Labor Market Success." *Labour Economics* 8 (2): 203–22.

Bryk, Anthony. 2002. "No Child Left Behind: Chicago Style. What Has Really Been Accomplished?" Paper presented at Harvard University, Kennedy School of Government, Program on Educational Policy and Governance (June).

Bryk, Anthony, Penny B. Sebring, David Kerbow, Sharon Rollow, and John Q. Easton. 1998. *Charting Chicago School Reform: Democratic Localism as a Lever for Change*. Westview Press.

Elmore, Richard F. 2002. "Unwarranted Intrusion." *Education Next* (Spring): 31–35.

Finnigan, Kara, Jennifer O'Day, and David Wakelyn. 2001. "Buddy, Can You Lend Us a Hand? The Provision of External Assistance to Chicago Elementary Schools on Probation." Unpublished report. University of Wisconsin-Madison, Department of Education.

Hanushek, Eric A., John F. Kain, and Steven G. Rivkin. 1999. "Do Higher Salaries Buy Better Teachers?" Working Paper 7082. Cambridge, Mass.: National Bureau of Economic Research.

———. 2001. "Why Public Schools Lose Teachers." Working Paper 8599. Cambridge, Mass.: National Bureau of Economic Research.

———. 2002. "Inferring Program Effects for Specialized Populations: Does Special Education Raise Achievement for Students with Disabilities?" *Review of Economics and Statistics* 84 (November): 584–99.

Hess, Alfred. 1991. *School Restructuring, Chicago Style*. Corwin Press.

———. 1995. *Restructuring Urban Schools: A Chicago Perspective*. Teachers College Press.

Jacob, Brian A. 2002. "Accountability, Incentives and Behavior: The Impact of High-Stakes Testing in the Chicago Public Schools." Working Paper 8968. Cambridge, Mass.: National Bureau of Economic Research.

Jacob, Brian A., and Lars Lefgren. Forthcoming a. "The Impact of Teacher Training on Student Achievement: Quasi-Experimental Evidence from Reform Efforts in Chicago." *Journal of Human Resources*.

———. Forthcoming b. "Remedial Education and Student Achievement: A Regression-Discontinuity Analysis." *Review of Economics and Statistics*.

Jacob, Brian A., and Steven D. Levitt. Forthcoming. "Rotten Apples: An Investigation of the Prevalence and Predictors of Teacher Cheating." *Quarterly Journal of Economics*.

Klein, Stephen, Laura Hamilton, Daniel McCaffrey, and Brian Stecher. 2000. "What Do Test Scores in Texas Tell Us?" Issue Paper 202. Santa Monica, Calif.: Rand Corporation.

Koretz, Danieal M., and Sheila I. Barron. 1998. "The Validity of Gains on the Kentucky Instructional Results Information System (KIRIS)." Santa Monica: Calif.: Rand Corporation.

Krueger, Alan B. 1999. "Experimental Estimates of Education Production Functions." *Quarterly Journal of Economics* 114 (2): 497–532.

Loeb, Susanna, and Marianne E. Page. 2000. "Examining the Link between Teacher Wages and Student Outcomes: The Importance of Alternative Labor Market Opportunities and Non-Pecuniary Variation." *Review of Economics and Statistics*: 393–408.

Murnane, Richard J. 1975. *The Impact of School Resources on the Learning of Inner City Children.* Ballinger.

National Center for Trends in Educational Statistics (NCES). 2000. *Trends in Academic Progress: Three Decades of Student Performance.* NCES 2000-469. Office of Research and Improvement, U.S. Department of Education.

Rivkin, Steven G., Eric A. Hanushek, and John F. Kain. 2001 (revised). "Teachers, Schools, and Academic Achievement." Working Paper 6691. Cambridge, Mass.: National Bureau of Economic Research.

Roderick, Melissa, and Mimi Engel. 2001. "The Grasshopper and the Ant: Motivational Responses of Low-Achieving Students to High-Stakes Testing." *Educational Evaluation and Policy Analysis* 23 (3): 197–227.

Roderick, Melissa, Brian A. Jacob, and Anthony Bryk. Forthcoming. "Summer in the City: Achievement Gains in Chicago's Summer Bridge Program." In *Summer Learning: Research, Policies and Programs*, edited by Geoffrey Borman and Matthew Boulay. Erlbaum.

Roderick, Melissa, Anthony S. Bryk, Brian A. Jacob, John Q. Easton, and Elaine Allensworth. 1999. "Ending Social Promotion: Results from the First Two Years." Research Report, Consortium on Chicago School Research.

Roderick, Melissa, Brian A. Jacob, and Anthony Bryk. Forthcoming. "The Impact of High-Stakes Testing in Chicago on Student Achievement in the Promotional Gate Grades." *Educational Evaluation and Policy Analysis.*

Rosenkranz, Todd. 1994. "Reallocating Resources: Discretionary Funds Provide Engine for Change." *Education and Urban Society* 26 (3): 264–84.

Rotherman, Andrew. 2002. "A New Partnership." *Education Next* (Spring): 37–41.

Smylie, Mark A., Elaine Allensworth, Rebecca Greenberg, Rodney Harris, and Stuart Luppescu. 2001. "Teacher Professional Development in Chicago: Supporting Effective Practice." Research Report, Consortium on Chicago School Research.

Tepper, Robin. 2001. "The Influence of High-Stakes Testing on Teacher Behavior and Instructional Practice in Chicago." Unpublished manuscript. University of Chicago.

Tepper, Robin, Susan Stone, and Melissa Roderick. Forthcoming. "Ending Social Promotion: The Response of Teachers and Students." Research Report. Consortium on Chicago School Research.

Thompson, Kenneth R. 1999. "A Conversation with Paul Vallas: Successful Leadership in the Chicago Public Schools." *Journal of Leadership Studies* (June 22):148.

Tyack, David, and Cuban, Larry. 1995. *Tinkering toward Utopia: A Century of Public School Reform.* Harvard University Press.

THOMAS J. KANE

DOUGLAS O. STAIGER

GAVIN SAMMS

School Accountability Ratings and Housing Values

DURING THE PAST DECADE, states have constructed elaborate systems for rating the performance of individual schools based on student test scores and then have released this information in the form of school "report cards." The federal No Child Left Behind Act of 2001 will accelerate that movement by requiring states to test all students in grades three through eight, publicly report each school's student test performance, and sanction schools when they fail to achieve specific standards. Earlier research has documented the cross-sectional relationship between housing values and student test scores at neighborhood schools.[1] Given the magnitude of the relationship between test scores and housing prices in the cross section, one might expect the release of school report cards to have important effects on housing values and, indirectly, to provide incentives for schools to improve performance. However, there are also reasons to believe that the housing market would downplay the information in school report cards. In particular, school test scores are noisy measures of school performance and may provide homeowners with little new information about which schools are the best ones.[2]

Kane and Staiger acknowledge the generous support of the Andrew W. Mellon Foundation. Jacqueline McNeil at the Charlotte-Mecklenburg School district and Gary Williamson at the North Carolina Department of Public Instruction provided data and graciously answered many questions. The authors are also indebted to the discussants, conference organizers, and conference participants for many helpful suggestions.

1. Black (1999); Bogart and Cromwell (1997); Weimer and Wolkoff (2001); P. L. 107-110.
2. Kane and Staiger (2002a, 2002b, 2002c).

In this paper, we explore how school test scores, changes in school test scores, and categorical ratings are related to housing values. To control for any correlation between scores and neighborhood amenities, we use the approach of Sandra E. Black and focus on homes near elementary school attendance boundaries.[3] The geographical detail in our data allow us to precisely determine the location of each home being sold and every school and school boundary and to focus our analysis on homes within a few thousand feet (or less) of school boundaries. Thus our empirical strategy is to compare sales prices for homes located in the same neighborhood and taxing municipality but that are assigned to different elementary schools. We control for a range of detailed observable characteristics of the house such as distance to school, lot and home size, and middle and high school assignments.

Our empirical analysis uses data from the housing market in Mecklenburg County, North Carolina, where various indicators of school quality were released by the state between 1993 and 2001 and reported each fall in the local paper. Between 1993 and 1996, average test scores were reported by grade level for the school overall and two racial categories (African Americans and whites/others). Beginning in August 1997, the state began explicitly placing schools in performance categories (ranging from "low performing" to "schools of excellence"), using a combination of the proportion of students that achieved proficiency on the test and a value-added measure (based on average improvement in each student's score from the prior year). With these data, we are able to explore how housing values are related to the variation in performance across schools, the year-to-year variation in performance for a given school, and the change to categorical performance measures in 1997.

We begin by estimating the relationship between long-run measures of school test performance (scores averaged over many years) and housing values using the regression discontinuity design proposed by Black— comparing sales prices of homes near elementary school boundaries. We find a significant positive relationship between test performance and housing values, somewhat larger than that found by Black, and which is robust across a variety of specifications.[4] Our estimates suggest that a one student-level standard deviation difference in mean school test score is associated with an 18 to 25 percentage point difference in house value,

3. Black (1999).
4. Black (1999).

controlling for neighborhood amenities and housing characteristics. A student-level standard deviation in test scores is quite large relative to the between-school differences. The implied impact of a school-level standard deviation is smaller, approximately 4 to 5 percentage points. Nevertheless, if year-to-year changes in school performance had effects of this magnitude, we would expect large swings in property values over time.

However, as just noted, there are reasons to believe that housing values may not respond strongly to the annual information that is released in school report cards. In previous work, we have highlighted the importance of year-to-year fluctuations in test performance, owing to sampling variation and other one-time factors affecting school test scores.[5] If the housing market were unaware of the importance of sampling variation and focused too heavily on annual announcements of test performance, there would be considerable regression to the mean in housing prices following short-term fluctuations in test scores up or down. Our results suggest that the market heavily discounts short-term fluctuations in school performance, focusing instead on long-term mean differences in school performance. We see no evidence of volatility in housing prices to match the annual volatility in test scores.

We further evaluate the housing market's response to the categorical rating of school performance created by school accountability systems, to see if this new source of information had a more pronounced impact on housing values. David Figlio found some evidence that public reporting of school "report cards" (giving schools grades of A–F based on test performance) had an impact on house values in Florida.[6] Using data from before and after the introduction of report cards in 1999, Figlio concluded that the assigned letter grades had large impacts on house values (approximately 10 percent for each full grade increment) in the months immediately following their release. In 1997, North Carolina labeled thirteen of the sixty-one public elementary schools in our sample as "low performing" based on the proportion of their students failing to achieve level III proficiency in the end-of-grade exams. In contrast to Figlio, we see no evidence that housing prices declined in response to the categorical rating from the state, probably because these schools had been low-performing schools for some time and were known to home buyers even without the state labels. Moreover, other categories that reflected the

5. Kane and Staiger (2002a, 2002c).
6. Figlio (2002).

schools' mean "value added" (controlling for baseline student test scores) also had no apparent impact on housing prices. Either home buyers were uninterested in value-added differences (and primarily focused on mean performance in evaluating schools), or they did not rely on any designation based on a single year's worth of value-added measures. Such caution may be justified. Consistent with the findings in Thomas J. Kane and Douglas O. Staiger, schools often cycled in and out of these value-added categories between 1997 and 2001: an average of 37 percent of the elementary schools rated in the highest value-added category one year appeared in the lowest value-added category the following year.[7]

Finally, we provide some evidence that school test scores in Charlotte are correlated with differences in measured housing characteristics, even when one focuses on houses near boundaries. This finding raises some concern over the extent to which school test scores may also be correlated with neighborhood quality differences for which we cannot control. Indeed, even if neighborhoods were similar on either side of school boundaries when the boundaries were originally drawn, it would be surprising if the two sides of the boundary did not evolve differently, as high-quality schools lead to higher housing prices and attract home buyers with different preferences. The concern primarily affects the interpretation of the coefficient on long-term test scores. Our main findings about the effects of the short-term test score fluctuations and the impact of school ratings by the state would be unaffected by such unobserved differences in neighborhood quality, since such effects are identified with changes over time.

The Charlotte-Mecklenburg Housing and Test Score Data

The following paragraphs briefly describe our data and empirical strategy, before we discuss the results of our analysis.

Housing Data

We began with data on 304,000 real estate parcels in Mecklenburg County, North Carolina (population 640,000), including commercial properties, apartments, and condo units as well as single-family homes. Of

7. Kane and Staiger (2002a, 2002c).

Figure 1. Trends in Real Sales Price at Various Percentiles

Real sales price
(thousands of 2001 dollars)

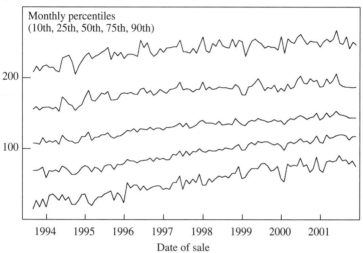

these, only 192,000 were single-family homes (including some vacant lots zoned for single-family use). We further limited the sample in two ways. First, we focused on the 138,000 parcels in the county with stable elementary school assignments between 1993 and 2001. This restriction eliminates parcels that experienced large changes in their school test scores because of changes in school assignment and allows us to focus on whether new test score information for a given school affects property values. Second, we focused on nonvacant parcels that were sold between 1993 and 2001 (for more than $14,000 and less than $674,000, roughly the first and ninety-ninth percentile in 2001 dollars). For each of these parcels, we were able to observe up to five sales.[8] After imposing these sample restrictions, we were left with a sample of 86,865 sales for 67,066 parcels.

In figure 1 we plot trends in the tenth through ninetieth percentile of the real home sales prices (2001 dollars) for each month in our data. Median real home values have risen about 3.6 percent per year in Meck-

8. Since less than 1 percent of the sample had a fifth sale after September 1993, very few transactions were truncated by the limit of five per property, and we have sales price data for virtually all single family sales transactions occurring between September 1993 and December 2001.

lenburg County. This growth has been somewhat faster for low-priced homes (5.7 percent per year at the tenth percentile) than for high-priced homes (3.1 percent per year at the ninetieth percentile). Additional descriptive statistics for this sample on sales price and housing character-istics are given in appendix table 1.

The Charlotte-Mecklenburg School District (CMS) provided us with detailed school boundary information beginning in the fall of 1993 through the fall of 2001. Not all districts maintain such sophisticated geographical data. However, during the period we are studying, the dis-trict was under court order to maintain African American representation in each school within a target range. As a result, it carefully weighed the implications of changes in school boundaries, by precisely locating school boundaries and combining those boundaries with demographic information on different neighborhoods.

Many of the school boundaries are irregularly shaped, reflecting the requirements of the court order to achieve a racial mix of students in the schools, To the extent that school assignment areas did not simply coin-cide with existing neighborhood boundaries, but crossed neighborhood boundaries, such irregularities will help us to separately identify the effects of school quality from other neighborhood amenities.

Because we were able to place each parcel in relation to the school boundaries, we calculated the distance of each parcel to the closest sin-gle-family parcel with a different school assignment. Parcels were cate-gorized by the closest boundary. For the parcels with stable school assignments between 1993 and 2001, there were sixty-one different ele-mentary schools and 143 distinct boundaries with each boundary identi-fied by a unique school pair. Owing to mandatory busing in Charlotte during the period we are studying, some school assignment areas were noncontiguous—that is, a given school may have school assignment areas in different parts of the city. In other words, a "boundary" between a pair of schools could be noncontinuous and located in different neigh-borhoods. Accordingly, we experimented with several other geographic controls—essentially allowing for different fixed effects on different sec-tions of a school boundary.

Figure 2 summarizes the geographic dimensions of the data. In the top left corner, we plot the coordinates of all the parcels in Mecklenburg County—commercial and residential—by their distance in feet from the southern and western edges of the county. In the top right corner, we plot

Figure 2. Geographic Dimensions

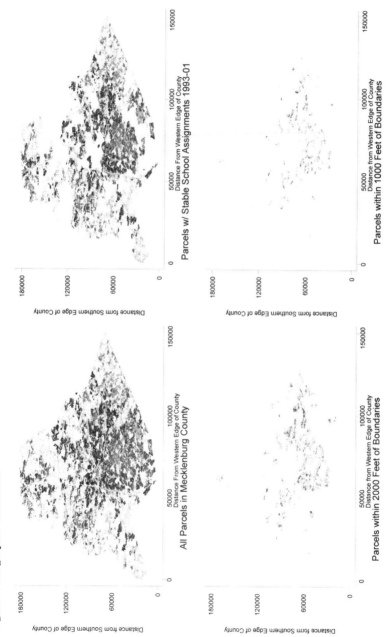

the locations of single-family homes that sold at some point between September 1993 and December 2001, which were located in areas with consistent school assignments from 1993 through 2001. The blank areas in the graph identify commercial districts as well as parts of the city where school assignment zones were redrawn at some point between 1993 and 2001. The bottom left figure plots the locations of all parcels that were located within 2,000 feet of the closest school boundary. Given the smaller lot sizes, a disproportionate share of the parcels close to boundaries was drawn from the central part of the county. In the bottom right, we plot the locations of all of the parcels within 1,000 feet of a school boundary. These parcels were disproportionately drawn from the central city for the same reason. However, it is also apparent from figure 2 that the effect of school assignments will be evaluated for properties in very close proximity to one another and that there are a large number of boundaries to exploit.

Test Score Data

Each July, between 1993 and 1996, the Charlotte-Mecklenburg school district identified schools that had achieved certain targets for improved test scores. In the fall (usually in October), the *Charlotte Observer* published mean test scores for schools in the district. The scores were reported by grade level for the school overall and by two racial categories (African Americans and whites/others). The reports included information on the percentage of students in each racial group and other student characteristics, such as the proportion of students on free or reduced price lunch and the proportion of students with both parents living at home. Although the reports did not include any direct measure of value-added differences among schools, home buyers could do their own "regression adjustment," adjusting test performance for the demographic composition of each school. Beginning in August 1997, the state began explicitly rating schools, using a combination of performance levels and value-added measures. Schools that achieved "expected" or "exemplary" scores on the state's growth composite—a value-added measure of the mean growth in individual students' performance from the end of one grade to the next—were singled out. In fact, teachers in schools with "expected" or "exemplary" value-added scores received bonuses from the state. Among those failing to achieve "expected" value added, schools were labeled "low performing" if fewer than half their students reached a specific level of proficiency in end- of-grade tests. Schools with very high levels of performance were identified as "schools of distinction" or "schools of excellence."

Our sample of parcels with stable assignments was assigned to one of sixty-one different elementary schools in the Charlotte-Mecklenburg school system. During our sample time period, all of the schools were kindergarten through grade five with students in grades three through five being tested. In 1999, the proportion of students in each of these schools achieving level III and above on the state's end-of-grade tests ranged from 39 percent at the lowest-performing schools to 95 percent in the highest-performing. The mean math score was .39 student-level standard deviations below the state mean for the lowest-performing school and was .70 student-level standard deviations above the state mean for the highest-performing school. The percentage of tested students in each school who were African American ranged from 1 percent to 94 percent. However, because of court-ordered busing, school boundaries were drawn so that most students attended schools in which between 33 and 54 percent of students tested were African American. (See appendix table 1 at the end of this chapter for more details on how these variables varied across our sample.)

The school district operates a number of magnet schools, which allow students to attend schools outside their attendance area. Such options may lead us to understate somewhat the housing market value of school quality. Four of the top ten elementary schools ranked by mean test performance in 2000 were magnet schools. (Magnet programs did not have assignment boundaries and are not included in our analysis.) However, entrance into the remaining six schools in the top ten was determined solely by residence. Moreover, the most desirable magnet programs were oversubscribed and subject to lotteries.

Before the state began providing categorical ratings for schools, test scores were generally released in the fall following each spring's test administration.[9] After the introduction of categorical ratings by the state

---

9. The *Charlotte Observer* reported lists of schools that had achieved targeted improvements in performance on August 26, 1993; July 14, 1994; July 12, 1995; and July 20, 1996. In addition, the *Charlotte Observer* contained special advertising supplements reporting school test scores and student characteristics on October 24, 1994; October 26, 1995; and October 30, 1996.

in the summer of 1997, ratings were usually reported in August.[10] In our analysis, we matched the test data from the spring of a given year—which would have been released the subsequent summer and fall—to the housing sales data from the subsequent September through August calendar year. Thus we associate each house sale with the most recently available test score. For example, the results from the spring 1997 test administration, released in August of 1997, were matched to the housing sales data from September 1997 through August 1998.

We have student-level microdata on math and reading performance and race in grades three through eight for schools in North Carolina for 1993 through 1999. (We do not have the microdata for 2000 and 2001.) Using the microdata, we constructed mean scaled test scores (standardized by grade) for 1993 through 1999 for all of the Charlotte-Mecklenburg schools. Data similar to these were published in the newspaper.

The North Carolina Department of Public Instruction provided us with data on school ratings and performance composites for each year from 1997 through 2001. The performance composite is the proportion of students scoring above a specific threshold in each grade and subject in a school. The performance composite seems to have been measuring the same attribute as the mean scaled score we calculated from the microdata: the correlation between the annual performance composite and the mean scaled score for 1997 through 1999 (the only three years in which we have both series) was .98.

Empirical Strategy

In the literature on school quality and housing values, the primary challenge has been to distinguish between the impact of school quality differences and other factors—such as neighborhood amenities and differences in the quality of other public services—which may be correlated with school quality. To address this issue, we focus on differences in housing values near school boundaries—parcels within 2,000, 1,000, or 500 feet of school boundaries—and control for housing characteristics

---

10. The stories reporting schools' ratings under North Carolina's ABC's program appeared on August 8, 1997; August 7, 1998; August 6, 1999; August 4, 2000; and October 5, 2001. The scores were reported unusually late in 2001 owing to the need for an equating study, given a change in the state testing program that year.

and fixed effects for the areas where the boundaries are located. Black employed an analogous strategy by including properties within .33, .20, and .15 of a mile (approximately 800-1,800 feet) on either side of a school boundary.[11]

To the extent that the school boundaries coincide with natural boundaries between areas with different amenities and public services, our estimates would still be conflating the effects of school quality and other characteristics. As a result, rather than simply include boundaries for pairs of schools, we sought other ways to identify differences between neighborhoods. The tax assessor's office has identified 1,048 different neighborhoods within Mecklenburg county. The typical neighborhood is rather small: half of all parcels are within 400 yards of the center of the neighborhood, and 95 percent of parcels are within 2,000 yards of the center of their neighborhood. We experiment with including fixed effects for each of these neighborhoods, thereby identifying the impact of school quality for properties in the same neighborhood assigned to different schools. Under this approach, when an entire neighborhood is assigned to the same school, none of the parcels in that neighborhood contributes to estimating the impact of school quality on housing values. The use of the neighborhood dummies also allows us to control for variation in housing prices along major roadways and other natural barriers, to the extent that bordering properties are recognized as being in different neighborhoods.

Besides using neighborhood boundaries, we overlaid the map of Mecklenburg County with grids of arbitrary sizes and included fixed effects for each square block on the grid. We report results using 2,500 foot square blocks (slightly less than a half-mile square) but found similar results using blocks from 1,000 to 10,000 feet square. Just as with neighborhoods, only those square blocks that cross a school boundary contribute to estimating the impact of school quality. We also explicitly test for a discontinuity in housing prices at the boundaries themselves.

Mecklenburg County includes the city of Charlotte and six additional municipalities (Cornelius, Davidson, Huntersville, Matthews, Mint Hill, and Pineville). Tax rates vary by municipality; the quality of city services may also vary. In most cases, the neighborhood definitions lie within municipality boundaries and, therefore, implicitly control for these factors too. However, some neighborhoods do cross municipality bound-

11. Black (1999).

aries. As a result, we include fixed effects for municipalities, implicitly controlling for tax rate differences and other differences between municipalities.

Results

We report the empirical results in four sections. In the first section, we estimate the relationship between long-run measures of school test performance (scores averaged over many years) and housing values using the regression discontinuity design proposed by Black, which compares sales prices of homes just situated on either side of elementary school boundaries.[12] We find a significant positive relationship between test performance and housing values, somewhat larger than that found by Black and which is robust across a variety of specifications. In the second section, we explore whether housing values respond to new information in the form of the current year's test scores or the new ranking system adopted in 1997. We find no evidence that year-to-year changes in test scores or the release of the new school rankings had any impact on housing values. In the third section of the results, we explore whether school test performance is related to property values simply because it proxies for racial mix at the school. The evidence suggests that test performance does not proxy for racial mix, and the test performance of white students has the strongest relationship to property values. The final section evaluates the validity of the regression discontinuity design for evaluating the housing market payoff to long-run differences in test scores, exploring whether differences in test scores at school boundaries proxy for unmeasured characteristics of the house or its neighborhood. The evidence suggests that test performance may proxy for unmeasured characteristics of the house or its neighborhood.

Long-Run Measures of School Test Performance and Housing Values

Table 1 presents the coefficients on elementary school test scores and housing characteristics. The dependent variable is the natural log of sales price. The school test score is the mean elementary school math and reading score over the period 1993 through 1999, after subtracting the

12. Black (1999).

Table 1. Housing Market Valuation and Math and Reading Scores, 1993–99

Sample	1 Full sample	2 Distance <2,000 feet	3 Distance <2,000 feet	4 Distance <2,000 feet	5 Distance <2,000 feet	6 Distance <1,000 feet	7 Distance <500 feet
Math and reading score, 1993–99	0.396	0.627	0.247	0.175	0.245	0.188	0.191
	(0.086)	(0.127)	(0.044)	(0.049)	(0.064)	(0.047)	(0.050)
Distance to school (miles)	−0.028	−0.065	−0.039	−0.022	−0.011	−0.044	−0.052
	(0.012)	(0.015)	(0.010)	(0.004)	(0.006)	(0.014)	(0.016)
Number of bedrooms	0.007	0.019	0.026	0.033	0.024	0.024	0.003
	(0.009)	(0.011)	(0.009)	(0.007)	(0.008)	(0.013)	(0.015)
Number of bathrooms	0.107	0.089	0.042	0.029	0.023	0.039	0.042
	(0.012)	(0.015)	(0.007)	(0.005)	(0.005)	(0.009)	(0.013)
Number of halfbaths	0.093	0.117	0.067	0.042	0.036	0.061	0.059
	(0.019)	(0.025)	(0.016)	(0.011)	(0.011)	(0.017)	(0.029)
Acreage	0.043	0.014	0.122	0.104	0.108	0.102	0.059
	(0.018)	(0.024)	(0.012)	(0.012)	(0.011)	(0.018)	(0.025)
Heated square feet/100	0.039	0.04	0.032	0.023	0.027	0.03	0.031
	(0.001)	(0.002)	(0.001)	(0.002)	(0.002)	(0.002)	(0.002)
Garage?	0.096	0.083	0.064	0.049	0.055	0.067	0.036
	(0.010)	(0.014)	(0.007)	(0.007)	(0.006)	(0.008)	(0.012)
Basement?	0.046	0.08	0.01	0.023	0.011	0.013	−0.002
	(0.034)	(0.037)	(0.027)	(0.016)	(0.020)	(0.022)	(0.036)
Air conditioning?	0.238	0.178	0.123	0.088	0.081	0.11	0.094
	(0.031)	(0.028)	(0.020)	(0.010)	(0.011)	(0.021)	(0.019)
Age/10	−0.006	−0.013	−0.086	−0.072	−0.092	−0.09	−0.11
	(0.017)	(0.024)	(0.013)	(0.012)	(0.011)	(0.014)	(0.015)
Age2/100	0.004	0.005	0.006	0.004	0.007	0.006	0.008
	(0.003)	(0.004)	(0.002)	(0.002)	(0.002)	(0.003)	(0.003)
Number of fixed effects							
Boundary	0	0	107	0	0	94	81
Neighborhood	0	0	0	316	0	0	0
2,500 feet square	0	0	0	0	553	0	0
Observations	83,056	28,168	28,168	28,101	28,168	10,975	3,104
R^2	0.74	0.71	0.81	0.85	0.85	0.81	0.81

Note: The dependent variable is ln(sale price). Each regression also included academic-year dummies, month dummies, and dummies for municipality. Huber-White standard errors were calculated allowing for clustering at the school level. Sample includes all single-family home sales between September 1, 1993, and December 31, 2001.

mean and dividing by the student-level standard deviation by grade. (The resulting score is in student-level standard deviation units.) Each specification includes indicators for municipality. Although we do not include a separate measure for property tax rate, the dummy variables for each municipality implicitly control for tax rates as well as any other differences between the municipalities in Mecklenburg County. Finally, to account for seasonality and general trends in the housing market in Charlotte, we include as regressors academic year and month dummies, although these are not reported separately.

Column 1 reports the results for the full sample without including fixed effects for neighborhoods. A one student-level standard deviation difference in school test scores is associated with a 39.6 percent increase in housing values. Column 2 reports the results for the sample of parcels within 2,000 feet of the boundary. A one student-level standard deviation difference in test scores is associated with a 62.7 percent difference in housing prices. Both of these specifications fail to account for neighborhood differences in housing values that are not captured by housing characteristics and are likely to be overstated as a result.

Column 3 includes fixed effects for each of the 143 boundaries between school assignment areas.[13] The coefficient on school test scores is cut in half after controlling for the variation between neighborhoods with the boundary fixed effects. The value of many other housing characteristics also changed after including the boundary fixed effects. For example, the coefficient on lot acreage increased eightfold, while the coefficient on the age of the building increased sixfold (while the coefficient on the quadratic term in age remained roughly constant). Presumably, these findings reflect the fact that the neighborhood dummies also implicitly control for distance from local business and entertainment districts, which is likely to be negatively related to housing prices and age of building but positively correlated with lot size. Although our purpose is to focus on the value of test score differences, the finding suggests that hedonic estimates of housing characteristics other than test scores may be subject to similar biases because of unmeasured neighborhood characteristics.

The impacts of school test scores in columns 1 and 2 are somewhat larger than similar estimates in Black, although the relative impact of

---

13. There were 143 boundaries in the full data set but only 107 in the sample of parcels within 2,000 feet of a boundary with stable school assignments.

including boundary fixed effects is the same. Black found that a school-level standard deviation in elementary school test scores was associated with a 4.9 and 2.2 percentage point difference in housing price respectively, before and after limiting the sample to houses near school boundaries.[14] In Charlotte, a school-level standard deviation is equal to .21 student-level standard deviations. Multiplying the coefficients in table 1 by .21 implies a percentage point difference of 13 and 5 percentage points per one school-level standard deviation respectively.

One reason for the larger estimated impact of school test score coefficient than in Black may be that we also included the straight-line distance to the elementary school in miles. (We have also tried including a quadratic in distance, but the quadratic term was generally indistinguishable from zero.) With boundary effects, an additional mile in distance from the elementary school was associated with a 1 to 5 percentage point decline in housing value. This is quite large—implying, for instance, that a few miles of distance has the same implication for home value as a school-level standard deviation difference in test scores. William T. Bogart and Brian A. Cromwell and Charles Clotfelter suggest that the value of a neighborhood school may be substantial.[15] Including the distance controls led to increases in the estimated impact of test scores (from roughly .17 to .25 in a specification otherwise similar to that in column 3), since distance and mean test scores are positively correlated.

In column 4, we included dummy variables for each of the 1,048 neighborhood definitions used by the county tax assessor's office (the parcels within 2,000 feet of the boundaries only fell within 316 such neighborhoods). The coefficient on test scores declines somewhat to 17.5 percent. The neighborhood definitions are used to distinguish among different areas for appraisal purposes and, as a result, presumably reflect differences in area amenities. We would expect such a decline if the neighborhood definitions were better at identifying when school boundaries coincided with informal neighborhood boundaries.

In column 5, we added fixed effects for 2,500 foot square blocks. This is cutting the data even more finely, allowing for different fixed effects along each segment of a school boundary. However, the result is largely

---

14. Black (1999).
15. Bogart and Cromwell (2000); Clotfelter (1975).

unchanged, with a coefficient of 24.5 percent per student-level standard deviation difference in test scores.

In columns 6 and 7, we focus even more stringently on schools near the boundaries—limiting the sample to parcels within 1,000 feet and within 500 feet of the closest parcel on the other side of the boundary. In many cases, this is limited to the first several of rows of parcels on each side of the boundary. The coefficients on mean test score in columns 6 and 7 are .188 and .191 respectively.

Table 2 reports results from the same specifications, using the mean performance composite for each school between 1997 and 2001. The school-level standard deviation in performance composites and mean scaled scores was 10.2 and .21 respectively. Multiplying the coefficients on school quality measures in tables 1 and 2 by their respective school-level standard deviation reveals very similar implied impacts on housing values. Moreover, the pattern of results in table 2 is similar to the results in table 1.

Satellite Zones

One of the more striking findings in table 1 is the magnitude of the effect of distance from one's elementary school on housing values. For example, the coefficients in column 3 imply that the impact on housing prices of a six-mile difference in distance is equivalent to the effect of moving from the school with the highest test scores in the county to a school with the lowest test scores. As already noted, the busing plan in Charlotte created "satellite zones" for fifteen of the elementary schools in our sample to achieve greater racial balance for schools in predominately white neighborhoods. The satellite zones were typically in low-income neighborhoods with high proportions of African American students (although for one of the schools in our sample, the satellite zone was created to boost white enrollments at a school in an African American neighborhood). The students from the satellite zones were required to travel longer distances to schools—the median distance to the school for parcels in satellite zones was 3.9 miles, compared with 1.0 mile for parcels in nonsatellite areas. To test whether the effect of distance in tables 1 and 2 was due to the correlation between distance and parcels in satellite zones (which tended to be low-income neighborhoods with lower housing values), we re-estimated each of the specifications above, excluding parcels located in the satellite zones. The results are reported

Table 2. Housing Market Valuation and Average Performance Composite, 1997–2001

Sample	1 Full sample	2 Distance <2,000 feet	3 Distance <2,000 feet	4 Distance <2,000 feet	5 Distance <2,000 feet	6 Distance <1,000 feet	7 Distance <500 feet
Performance composite/10, 1997–2001	0.073	0.154	0.054	0.055	0.046	0.058	0.068
	(0.020)	(0.042)	(0.015)	(0.015)	(0.016)	(0.015)	(0.017)
Distance to school (miles)	-0.027	-0.068	-0.039	-0.024	-0.01	-0.046	-0.055
	(0.012)	(0.014)	(0.011)	(0.006)	(0.007)	(0.014)	(0.016)
Number of bedrooms	0.006	0.01	0.025	0.032	0.024	0.023	0.001
	(0.009)	(0.013)	(0.009)	(0.007)	(0.008)	(0.013)	(0.014)
Number of bathrooms	0.116	0.098	0.043	0.029	0.024	0.039	0.042
	(0.011)	(0.014)	(0.007)	(0.005)	(0.006)	(0.009)	(0.013)
Number of halfbaths	0.095	0.103	0.066	0.041	0.036	0.06	0.057
	(0.019)	(0.025)	(0.016)	(0.011)	(0.011)	(0.017)	(0.029)
Acreage	0.043	0.015	0.122	0.105	0.107	0.101	0.057
	(0.018)	(0.023)	(0.012)	(0.012)	(0.012)	(0.018)	(0.024)
Heated square feet/100	0.04	0.044	0.032	0.023	0.027	0.03	0.032
	(0.002)	(0.002)	(0.001)	(0.002)	(0.002)	(0.002)	(0.002)
Garage?	0.099	0.083	0.064	0.05	0.055	0.067	0.036
	(0.010)	(0.015)	(0.007)	(0.006)	(0.006)	(0.009)	(0.012)
Basement?	0.045	0.076	0.01	0.023	0.01	0.014	-0.001
	(0.036)	(0.037)	(0.027)	(0.016)	(0.020)	(0.022)	(0.036)
Air conditioning?	0.256	0.193	0.125	0.089	0.083	0.111	0.096
	(0.033)	(0.028)	(0.020)	(0.010)	(0.011)	(0.021)	(0.019)
Age/10	-0.002	-0.007	-0.087	-0.073	-0.094	-0.091	-0.11
	(0.017)	(0.024)	(0.014)	(0.012)	(0.011)	(0.014)	(0.015)
Age2/100	0.004	0.005	0.006	0.004	0.007	0.007	0.008
	(0.004)	(0.004)	(0.002)	(0.002)	(0.002)	(0.003)	(0.003)
Number of fixed effects							
Boundary	0	0	107	0	0	94	81
Neighborhood	0	0	0	316	0	0	0
2,500 feet square	0	0	0	0	553	0	0
Observations	83,056	28,168	28,168	28,101	28,168	10,975	3,104
R^2	0.74	0.71	0.81	0.85	0.85	0.81	0.81

Note: The dependent variable is *ln*(sale price). Each regression also included academic-year dummies, month dummies, and dummies for municipality. Huber-White standard errors were calculated allowing for clustering at the school level. Sample includes all single-family home sales between September 1, 1993, and December 31, 2001.

in the top panel of table 3. Although the point estimates are somewhat smaller than in table 1, distance from the assigned elementary school continued to have a large impact on housing values, even after excluding the parcels in satellite zones.

Interactions with Household Income

We were interested in any differences in the valuation of school performance and distance by high- and low-income home buyers. Unfortunately, we did not have the household incomes of those families living in individual parcels. Instead, we used the median household income in the 2000 census for the census tracts in which the parcels were located. The bottom two panels of table 3 report the results of analyzing differences separately for those parcels with income above and below the county-wide median. Although the point estimates of the value of school quality are larger in columns 1 and 2 for low-income tracts, the estimates are similar in columns 3 through 7 in which a more complete set of geographic controls is included. Interestingly, the coefficient on distance from the assigned elementary school is indistinguishable from zero for high-income tracts but remains sizable for the parcels in lower-income tracts. This may reflect the fact that it takes longer to travel a given distance in more densely populated neighborhoods where the lower-income households live, than in suburbs, where the higher-income households live. (We are using straight-line distances, which may differ from travel time distances.)

Controlling for Middle School and High School Assignments

Besides the elementary school assignments, we were able to attain information on middle school and high school assignments as well as for each parcel in the county. Although we did not have ready access to middle school and high school test scores to separately estimate the payoff to middle school and high school test scores, we were able to include fixed effects for middle schools and high schools in the sample to test the extent to which the observed value of elementary school performance may be reflecting middle school and high school assignments. We re-estimated the specification in column 3 of table 1 with middle school and high school fixed effects respectively. Since most of the students from a given middle school were assigned to the same high school, we did not

Table 3. Housing Market Valuation, Test Scores, and Robustness to Alternative Samples, 1993–99

Sample	1 Full sample	2 Distance <2,000 feet	3 Distance <2,000 feet	4 Distance <2,000 feet	5 Distance <2,000 feet	6 Distance <1,000 feet	7 Distance <500 feet
Excluding parcels in satellite zones							
Math and reading score, 1993–99	0.377	0.594	0.226	0.165	0.267	0.226	0.142
	(0.087)	(0.130)	(0.041)	(0.055)	(0.066)	(0.041)	(0.041)
Distance to school (miles)	0.003	−0.034	−0.017	−0.026	−0.010	−0.017	−0.030
	(0.013)	(0.014)	(0.006)	(0.007)	(0.007)	(0.006)	(0.012)
Observations	78,036	25,799	25,799	25,732	25,799	25,799	2,757
Parcels in census tracts with above-median income							
Math and reading score, 1993–99	0.143	0.105	0.160	0.181	0.207	0.160	0.203
	(0.088)	(0.174)	(0.047)	(0.095)	(0.070)	(0.047)	(0.035)
Distance to school (miles)	0.026	−0.020	−0.001	−0.012	0.013	−0.001	−0.016
	(0.019)	(0.030)	(0.014)	(0.018)	(0.014)	(0.014)	(0.026)
Observations	43,430	9,584	9,584	9,584	9,584	9,584	840
Parcels in census tracts with below-median income							
Math and reading score, 1993–99	0.396	0.459	0.147	0.183	0.231	0.147	0.123
	(0.115)	(0.138)	(0.040)	(0.051)	(0.056)	(0.040)	(0.053)
Distance to school (miles)	−0.037	−0.046	−0.023	−0.025	−0.015	−0.023	−0.026
	(0.012)	(0.015)	(0.006)	(0.004)	(0.006)	(0.006)	(0.009)
Observations	39,626	18,584	18,584	18,517	18,584	18,584	2,264

Note: The dependent variable is *ln*(sale price). Each regression also included the same control variables as in table 1. Top panel regressions excluded parcels in satellite zones from which students were bused. Regressions in bottom two panels split the sample into parcels from census tracts with above and below-median income, based on 1990 census. Huber-White standard errors were calculated allowing for clustering at the school level. Samples include all single-family home sales between September 1, 1993, and December 31, 2001.

include both the middle school and high school effects in the same specification.

Although they remain statistically different from zero, the point estimates of the value of test performance is slightly smaller with the inclusion of middle school and high school effects– .164 and .192, respectively, rather than .247. As a result, only a portion of the value of student performance attributed to elementary schools appears to be due to middle school and high school assignments.

Do Housing Values Respond to New Test Score Information?

If short-term fluctuations in test scores are reliable indicators of changes in school quality, then real estate prices should be influenced by the most recently available scores. However, short-term fluctuations in test scores may be unreliable for at least two reasons. The first is sampling variation. The median elementary school in the United States has only sixty-nine students per grade level.[16] Even if schools are drawing from the same neighborhoods, a few particularly bright or rowdy children can have a large impact on test scores. The second source of volatility is one-time factors—such as a dog barking in the parking lot on the day of the test, interactions between a particular school's curriculum and the test form being used, or other factors—whose variance does not shrink with sample size. If sampling variation and other one-time factors account for most of the short-term fluctuations in test scores, then real estate markets should ignore year-to-year changes in test scores and focus on estimates of persistent performance differences such as long-run averages of test scores.

Based on test performance in North Carolina for a single grade (fourth grade), Kane and Staiger estimate that 14 percent of the variance in test score levels for the median-sized school is attributable to the combination of sampling variation and other one-time factors.[17] The proportion of variance owing to one-time factors is much higher when the focus is on changes in performance from one year to the next (73 percent) or when one is measuring "value-added" differences between schools (49 per-

16. In the 1999 Common Core of Data, among schools with a fourth grade classroom, the median school contained sixty-nine students in the fourth grade and the mean number of students was seventy-four.
17. Kane and Staiger (2002a, forthcoming).

cent).[18] The latter fact is reflected in substantial year-to-year fluctuation in the proportion of schools achieving "expected" or "exemplary" value added under the rating system started in 1997. North Carolina has been testing in grades three through eight since 1993. As a result, the averaging across grade levels may reduce the variance because of one-time factors somewhat from the estimates just mentioned.[19] Nevertheless, these estimates suggest that short-term fluctuations in test scores are likely to be unreliable and, therefore, should have little impact on housing values if housing markets are cognizant of their volatility.

In table 4, we investigate the impact of short-term fluctuation in test scores on housing values. In columns 1 and 5, we replicate the earlier specifications for mean scaled scores (1993–99) and for mean performance composite (1997–2001). In columns 2 and 6, besides the long-term mean performance, we include the difference between the single-year test score released that year and the long-term score. (Recall that we have matched test scores released in July or August to housing sale prices for the subsequent September through August period.) In both specifications, when both the long-term score and the annual deviation from the long-term score are included, it is only the coefficient on the long-term score that is statistically distinguishable from zero. In columns 3 and 7, we include fixed effects for 2,500-square-foot areas, with little impact on either set of estimates. In columns 4 and 8, we include fixed effects for each of the schools. Although the coefficient on the long-term mean test score is no longer identified since it does not vary for a given school, the coefficient on the annual deviation from the long-term mean remains small and statistically indistinguishable from zero.

In other words, the housing market seems to downplay short-term fluctuations in test scores and focus on long-term means. This is precisely what we would expect if home buyers have prior beliefs about school quality—based on a history of test scores or other information—and if they are aware of the short-term volatility in the schools they are following. The more noise they expect to find in short-term fluctuations,

---

18. The value-added measure used was the average gain in student performance in combined reading and math scores between the end of third and fourth grades.

19. It is a nontrivial exercise to estimate how much the averaging across grades would affect year-to-year volatility, since it requires estimating the possible persistence in shocks at the cohort level, for instance, as the third grade students this year become fourth grade students next year.

Table 4. Housing Market Valuation of Alternative Test Score Measures, Various Time Periods

Test measure:	*1*	*2*	*3*	*4*	*5*	*6*
	Average math and reading, 1993–99			*Performance composite/10, 1997–2001*		
Sample: (see note)	*1993–96*	*1997–99*	*2000–01*	*1993–96*	*1997–99*	*2000–01*
Average test score	0.232	0.269	0.291	0.054	0.053	0.068
	(0.041)	(0.053)	(0.051)	(0.015)	(0.017)	(0.017)
Distance to school	−0.041	−0.039	−0.034	−0.041	−0.038	−0.037
(miles)	(0.011)	(0.009)	(0.009)	(0.012)	(0.010)	(0.009)
Number of bedrooms	0.023	0.029	0.037	0.022	0.028	0.035
	(0.010)	(0.011)	(0.011)	(0.010)	(0.011)	(0.011)
Number of bathrooms	0.042	0.045	0.054	0.043	0.046	0.054
	(0.009)	(0.008)	(0.015)	(0.009)	(0.009)	(0.016)
Number of halfbaths	0.069	0.068	0.067	0.07	0.067	0.063
	(0.020)	(0.019)	(0.021)	(0.020)	(0.019)	(0.021)
Acreage	0.087	0.138	0.155	0.088	0.138	0.154
	(0.011)	(0.020)	(0.025)	(0.012)	(0.020)	(0.026)
Heated square feet/100	0.032	0.03	0.031	0.032	0.031	0.032
	(0.001)	(0.002)	(0.002)	(0.001)	(0.002)	(0.002)
Garage?	0.068	0.065	0.051	0.069	0.065	0.048
	(0.007)	(0.010)	(0.013)	(0.007)	(0.010)	(0.013)
Basement?	0.014	0.013	−0.007	0.014	0.015	−0.006
	(0.029)	(0.032)	(0.022)	(0.029)	(0.031)	(0.023)
Air conditioning?	0.121	0.135	0.126	0.122	0.138	0.126
	(0.016)	(0.029)	(0.025)	(0.016)	(0.029)	(0.025)
Age/10	−0.088	−0.075	−0.062	−0.089	−0.076	−0.062
	(0.016)	(0.013)	(0.016)	(0.016)	(0.014)	(0.016)
Age2/100	0.004	0.005	0.004	0.004	0.006	0.004
	(0.003)	(0.002)	(0.003)	(0.003)	(0.002)	(0.003)
Number of fixed effects						
Boundary	105	105	104	105	105	104
Observations	12,768	10,870	4,530	12,768	10,870	4,530
R^2	0.83	0.8	0.82	0.83	0.8	0.82

Note: The dependent variable is *ln*(sale price). Each regression also included academic-year dummies, month dummies, and dummies for municipality. Huber-White standard errors were calculated allowing for clustering at the school level. Sample includes only parcels within 2,000 feet of an enrollment boundary. Years refer to academic year beginning on September 1 of the given year.

the more slowly they will update these beliefs based on current test scores. Kane and Staiger formalize such intuition with a method for "filtering" test scores over time, by constructing a weighted average of recent performance in which the weights are functions of school sample size, the estimated variance in long-term school quality, and the variance in one-time shocks to performance.[20] The fact that home buyers downweight recent test scores suggests that they may be implicitly applying some similar intuition to annual test score releases.

Impact of Test Performance in Different Time Periods

In the preceding analysis, we used the long-term mean test score as our measure of school performance and pooled observations over several years. In other words, even for transactions occurring in 1993, we used the long-term mean test score for the 1993–99 period in table 1 and for the 1997–2001 period in table 2. We calculated the long-term means in order to minimize the error in identifying school quality resulting from annual fluctuations in school mean scores.[21] Implicitly, we are assuming that performance differences between schools are largely fixed and that home buyers form impressions of schools over long periods. Although the test was different before 1993, scores were being published for each school in Charlotte several years before the beginning of our sample. If that is the case, then each year's test score contributes equally to the estimation of long-term performance differences. In our analysis, future test scores are essentially "standing in" for the past test scores (and other less quantitative information that forms the basis of a school's reputation in the community) that we did not have in allowing us to calculate the long-term mean. By including only the long-term mean, we are imposing the constraint that the coefficient on each year's mean score was the same. To test this hypothesis, we ran separate regressions for each year from 1993 through 2001, including as regressors the mean scores of all seven years separately (1993 through 1999), and tested whether the evidence would lead us to reject that constraint. For eight out of nine years, we could not reject the hypothesis that the coefficients on all the years' scores were the same. In other words, we could not reject the hypothesis

---

20. Kane and Staiger (2002a).
21. See Kane and Staiger (2002c) for more on volatility in school-level test score measures.

that even future years' test performance provides the same information as past years' performance. Each contributes similarly to forming the long-term impressions that home buyers are using.

In table 5, we use the mean performance measures to study the relationship between test scores and housing values during different periods—1993–96, 1997–99, and 2000–01. All columns of results use the same specification in column 3 of tables 1 and 2 above. The school performance measures are not varying across periods—for each school, we are using the 1993–99 mean scaled score and 1997–2001 mean performance composite respectively. The coefficient on long-term mean test performance in each period is similar. In fact, it seems to increase slightly over time for both measures of mean school performance—possibly reflecting the rise in the labor market value of education and pre-market skills.

Introduction of Categorical Ratings in 1997

In 1997, the state of North Carolina began rating schools statewide based on a combination of measures reflecting their students' performance as well as the school's mean value added. To measure performance level, they used the same "performance composite" measure we are using, which is a weighted average of the proportions of students achieving proficiency of "level III" or above in the reading and mathematics end-of-grade tests. (The performance composites also include writing in grades four and seven.) The state's value-added measure or "growth composite" is a function of the change in performance for the students currently enrolled in school over the same students' performance in the previous year.[22] Table 6 summarizes the possible ratings.

Schools achieving their expected growth targets could not be labeled low performing, even if fewer than 50 percent of their students are performing at level III and above. Moreover, schools with performance composite greater than 90 were recognized as "schools of excellence" if they met the expected value-added standard and "schools of distinction" if they did not. A school could also earn the label "school of distinction"

---

22. The growth composite is the school-level mean of the following function at the individual student level: $\alpha_g + \beta_{1g}M_t - \beta_{2g}M_{t-1} + \beta_{3g}R_t - \beta_{4g}R_{t-1}$, where M_t, M_{t-1}, R_t, and R_{t-1} represent the math and reading scores this year and last year and the parameters β_{1g}, β_{2g}, β_{3g}, and β_{4g} vary by grade level, g, and are greater than zero and less than 1.

Table 5. Housing Market Valuation of Alternative Test Score Measures[a]

Test measure:	Math and reading (1993–99)				Performance composite/10 (1997–2001)			
	1	2	3	4	5	6	7	8
Years in sample:	1993–99	1993–99	1993–99	1993–99	1997–2001	1997–2001	1997–2001	1997–2001
Average test score	0.244	0.24	0.247		0.057	0.056	0.052	
	(0.045)	(0.044)	(0.067)		(0.016)	(0.016)	(0.018)	
Single-year test score – average test score		−0.02	0.008	−0.022		−0.003	−0.001	0
		(0.046)	(0.046)	(0.047)		(0.009)	(0.008)	(0.009)
Distance to school (miles)	−0.04	−0.038	−0.009	−0.082	−0.037	−0.038	−0.011	−0.08
	(0.010)	(0.010)	(0.006)	(0.012)	(0.009)	(0.009)	(0.007)	(0.012)
Number of fixed effects								
Boundary	106	106	0	106	106	106	0	106
2,500 feet square	0	0	540	0	0	0	534	0
School	0	0	0	50	0	0	0	49
Observations	23,638	23,416	23,416	23,416	15,400	15,370	15,370	15,370
R^2	0.82	0.82	0.85	0.82	0.8	0.8	0.84	0.81

Note: The dependent variable is ln(sale price). Each regression also included academic-year dummies, month dummies, and dummies for municipality. Huber-White standard errors were calculated allowing for clustering at the school level. Sample includes only parcels within 2000 feet of a school boundary sold in the years indicated. Years refer to academic year beginning on September 1 of the given year.

a. Long-run averages versus annual deviations from average.

Table 6. School Rating Definitions, North Carolina

	Performance composite:				
Growth composite	*Statistically significant, <50*	*<50 but not statistically significant*	*≥50, < 80*	*≥80, <90*	*≥90*
Below expected	Low-performing	No recognition	No recognition	School of distinction	School of distinction
≥ Expected, < exemplary	Expected growth	Expected growth	Expected growth	School of distinction	School of excellence
≥ Exemplary	Exemplary growth	Exemplary growth	Exemplary growth	School of distinction	School of excellence

if it achieved a performance composite between 80 and 90 and also achieved at least expected value added. Schools were designated low performing if their performance composite was statistically significantly below 50 and if they failed to meet the growth target. Teachers in schools achieving "exemplary" growth received $1,500 bonuses (raised from $1,000 in 1998), and those in schools achieving "expected" growth received $750 bonuses (beginning in 1998).

Table 7 summarizes the proportion of elementary schools serving our sample in Charlotte moving from one category to another from year to year. There is considerable year-to-year change in the schools' performance categories. There were thirteen schools identified as low performing in Charlotte in 1997. Two of these remained low performing in 1998. Six of the initially low-performing schools achieved "exemplary" growth in 1998. The "exemplary" and "expected" categories tend to be the most volatile, given that they are based solely on the value-added measures. For instance, 58 percent of the schools that achieved "exemplary" growth in 1998 did not even achieve their expected growth targets in 1999.

Table 8 reports the coefficients on each of the categories after controlling for the performance composite level. The labels reflect a mixture of performance levels and value-added measures. All schools were identified as having achieved "expected" or "exemplary" growth based on their value-added measure. Those same schools were also identified if they achieved other distinctions, such as "schools of excellence" or "schools of distinction." In other words, the coefficients on the indicators for distinction and excellence measure the marginal impact of having high performance over and above reaching the expected or exemplary growth tar-

Table 7. Changes in Charlotte-Mecklenburg Elementary School Ratings, North Carolina ABC Program

Schools in each row in 1997 achieving rating in 1998 (percent)

	Low performance	Below expected	Expected	Exemplary	Distinction/ excellent
Low performance	15	8	31	46	0
Below expected	0	33	42	25	0
Expected	0	8	15	54	23
Exemplary	0	25	13	63	0
Distinction/ excellent	0	0	0	0	100
Percent	3	20	28	39	10

Schools in each row in 1998 achieving rating in 1999 (percent)

	Low performance	Below expected	Expected	Exemplary	Distinction/ excellent
Low performance	50	0	0	50	0
Below expected	0	50	42	8	0
Expected	0	41	41	12	6
Exemplary	0	58	8	29	4
Distinction/ excellent	0	17	0	0	83
Percent	2	46	23	18	11

Schools in each row in 1999 achieving rating in 2000 (percent)

	Low performance	Below expected	Expected	Exemplary	Distinction/ excellent
Low performance	100	0	0	0	0
Below expected	0	57	29	14	0
Expected	0	64	14	21	0
Exemplary	0	45	18	36	0
Distinction/ excellent	0	0	0	0	100
Percent	2	49	20	18	11

Schools in each row in 2000 achieving rating in 2001 (percent)

	Low performance	Below expected	Expected	Exemplary	Distinction/ excellent
Low performance	0	0	0	100	0
Below expected	0	30	43	20	7
Expected	0	33	25	17	25
Exemplary	0	18	27	45	9
Distinction/ excellent	0	14	0	0	85
Percent	0	26	31	23	20

Note: Limited to nonmagnet elementary schools with stable school assignments between 1993 and 2001.

Table 8. Housing Market Valuation of Alternative Test Score Measures[a]

Rankings for which years?	1	2	3	4	5	6
		Annual	Annual	Average	As indicated	As indicated
Sample years:	1997–2001	1997–2001	1997–2001	1997–2001	1997	1998–2001
Average performance composite/10, 1997–2001	0.057	0.055		0.053	0.033	0.049
	(0.016)	(0.017)		(0.025)	(0.023)	(0.017)
North Carolina ranking:						
Low performing		−0.018	0.005	−0.132		
		(0.028)	(0.020)	(0.061)		
Expected growth		0.003	0.006	−0.023		
		(0.008)	(0.006)	(0.054)		
Exemplary growth		0.001	0.004	0.021		
		(0.008)	(0.007)	(0.042)		
Distinction		−0.025	0.011	−0.125		
		(0.021)	(0.011)	(0.072)		
Excellence		−0.009	−0.066	−0.084		
		(0.053)	(0.031)	(0.106)		
Low performing in 1997 only					−0.021	−0.006
					(0.038)	(0.026)
Low performing in 1997 and at least one other year					−0.116	−0.119
					(0.069)	(0.038)
F test for all rank coefficients = 0		0.41	1.79	1.66	1.48	5.78
p value		0.84	0.11	0.14	0.23	0.003
Distance to school (miles)	−0.037	−0.037	−0.08	−0.036	−0.037	−0.038
	(0.009)	(0.010)	(0.007)	(0.010)	(0.015)	(0.009)
Number of fixed effects						
Boundary	106	106	106	106	106	106
School	0	0	49	0	0	0
Observations	15,400	15,400	15,400	15,400	15,400	15,400
R^2	0.8	0.8	0.81	0.8	0.8	0.81

Note: The dependent variable is *ln*(sale price). Each regression also included academic-year dummies, month dummies, and dummies for municipality. Huber-White standard errors were calculated allowing for clustering at the school level. In column 3 only, standard errors were clustered at school-by-year level, to avoid bias in clustered standard errors for small cells. Sample includes only parcels within 2,000 feet of a school boundary sold in the years 1997–2001. Years refer to academic year beginning on September 1 of the given year.

a. Long-run averages versus North Carolina rankings.

gets. Each specification is estimated only for those parcels within 2,000 feet of a school boundary and was limited to 1997–2001, the years in which the award program operated. Column 1 includes the annual performance composite as well as boundary fixed effects. Column 2 adds indicators for each of the rating categories—which are allowed to vary by year for each school. The left-out category includes schools that were not recognized in that year, because they failed to achieve expected growth but did not have fewer than 50 percent of their students scoring at level III or above.

Conditional on the performance composite measure, none of the coefficients on the categorical ratings in column 2 were statistically significantly different from zero individually. Table 8 also reports the test of the null hypothesis that the coefficients on all of the categorical dummies are equal to zero. Given the *p* value in column 2 of .84, there is little evidence to reject the hypothesis that none of the categories matter. In column 3, we included fixed effects for all of the schools, essentially identifying the effect of categories for those who switch categories from year to year. The *p* value on the test of joint significance is closer to the standard level for rejection (.11) but largely because of a *negative* estimated coefficient for schools of "excellence" (perhaps reflecting some nonlinearity in the relationship with the performance composite at the top end).

Perhaps the failure to find an effect of the ratings is because the ratings are volatile from year to year. As a result, in column 4 we include each school's *average* ranking between 1997 and 2001 (for example, if a school was low performing for one out of five years, the value of the low-performing measure would be equal to .2) as well as their average score on the performance composite for those years. Again, we could not reject the hypothesis that the coefficients on all of the categories were jointly equal to zero, and the estimated coefficients for schools of "distinction" and "excellence" are unexpectedly negative.

The failure to find a relationship in any of these specifications between "exemplary" or "expected" growth and housing prices is particularly interesting for two reasons. First, the state focused the lion's share of the financial rewards on the schools identified as meeting "exemplary" or "expected" growth targets. Apparently, housing markets did not share state policymakers' enthusiasm for these measures. Second, while housing markets had available measures of students' performance before 1997, the "expected" and "exemplary" measures were the first explicit measures of value-added differences that were made available. Thus one might have expected a larger response to this new information.

Although most of the coefficient estimates for the school rankings are insignificant or have unexpected signs, the coefficient for the proportion of years between 1997 and 2001 that a school was labeled "low perform-ing" in column 4 is negative and marginally significant. However, the lower property values associated with these schools seems to have been pre-existing, rather than the result of being labeled "low performing." In our sample, eleven schools were low performing in 1997 only, while two other schools were low performing in both 1997 and 1998 (one of these continued to be low performing through 2000). In columns 5 and 6 of table 8, we include dummy variables for the schools that were low per-forming in 1997 only and for the schools that were low performing in 1997 and 1998. Column 5 includes only sales that occurred after release of the 1997 ratings but before the 1998 ratings were known (September 1997 through August 1998). In column 6 we include only sales after the 1998 ratings were released (September 1998 onward). The estimated coefficients are nearly identical in the two samples and imply that home prices for the two schools that continued to be low performing in 1998 were about 12 percent lower than schools never identified as low per-forming—but this difference existed even before the 1998 ratings had been released.

A simple plot of sales prices over time also suggests that the lower property values associated with low-performing schools were pre-existing, and there was no apparent impact of being so labeled. Figure 3 reports real median housing prices by three-month interval, beginning in September 1993 and running through December 2001 (using September-November, December-February, and so aligns with the release of test score data in August). We plot trends for houses assigned to three differ-ent groups of schools: those never identified as low performing (the top line), those identified as low performing only in 1997 (the second line), and those identified as low performing in both 1997 and 1998 (the bot-tom line). Homes assigned to schools identified as low performing (par-ticularly the two schools that continued to be low performing after 1997) have sold for lower prices throughout our sample period, with no obvi-ous change in sales price occurring at the time of being identified as low performing. The first vertical line identifies the housing sales in Septem-ber 1997, when the schools would have been originally identified as low

Figure 3. Trends in Median Real Sales Price according to School Performance, 1994–2002

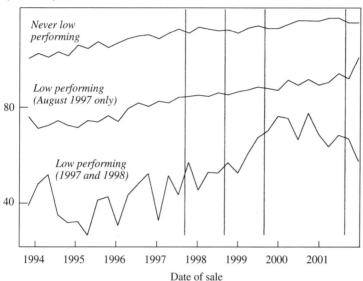

Median sale price
(thousands)

performing. There is no apparent change in the bottom two lines relative to the top line, which we would have expected if the "low-performing" ranking had an impact on housing values. The second vertical line identifies September 1998, when the eleven school assignment areas represented by the middle line were taken off low-performing status. The remaining vertical lines identify September 1999 and 2001, when the remaining two schools represented by the bottom line were taken off low-performing status. Again, there is no evidence of any systematic change in existing trends.[23]

Do Test Scores Proxy for Racial Differences between Schools?

There is a general concern that differences between schools in test score measures are more the result of differences in the socioeconomic

---

23. Note that the percentage increase in prices was higher in the bottom two groups of neighborhoods over much of the period. Recall that prices for the lower percentiles of the housing price distribution rose more quickly than the median prices over this time period.

Figure 4. Plot of Average Test Score and Percent Black in School[a]

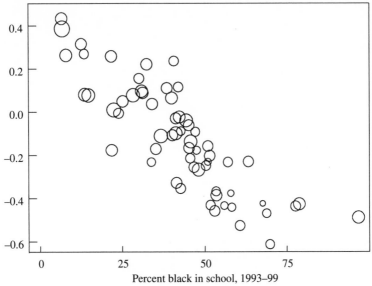

Average math + reading
score, 1993–99

Percent black in school, 1993–99

a. Size of circle proportional to school size.

status of their students rather than the value added of the school. A related question is whether homeowners are paying a premium for schools with high value added or simply buying into a school with students of high socioeconomic status (and, as a result, high test scores).

In our data, most of the difference between schools in average test scores is attributable to racial composition. Figure 4 reports the average test score and the percent of students who are African American.[24] In Charlotte, the correlation between a school's average test score and the proportion of the students in the school who are African American is –.8. In other words, more than 60 percent of the variance in test scores is associated with racial composition alone. Some part of this association may be because schools with a high proportion of African American stu-

24. The relationship in figure 4 reflects more than the fact that there is a difference in average scores between African American students and whites. The mean test scores for both whites and African Americans are lower in schools with a high percentage of African American students.

Table 9. Housing Market Valuation of Alternative Test Score Measures: Racial Mix of School

	1	2	3	4	5	6	7
Math and reading score, 1993–99	0.222 (0.052)				0.281 (0.106)	–0.115 (0.119)	0.356 (0.049)
Average % of students black	–0.064 (0.082)						
Fixed-weight score, 1993–99		0.282 (0.052)			–0.044 (0.126)		
White students' score, 1993–99			0.261 (0.037)			0.353 (0.107)	
Black students' score, 1993–99				–0.058 (0.078)			–0.288 (0.065)
Distance to school (miles)	–0.039 (0.010)	–0.036 (0.010)	–0.038 (0.010)	–0.032 (0.010)	–0.039 (0.010)	–0.037 (0.011)	–0.041 (0.010)
Number of fixed effects							
Boundary	107	107	107	107	107	107	107
Observations	28,168	28,168	28,168	28,168	28,168	28,168	28,168
R^2	0.81	0.81	0.82	0.81	0.81	0.82	0.82

Note: The dependent variable is *ln*(sale price). Each regression also included academic-year dummies, month dummies, a monthly trend, and dummies for municipality. Huber-White standard errors were calculated allowing for clustering at the school level. Sample includes only parcels within 2,000 feet of a school boundary sold in 1993–2001. Years refer to academic year beginning on September 1 of the given year.

dents are low value-added schools, but a larger part simply reflects the achievement gap: African American students in Charlotte score about two-thirds of a standard deviation below white students. In this section, we explore whether the housing market makes any attempt to account for the percentage of students in a school who are African American in drawing inferences about school quality.

In column 1 of table 9, besides average test score and distance measures, we include as a regressor the proportion of African American test takers in each school between 1993 and 1999. Holding a school's average test score constant, a school with a higher proportion of African American students seems to be providing more value added to its students—they are doing just as well with a student population of lower socioeconomic status. Therefore, if homeowners are paying for value added, we would expect a positive coefficient on the proportion of students in a school who are African American. In fact, the point estimate of the coefficient on the percentage of students who are African American is negative and indistinguishable from zero, suggesting that homeowners are paying for peers rather than value added at a school.

But there are other reasons that the percentage of students who are African American may not have a positive effect on housing values, holding test scores constant. In particular, homeowners may have direct preferences for racial composition in the school. For instance, suppose that home buyers were adjusting scores to reflect value added but also attached negative value to the proportion of students who were African American. The two effects could simply be offsetting each other.

An alternative approach to discerning whether home buyers account for racial composition when interpreting school mean test scores is to construct a test score measure that does not suffer from any composition bias, that is, a fixed-weight average of performance for various racial groups—so that none of the variation in the measure comes from different racial composition across schools. There are three common-sense options for choosing the weights:

—Use the average test scores among white students (all the weight on whites);

—Use the average test scores among African American students (no weight on whites);

—Use fixed weights, weighting the test scores of whites and African Americans by the overall proportion of each racial group in the Charlotte schools (roughly 60 percent to 40 percent).

In the remaining columns of table 9, we report results of using each of these measures in place of (columns 2,3, and 4) or in combination with (columns 5, 6, and 7) the actual average test score in the school. We calculated mean test scores by school by race for the years 1993–99, using the microdata on individual students' performance (similar racial breakdowns of test scores were available to parents over this time period in Charlotte).

There are several results in these columns suggesting that the people in the market for housing do indeed adjust for racial composition when they are judging the quality of schools. When used in place of overall test scores in columns 2 and 3, the association of the fixed-weight and the white test scores with housing values is roughly of the same magnitude and significance as when the actual test score is included—so the relationship between school quality and test scores is not simply being driven by racial composition in the school. When the overall test score is included along with the fixed-weight test score in column 5, the fixed-weight test score is no longer significant. However, in column 6 the white test score continues to have a large positive and significant effect, while the overall test score is insignificant. Thus these columns suggest that real estate values are not being driven by differences in the racial composition of schools, and that homeowners' perceptions of school quality are most strongly associated with test scores among white students.

However, there are some puzzling results in table 9. It is somewhat perplexing that the coefficient on the mean test score for African American students in column 4 is not statistically distinguishable from zero. One might question why test score results for African American students—roughly 40 percent of the students in Charlotte—are being ignored in evaluating school quality. Moreover, the results in column 7 suggest that holding constant a school's overall score, the mean test score for African American students is actually negative and statistically significant. If high test scores among white students are an indicator of a good school, why should housing markets ignore, or even draw the opposite inference from, high test scores among African American students?

One possible clue in this puzzle is that average test scores by race are not correlated within schools. This is because some of the highest-scoring white students were attending several schools with some of the lowest-scoring African American students. Based on the differences in travel distance within the school, the minority students in these schools seem to have been bused into largely white neighborhoods from neighborhoods with high concentrations of African American students. One possible hypothesis that would reconcile the anomalies is that there are some low-scoring African American students being bused to attend a handful of the most desirable schools in the district. If that were the case, then even after conditioning on overall test scores, the presence of African American students from very poor neighborhoods could be positively correlated with unobserved school quality. This is a finding we intend to explore in future work that directly evaluates the patterns and implications of busing in Charlotte.

Validity of the Regression Discontinuity Identification Strategy

As we saw with the change in coefficient on test scores after including boundary and neighborhood fixed effects, there are a number of *unob-*

served factors determining housing values that are correlated with test scores between different school boundary areas. The identification strategy used throughout the paper assumes that such unobserved factors change "smoothly" across space and are not systematically correlated with school test scores across the boundaries themselves. Although we cannot test whether the unobserved factors systematically differ across school boundaries without an instrument, we can test whether those factors we do observe—acreage, number of bedrooms, number of bathrooms, number of half-bathrooms, heated square footage, the presence of air conditioning and a garage—differ for those properties in areas assigned to higher-performing schools.

In table 10, we report the coefficient on school mean test scores and distance to the school using the same sample definitions and fixed effects as in tables 1 and 2, with and without including the housing characteristics as controls. If the housing characteristics were not systematically different on either side of the school boundaries, we would expect to estimate a similar relationship between test scores, distances to school and housing values without the controls, though with slightly higher standard errors. In most specifications, the estimated coefficients on test scores and on distance roughly double when one excludes the housing characteristics—suggesting that the observed characteristics are indeed correlated with test scores at the boundaries, and homes are of higher quality on the side of the boundary with the better school.

In table 11, we directly examine which of the housing characteristics seem to differ across boundaries. Each regression used a housing characteristic as the dependent variable and estimated the coefficient on test scores and distance for parcels within 2,000 feet of school boundaries, controlling for boundary fixed effects, a trend, year and month dummies, and municipality dummies. With the notable exception of lot acreage (which is difficult to alter), many of the characteristics are related to test scores even when the sample is limited to schools near the borders.

These findings are not inconsistent with Black, who also found differences in observed housing characteristics between homes on the high- versus low-scoring side of school boundaries.[25] However, the magnitude of these differences and the sensitivity of the estimates to controlling for

25. Black (1999, table 3).

Table 10. Housing Market Valuation of School Test Scores with and without Controlling for Housing Characteristics

Sample	1 Full sample	2 Distance <2,000 feet	3 Distance <2,000 feet	4 Distance <2,000 feet	5 Distance <2,000 feet	6 Distance <1,000 feet	7 Distance <500 feet
With controls							
Math and reading score, 1993–99	0.396	0.627	0.247	0.175	0.245	0.188	0.191
	(0.086)	(0.127)	(0.044)	(0.049)	(0.064)	(0.047)	(0.050)
Distance to school (miles)	−0.028	−0.065	−0.039	−0.022	−0.011	−0.044	−0.052
	(0.012)	(0.015)	(0.010)	(0.004)	(0.006)	(0.014)	(0.016)
R^2	0.74	0.71	0.81	0.85	0.85	0.81	0.81
No controls							
Math and reading score, 1993–99	1.339	1.559	0.498	0.295	0.443	0.459	0.385
	(0.114)	(0.179)	(0.105)	(0.100)	(0.106)	(0.115)	(0.106)
Distance to school (miles)	−0.041	−0.127	−0.081	−0.025	−0.027	−0.094	−0.104
	(0.025)	(0.020)	(0.024)	(0.007)	(0.010)	(0.029)	(0.031)
R^2	0.37	0.41	0.66	0.79	0.78	0.69	0.7
Number of fixed effects							
Boundary	0	0	107	0	0	94	81
Neighborhood	0	0	0	316	0	0	0
2,500 feet square	0	0	0	0	553	0	0
R^2	0.74	0.71	0.81	0.85	0.85	0.81	0.81
Observations	83,056	28,168	28,168	28,101	28,168	10,975	3,104

Note: The dependent variable is *ln*(sale price). Each regression also included academic-year dummies, month dummies, a monthly trend, and dummies for municipality. Top panel regressions also included housing characteristics listed in tables 1–3. Huber-White standard errors were calculated allowing for clustering at the school level. Sample is all sales 1993–2001, restricted as stated at the top of each column.

Table 11. Housing Characteristics and School Test Scores

Dependent variable:	1 Number of bedrooms	2 Number of bathrooms	3 Number of halfbaths	4 Acreage	5 Heated square feet/100	6 Garage	7 Basement	8 Air conditioning	9 Age/10
Math and reading	0.232	0.453	0.035	-0.005	4.049	0.085	0.052	0.198	-1.033
score, 1993–99	(0.120)	(0.108)	(0.040)	(0.037)	(1.293)	(0.084)	(0.047)	(0.066)	(0.472)
Distance to school	-0.067	-0.049	-0.017	-0.011	-0.77	-0.021	-0.001	-0.032	0.112
(miles)	(0.015)	(0.019)	(0.007)	(0.005)	(0.192)	(0.017)	(0.004)	(0.011)	(0.094)
Number of fixed effects									
Boundary	107	107	107	107	107	107	107	107	107
R^2	0.29	0.38	0.15	0.14	0.5	0.35	0.1	0.21	0.57
Observations	28,168	28,168	28,168	28,168	28,168	28,168	28,168	28,168	28,168

Note: The dependent variable is given at the top of each column. Each regression also included academic-year dummies, month dummies, a monthly trend, and dummies for municipality. Huber-White standard errors were calculated allowing for clustering at the school level. Sample includes only parcels within 2,000 feet of a school boundary sold in the years 1993–2001.

Figure 5. Is There a Discontinuity in Sales Price at the Boundary?[a]

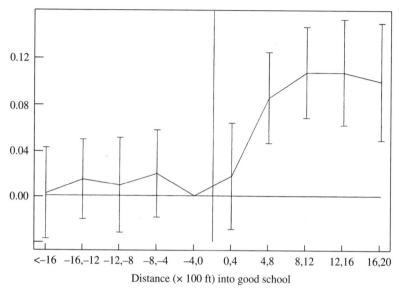

Sales price relative
to (–4,0)

Distance (× 100 ft) into good school

a. Regression-adjusted sales price in 400-foot intervals from school boundary for sample in which average test scores improve by at least 0.25 S.D.s at boundary (distance > 0 indicates inside good school attendance area.

these differences in observed housing characteristics are somewhat more pronounced in our data. One potential reason for this difference may be our focus on parcels with stable school assignments throughout the sample period. One could argue that school boards are less likely to change school boundaries where housing quality is starkly different on either side of the boundary (because of pressure from homeowners), or that housing quality differences are more likely to arise in areas with stable boundaries (as high-income families move into areas with good schools). In either case, school boundaries in which differences in school test scores are more strongly correlated with differences in housing and neighborhood characteristics would tend to be overrepresented in our sample.

Evaluating the Abruptness of the Change in Housing Prices

In figure 5, we investigate the abruptness of the change in housing prices at school boundaries. If school assignment is the primary factor underlying the increase in property values, then housing prices should rise abruptly at the boundary. To test whether there is such a discontinuity in house prices, in figure 5 we report the estimated log sales price of homes at 400-foot intervals on either side of school boundaries. We estimate the price for each interval from a regression with the same specification as in table 1, column 3 (with boundary fixed effects), except rather than including test scores we include dummy variables for 400-foot intervals. The interval 0-400 feet from the boundary with a better school is the omitted reference category. The intervals were defined so that, for example, a home that is 350 feet from the boundary with a better school is assigned a distance of *negative* 350, and a home 350 feet within the better school's boundary is assigned a distance of *positive* 350. We limited the analysis to boundaries where there was at least a .25 student-level standard deviation difference in mean test scores between the schools on the high-scoring and low-scoring side of the boundaries. There were roughly 3,000 home sales in each interval, except for the two intervals within 400 feet (either side) of the boundary that each had roughly 1,000 home sales.[26]

According to the results in figure 5, there were small differences in housing prices for houses within 400 feet of the boundary (or, more precisely, 400 feet from the closest house on the other side of the boundary). However, housing prices were sharply higher—about 8 percent—for the houses 400 to 800 feet into the high-scoring district. The magnitude of this effect is consistent with our earlier estimates: the average difference in scores between the high-scoring school and the low-scoring school was .32, which multiplied by the coefficient from column 3 of table 1 (.247) would yield an effect on house prices of 0.08. Thus we do observe an effect of about the expected magnitude *near* the boundary. However, the fact that the effect does not appear for homes 0-400 feet within the boundary of the better school raises additional questions of whether this is a causal effect of school quality.

Although these results do call into question the practicality of disentangling the effect of school quality from other neighborhood variables, perhaps they should not be surprising. Families who are willing to pay more to live in a school attendance area with higher test scores may also

---

26. The lower numbers of sales within 400 feet of the boundary is an artifact of the way in which we define distance to the boundary. We actually measure distance to the nearest house that sold in a different school attendance area. So 400 feet is an overestimate of how far these homes are from the boundary.

invest more in their homes. Even if houses are very similar on either side of a school border *when the boundary is originally drawn*, the similarity may not last long as properties are bought and sold, and as houses depreciate and are improved. Areas very near the boundary may not do as much of this upgrading, either because there is less return to doing so (because of neighborhood externalities from nearby homes on the less desirable side of the boundary) or because of the possibility of boundaries being moved in the future.

Note that the finding suggesting potentially unobserved differences in neighborhoods near school boundaries is primarily relevant for the cross-sectional effects of test performance on housing values. Studies that have tried to estimate the cross-sectional relationship between test performance and housing values may be overstating the importance of test performance, even if they limit themselves to properties near school boundaries. The primary results of this paper, which focus on the effect of changes of test scores and the creation of the state's rating system, would not be affected by unobserved differences between neighborhoods, as long as those differences were stable over time.

Conclusion

In the housing literature, there is a long tradition of attempting to disentangle the value of school test scores from other neighborhood amenities. Although such studies typically control for standard housing characteristics (such as number of bedrooms, square footage, lot size, and so on) and other neighborhood characteristics (such as mean income and local tax rates), readers of that literature appropriately worry that such studies fail to control for all the relevant characteristics that might be correlated with school test scores. Black proposed a novel approach by focusing on the values of properties near school boundaries, arguing that any differences in unmeasured neighborhood amenities would be minimized for properties that were in such close proximity.[27] Using data from Mecklenburg County, North Carolina, and focusing on properties within 500 to 2,000 feet of school boundaries, we replicate that approach and find similar results, suggesting that a one student-level standard deviation

27. Black (1999).

difference in a school's mean test score was associated with an 18 to 25 percentage point difference in house value. Nevertheless, we remain cautious in interpreting these estimates as reflecting the value of school quality alone, since there seemed to be changes in observable housing characteristics at the school boundaries in our data. One might be concerned that there are other unobserved differences in housing characteristics, even among properties near the school boundaries.

We also studied housing market reactions to the release of new information on the quality of schools, which state departments of education around the country are currently publishing. Although most states were already publishing some information on school mean test scores by the spring of 2001, the No Child Left Behind Act of 2001 will require most states to publish even more detailed information at the school level than they currently provide. We are much more confident in our ability to isolate the impact of new information, because we can look at changes in housing values within school assignment zones as new information is released over time. Earlier work by Figlio and Lucas in Florida suggested large housing price swings following the announcement of school ratings in 1999.[28] In North Carolina, we found no impact of annual changes in test scores on housing values. Moreover, we found no impact of the categorical rating system, which sorted schools into categories of "low performing" or "exemplary" based on a combination of baseline scores and "value-added" measures, which controlled for incoming students' baseline performance. The failure to find an impact of value-added ratings was particularly important, given that it would have been difficult for parents to have controlled for students' baseline scores with the data available to them previously.

Our findings have two potentially important implications for the education policy debate. First, even relative to the estimate of the value of school mean test score differences that we fear may be overstated, parents—particularly low-income parents—attach a large value to the proximity of the local school. A six- to eight-mile difference in the distance to the local school had a similar effect on housing values as a full student-level standard deviation in school mean test scores (roughly equivalent to moving from the highest to lowest scoring school in the district). Attempts to model the likely effect of school vouchers on the market for

28. Figlio and Lucas (2002).

schooling typically focus on differences in school quality alone. However, to the extent that they ignore the interplay between school siting and neighborhood segregation by race and family income, such models may underestimate the amount of income segregation that would remain in a voucher system. (Housing values would continue to capitalize distance to good schools even if school assignment boundaries were erased.)

Second, the housing markets seem to respond slowly to new information about school quality. Given the potential for free riding by some homeowners on the efforts of others to intervene in local schools, the housing market was already an unlikely source of pressure on local school officials to improve. Although some homeowners may be compelled to attend their local parent-teachers' association meeting in order to protect their property values, this is unlikely to lead to an efficient solution, even with high-quality measures of school performance. Regardless of this free-rider problem, our results suggest that short-term changes in test scores seem to be discounted. In other words, a school that is improving has a difficult time signaling that improvement to the housing market. This could be because there is so much other volatility in test scores that is difficult for home buyers to distinguish the signal from the noise, or because home buyers are primarily interested in the socioeconomic characteristics of schools, which are unlikely to change so quickly. In either case, short-term fluctuations in test scores and state accountability ratings have little effect on housing values.

In September 1997, William Capacchione sued the school district, claiming that his daughter was denied enrollment to a magnet school simply because of race. The case eventually led the courts to revisit the original court case requiring busing students in Charlotte on the basis of race. That case was not resolved until April 15, 2002, when the U.S. Supreme Court announced that it would let stand a lower court decision ending required busing in Charlotte.[29] By the fall of 2002, mandatory busing on the basis of race had been terminated, and many of the existing school boundaries had lost their importance as a public school choice program was implemented. The experience with the new school choice plan in Charlotte may yet yield valuable lessons on the interaction between housing markets and school quality.

29. Despite any uncertainty the legal proceedings may have created, we saw no evidence of a decline in values associated with high scoring schools between 1997 and the end of 2001.

Appendix Table 1. Summary Statistics

Variable name	Full sample					Within 2,000 feet of boundary		
	Observations	Mean	Standard deviation	Minimum	Maximum	Observations	Mean	Standard deviation
House price								
Real sale price (2001 dollars)	86,865	156,736	96,300	12,000	672,500	28,832	139,072	94,809
ln(Real sale price)	86,865	11.81	0.56	9.39	13.42	28,832	11.66	0.59
Test score measures								
Annual math and reading score	71,061	-0.02	0.29	-0.79	0.81	23,950	-0.12	0.27
Average math and reading score, 1993–99	86,865	-0.04	0.25	-0.62	0.44	28,832	-0.13	0.23
Average math + reading score, whites, 1993–99	86,865	0.24	0.24	-0.37	0.83	28,832	0.22	0.28
Average math + reading score, African Americans, 1993–99	86,865	-0.52	0.18	-0.80	-0.02	28,832	-0.57	0.14
Percent of students African American, 1993–99	86,865	0.37	0.17	0.07	0.96	28,832	0.45	0.14
Annual performance composite/10	49,926	6.89	1.18	3.63	9.76	15,737	6.44	1.03

Average performance composite/10, 1997–2001	86,865	7.00	1.06	4.19	9.46	28,832	6.53	0.82
School achieved exemplary growth	49,996	0.29	0.45	0	1	15,767	0.26	0.44
School achieved expected growth	49,996	0.33	0.47	0	1	15,767	0.27	0.45
School achieved score of distinction	49,996	0.11	0.31	0	1	15,767	0.04	0.21
School achieved score of excellence	49,996	0.06	0.24	0	1	15,767	0.02	0.14
School was low performance	49,996	0.16	0.36	0	1	15,767	0.21	0.40
Travel distance								
Distance to school (miles, straight line)	83,056	1.42	1.17	0.04	9.58	28,168	1.39	1.36
Characteristics of house								
Number of bedrooms	86,865	3.28	0.62	1	9	28,832	3.16	0.61
Number of bathrooms	86,865	1.96	0.58	1	6	28,832	1.80	0.63
Number of halfbaths	86,865	0.26	0.26	0	3.5	28,832	0.22	0.26
Acreage (acres)	86,865	0.37	0.40	0	5	28,832	0.36	0.31
Heated square feet / 100	86,865	19.54	8.03	4.14	100.61	28,832	17.56	7.27
House has garage	86,865	0.58	0.49	0	1	28,832	0.35	0.48
House has basement	86,865	0.07	0.25	0	1	28,832	0.08	0.28
House has air conditioning	86,865	0.93	0.26	0	1	28,832	0.88	0.33
Age of house in years / 10	86,865	1.64	1.91	0	10.10	28,832	2.60	1.96

Comments

Edward W. Hill: Thomas J. Kane, Douglas O. Staiger, and Gavin Samms make a contribution to our understanding of how Charlotte's housing market responds to new information about school quality. The results from their models indicate that long-term measures of school quality exert large positive effects on the value of housing after controlling for independent neighborhood effects. They find that annual fluctuations in school test performance do not affect housing values—the market treats them as noise. Surprisingly, the average educational attainment of an elementary school (as measured by the average reading and mathematics achievement scores of third and fifth graders) for whites influences house values while the scores of African American children do not. They also find that the presence of neighborhood schools increases the value of housing, especially for lower-income families.

The statistical work of Kane, Staiger, and Samms incorporates aspects of two literatures: the impact of public school quality on the asset value of housing and the evaluation of public school performance. There are five stylized facts about these linked investments.

First, education is funded through local taxes. Second, a child's placement in both the public school district and building is based on a family's residential location. Third, families have varying tastes for school quality. The literature links the asset value of housing to the quality of public schooling through a family's utility function in the tradition of Charles M. Tiebout.[30] Consumption is restricted by the tax price of the good, and

30. Tiebout (1956).

families make trade-offs between school quality and other goods. This assumption places the locational decision in a cross-sectional or static framework, turning education from an investment into a good that is consumed. Fourth, education is a merit good, and consumption is subsidized. Fifth, school-related tax payments are negatively capitalized in the value of residential land while the quality of education is positively capitalized.

There are three real-world problems with these stylized facts. First, not all metropolitan areas are composed of a large number of competing public school districts. Second, tax price is not the only determinant of school quality. Third, a family with school-age children frequently makes two investment decisions when it chooses a residential location. The first is a private market investment in housing. The second is a quasi-market investment in the human capital of their child. The last two problems are the subject of the remainder of the comment. Nothing that I write is a criticism of the work of Kane, Stagier, and Samms; these are thoughts triggered by their research.

Socioeconomic Status and the Education Production Function

The stylized facts imply that schools produce educational services that vary in quality with the one variable that is available in the model—the tax price of education. It does not. The education product function should correlate with property tax rates but not perfectly because of redistributive federal, state, and local funding and of the role that socioeconomic status (SES) plays in educational attainment.

That status enters the production function in two ways. The largest influence is between the SES of the student's family and achievement. The second is between some measure of classroom or schoolwide SES and achievement. Although SES is not solely a matter of money, family money income is the strongest correlate with educational achievement and is a major factor in determining a family's SES. Therefore, neighborhood housing values are based in part on the quality of educational outcomes; the quality of educational outcomes depends in part on the SES of the child's family and the SES of other children in the school; and neighborhood house values depend on the SES of existing residents.

Kane, Staiger, and Samms do not estimate educational production functions for individual students because the required data are not part of their data set. Instead, the authors estimate the effect of the racial composition of the student body on house values. Although SES is not directly entered into the equations, the assumption is made that the percentage of the student body that is African American is negatively correlated with the school's SES. The authors make the uncomfortable assumption that the percentage of African American children in the school proxies SES because they only have data on the average racial makeup of each school as a proxy for SES. The authors are clearly not thrilled with this assumption. This is most likely a reasonable assumption for statistical purposes, but it is troubling given that Charlotte does have a sizable middle-class African American community.

The authors ask the question: are people investing in schools that create an atmosphere for achievement, or are they purchasing entry rights into schools with high SES and through SES higher test scores? Or are white parents buying entry rights into schools with small proportions of African American students, thereby exercising a taste for discrimination and willingness to pay a premium to exercise that taste?

The statistical results are stark. The correlation between a school's average test score and the percent of the student body that is African American is –0.8 (figure 4). More than 60 percent of the variance in the test score is associated with racial composition alone. The authors note the average racial achievement gap in the school district: "African American students in Charlotte score about two-thirds of a standard deviation below white students." This result is from one of the most integrated urban school districts in the nation. The percentage of the student body of the elementary schools examined that is African American ranges from 1 to 94 percent, but the authors calculate that most schools range from 33 to 54 percent African American. To provide context to these data it is helpful to know that the Charlotte-Mecklenburg School District is the twenty-fourth largest in the nation, enrolling approximately 100,000 students in 135 schools. The overall system is 48 percent white, 43 percent African American, 4 percent Hispanic, and 5 percent other; 38 percent are eligible for free lunch.[31]

The statistical result is somewhat encouraging; the housing market is not directly discounting schools based on race. But it is doing so indirectly. When the schoolwide average test score is entered into sales price equations with the racial composition variable, the coefficient for the racial composition variable is negative and statistically indistinguishable

31. Snipes, Doolittle, and Herlihy (2002).

from zero. From this result it appears that homeowners are purchasing average test scores, which are most likely correlated with SES. Other specifications of the base model reinforce this interpretation. Real estate values are not being driven by the racial composition of schools but are driven by average school test scores and the test scores of white students. The authors ask: "if high test scores among white students are an indicator of a good school, why should housing markets ignore, or even draw the opposite inference, form high test scores among African Americans?"

The authors find clues in the pattern of busing and the fact that test scores by race are not correlated within schools. Some of the highest-scoring white students attend schools with some of the lowest-scoring black children. Differences in travel distances to school indicate that African American children are being bused into majority white schools. It appears that low-achieving minority children are going to schools with the region's best-performing white students, and the housing values are not being discounted as a result. The statistical results indicate that numbers of low-performing students are not affecting average scores in a major way, and therefore a balance between racial integration, putting low-achievement students in a high-achievement environment, and maintaining high average test scores must have been sought and reached by school administrators.

The Tie That Binds: Investing in Housing and Your Child's Human Capital

The third problem with the standard model lies in the way families make their educational choices. Both housing and education have current consumption aspects and investment aspects. Owing to the institutional constraints of the American market for primary and secondary education, these two investment decisions are not made independently. In portfolio terms their systematic risks covary. Making investment decisions that tie together quasi-market investments in public education with market decisions of investing in housing is a critical component of a family's investment portfolio. Therefore, one possible reason for changes in the relative prices of houses may be the increased rate of return from human capital investment.

The authors hint at the existence of path dependencies in their discussion of figure 5. In this figure they plot the log of the sales prices of houses in 400-foot increments on both sides of school catchment area borders, with the distance inside the high-performing school boundary on the right side and distance away from the high-performing school boundary heading to the left. The sale price is estimated from the hedonic regression with neighborhood dummy variables. The graph shows small differences within 400 feet of the boundary, followed by a rapid increase in value at 400 to 800 feet inside the high-performing school's catchment area (the prices climb by 8 percent). Why does it take 400 feet for prices to begin their climb? The authors speculate that "families who are willing to pay more to live in a school attendance area with higher test scores may also be willing to invest in their homes." In other words, they are investing in their linked capital assets. The authors then present the possibility of path dependencies. "Even if houses are very similar on either side of a school border *when the boundary is originally drawn* [emphasis in the original], the similarity may not last long as properties are bought and sold, and as houses depreciate and are improved." Incumbent upgrading will take place when rates of return justify the investment.

A second tie between the investment characteristics of housing and education is shown by the way the housing market ignores annual variations in test data. The authors conclude that housing markets incorporate long-term data on school performance and heavily discount annual fluctuations in test performance. In tests in which both long-term performance and the annual deviation from the long-term average are included, only the long-term average score is statistically different from having no effect on sales prices. The authors found that there was wide annual variation in the data reflecting sample variation and one-time factors that can affect test results. These results were repeated when the authors introduced the state of North Carolina's annual measures of value added in the educational process.

Is the housing market more rational than the research and evaluation unit of North Carolina's Department of Education? It is tempting to declare the bureaucrats test and measurement happy, praise the rationality of markets, and move on. Unfortunately, we cannot do this. Families that are simultaneously investing in housing and education are making long-term, illiquid, portfolio investments and are risk averse. They do not care about annual fluctuations in attainment. They are interested in long-term, risk-adjusted rates of return—just as in any other investment. This means that the only data of interest about educational performance are on long-term average achievement. The housing market is acting on the data of interest to investors while the bureaucrats are trying to measure change and improvement in outcomes, which is the objective given to them by the legislature and popular political pressure.

The research team has obtained its main objective. It has measured the influence of public school quality at the elementary school level on house price appreciation. It has also opened up an interesting set of questions on educational policies that will be able to inform public policy in the coming years, especially now that court-mandated busing has ended in the school district.

David L. Weimer: Public school districts in the United States almost universally enjoy local monopolies over the provision of publicly funded primary and secondary education. District policies often force parents to choose schooling through residential choice. As anyone who has bought or sold a house almost certainly knows from experience, the quality of the local elementary school tied to the residential property is one of the most important considerations in assessing the trilogy of "location, location, location." Economists and policy analysts who have looked for the impact on housing prices of elementary school quality, at least as measured by test scores, have found it. Thomas J. Kane, Douglas O. Staiger, and Gavin Samms add a particularly well-conceived analysis to this line of research that addresses several new questions: do housing markets capitalize long-term trends or short- term fluctuations in school performance? Do these markets capitalize the overall performance of schools or their value added in terms of test score gains? Do they capitalize labels attached to schools by the state?

These are important questions for two reasons. First, the greater demands for accountability being placed on school districts and schools by state and federal governments suggest that parents, and prospective home buyers, are likely to receive more information in the future about the annual performance of schools. Second, the findings of Kane and Staiger that assessments based on annual tests are highly volatile raise the possibility of the public receiving signals so noisy as to often mislead.[32] The answers provided by Kane, Staiger, and Samms to these ques-

---

32. Kane and Staiger (2002a).

tions are at least somewhat reassuring: housing markets seem to take an appropriately long-term view even if our policymakers do not.

Empirical Approach

Efforts to estimate the marginal impact of school quality on housing prices confront two difficulties. First, schooling is only one of a basket of public services attached to any particular residential location. Second, the immediate neighborhood of a residential property is likely to influence its price, and the factors that determine neighborhood quality are difficult to specify and measure.

The choice of Mecklenburg County, North Carolina, enables Kane and coauthors to deal effectively with the problem of multiple public services. It has a single school district with geographic catchments for elementary schools that cross the boundaries of Charlotte and six other municipalities. Consequently, the authors can adequately control for the provision of public services other than education with the inclusion of fixed effects for these political jurisdictions.

In order to control for neighborhood effects, the authors follow the very creative approach of Sandra Black.[33] She reasoned that, by restricting the sample to residential properties close to the boundaries of school catchments, models could be estimated with indicators for boundaries, so that comparisons would effectively be made holding neighborhood quality constant. Kane, Staiger, and Samms implement Black's general approach with a variety of specifications and sample restrictions. Their effort is exemplary. They make excellent, and even clever, use of the available data to allay concerns about their modeling, the appropriateness of their data, and the robustness of their findings. Although one might raise a few quibbles, I think most experienced empirical researchers will be impressed with the balanced and thorough analysis provided.

Findings and Policy Implications

Perhaps the most important finding is the absence of an effect of the yearly deviation of the test score from its long-run average. That is, the average test score over the estimation period provides the full school quality effect. In view of the concern warranted by the volatility in yearly

33. Black (1999).

test score and value-added measures, this finding is somewhat reassuring at least on the surface—the market seems to ignore what are likely to be very noisy signals. Yet why does the market fail to pay attention to the short-run fluctuations?

One possibility is that market participants assess school quality based on reputation, perhaps perceived in information provided by friends and real estate agents. The latest test score is simply one piece of information used to update the reputations. If initial beliefs (prior probabilities) were very strong, or real estate agents provide corrective information about the longer run, then Bayesian updating would result in relatively little change in the assessment of school quality.

Of course, the relative stability of opinion may be a two-edged sword. Besides cutting down reliance on noisy signals, it may also cut the market effect of real improvements in school quality. The result may be a long lag between the improvements in schools and the corresponding appreciation in housing values predicted by looking at yearly achievement levels.

Another finding of importance is the absence of an effect for the North Carolina categorical ratings. Here again, to the extent that these categories are based on highly volatile measures, the absence of a market effect might be judged positive. Alternatively, however, it could be that market participants care only about levels of output (average test scores) rather than school performance (changes in test scores). The direct interest of parents in putting their children in high-performing schools is likely to be stronger than their indirect interest in seeing the effective use of tax dollars by schools. If this is the case, then it suggests that these categorical rankings must operate top-down through administrative incentives rather than bottom-up through report cards.

Another interesting finding is that the market does not seem to value higher scores by African American students. The scores for white students appear to dominate. Is it possible that white participants make up so large a share of the market that their preferences dominate? In the absence of direct measures of market participation by race, perhaps a proxy could be based on changes in white and African American home-ownership rates over the time period of the study.

Finally, the apparently large negative effect of the distance to the assigned school on housing prices is noteworthy. Certainly, the time costs of travel provide an explanation, one consistent with the larger effect for poorer, and therefore more congested, neighborhoods. A reinforcing factor, however, may be that closeness to a school increases the perceived credibility of remaining in the catchment of that school. This factor might also help explain why the authors find a discontinuity inside, rather than at, the enrollment boundary.

In conclusion, Kane, Staiger, and Samms offer a very interesting, careful, provocative, and policy relevant analysis. The elimination of school catchment boundaries in Charlotte noted in the paper indeed provides a wonderful natural experiment for checking the predictive powers of the authors' models.

References

Black, Sandra E. 1999. "Do Better Schools Matter? Parental Valuation of Elementary Education." *Quarterly Journal of Economics* 114 (May): 577–99.

Bogart, William T., and Brian A. Cromwell. 1997. "How Much Is a Good School District Worth?" *National Tax Journal* 50 (June): 215–32.

———. 2000. "How Much Is a Neighborhood School Worth?" *Journal of Urban Economics* 47 (March): 280–305.

Clotfelter, Charles. 1975. "The Effect of School Desegregation and Housing Prices." *Review of Economics and Statistics* 57 (November): 446–51.

Figlio, David, and Maurice Lucas. 2002. "What's in a Grade? School Report Cards and House Prices." Working Paper 8019. Cambridge, Mass.: National Bureau of Economic Research..

Gormley, William T., and David L. Weimer. 1999. *Organizational Report Cards.* Harvard University Press.

Kane, Thomas J., and Douglas O. Staiger. 2002a. "Improving School Accountability Measures." Working Paper 8156. Cambridge, Mass.: National Bureau of Economic Research.

———. 2002b. "The Promise and Pitfalls of Using Imprecise School Accountability Measures." *Journal of Economic Perspectives* 16 (Fall): 91–114.

———. 2002c. "Volatility in School Test Scores: Implications for Test-Based Accountability Systems." *Brookings Papers on Education Policy.* Brookings.

———. Forthcoming. "Racial Subgroup Rules in School Accountability Systems." In *No Child Left Behind? The Politics and Practice of School Accountability*, edited by Paul E. Peterson and Morton R. West. Brookings.

Snipes, Jason, Fred Doolittle, and Corinne Herlihy. 2002. *Foundations for Success: Case Studies of How Urban School Systems Improve Student Achievement.* Washington, D.C.: Council for Great City Schools.

Tiebout, Charles M. 1956. "A Pure Theory of Local Expenditures." *Journal of Political Economy* 65 (October): 416–24.

Weimer, David L., and Michael J. Wolkoff. 2001. "School Performance and Housing Values: Using Non-Contiguous District and Incorporation Boundaries to Identify School Effects." *National Tax Journal* 54 (June): 231–53.

THOMAS NECHYBA
Duke University

Public School Finance and Urban School Policy: General versus Partial Equilibrium Analysis

THE EFFECTS OF ALTERNATIVE APPROACHES to educational finance on public school quality have attracted substantial attention from researchers and policymakers. Much of this analysis, however, focuses narrowly on the effects of financial resources on school quality in the absence of behavioral adjustments to policy changes. In contrast, this paper examines the relationship between school financing methods and school quality in a framework that explicitly links public finance issues, housing markets, and school quality. In the framework employed here, the quality of a school varies with its financial resources and the quality of students (and their families) that attend the school. Student and family quality in turn depend on both the abilities with which schoolchildren arrive at school as well as the economic status of their parents, who may be able to contribute in other ways to local schools. Households vote for public school spending and pay taxes to support schools, and they may respond to changes in school financing policy by moving or placing their children in private schools. Thus household responses to policy changes not only cover a broad range of options but also interact with the choices of other households, because school quality depends on who else attends local

Financial support from the National Science Foundation (SBR-9905706) is gratefully acknowledged, as are comments from participants at the conference, particularly the comments by discussants Rick Hanushek and Susanna Loeb, as well as those of the editors.

139

schools, local housing prices and private school markets reflect overall changes in demand, and local voting on public school spending is affected by all these changes.

Using this framework, this paper focuses on three widely examined policy changes: shifts from local to state financing, changes in state aid formulas, and the introduction of state-funded vouchers. The main finding is that the indirect (general equilibrium) effects of policy changes on school quality—for example, those that arise from households moving and thus alter the quality of neighborhoods and students, or those that arise from parents choosing to shift their students from public to private school or vice versa—tend in many cases to dominate the direct (partial equilibrium) effect on the amount of financial resources devoted to schools. In many ways, this should not be surprising. Public school institutions shape the way many households decide where to live and where to send their children to school, and changes in these institutions alter the fundamental trade-offs faced by families as they make these choices.

This principal finding has several implications for the analysis of educational finance issues. First, urban housing markets and residential mobility play an important role in determining the impact of many school finance policies. Given the strong link between housing markets and access to public schools, an analysis of policy should include an explicit recognition of changes in these markets brought about by household mobility. Second, the existence of private schools, and the extent to which parents are willing and able to shift their students from the public to the private sector, imposes constraints on the impacts of public school policies. In the presence of an active private school market that might respond to changes in public school policies, a focus on only public schools is furthermore incomplete because it ignores the impact of public school policies on a significant number of children. Third, the existence of likely behavioral responses to policies and the link of schools to neighborhoods place severe limits on the extent to which equalizing school financial resources will result in equalizing school quality. This implies that the court-driven focus on spending inequalities may have excessively narrowed policy discussions to only one dimension of a multidimensional problem. Finally, the results in this paper suggest that to the extent they accurately forecast the general equilibrium effects of school finance policies, many households will be more affected by changes in their wealth (through changes in housing values) from changing school finance policies than through changes in educational opportunities for their children. This adds an important dimension to the political economy analysis of proposals such as school vouchers that would adversely affect the wealth of those who are likely to be disproportionately influential in the political process. In many cases, the politics behind school policymaking may thus have less to do with schools and more with property values.

The advantages of the framework employed in this analysis include the ability to examine effects of alternative policies within a single, internally consistent model and to isolate the relative importance of each channel through which effects occur. With key structural parameters of the model matched to real-world data in order to successfully replicate important features of actual communities and schools, the resulting computational model is used to conduct policy experiments that explicitly trace out not only the immediate impact of large policy changes but also the long-run impact of changes in the economic environment in which households make choices about schooling. Although this makes possible an explicit comparison of partial equilibrium and general equilibrium effects within a single framework, the assumptions made are in some cases tenuous enough to recommend caution in interpreting results as absolute predictions.

The analysis begins by outlining the main features of the modeling framework. The next section examines the effects of the three types of policies and breaks down the results into direct and indirect effects. I then discuss a series of caveats to interpreting the model.

An Economic Model of Equilibrium Differences in Public School Quality

The effects of school reform depend in part on the underlying causes for current public school differences in quality. Two such possible causes are differences in parental tastes for education and in parental information regarding public schools, either of which could cause parents to choose different types of schools. This paper takes another approach in that it explains differences in public school quality by incorporating explicitly the political and economic environment within which parents make educational choices.[1]

Although public schools are free in the sense that they do not charge tuition, access to each public school is typically restricted to those who reside within the attendance zone (or district) of that school.[2] Housing markets are such that not all house qualities are available in all school districts, thus limiting options for some families. Furthermore, the housing market capitalizes public school quality, thus explicitly introducing "tuition" to public schools through a housing price premium in the better school districts. Finally, public school inputs are at least partially linked to local community characteristics, with higher-income communities likely to spend more for each pupil as well as contribute more to the local public school in nonpecuniary inputs such as teacher quality, peer quality, and parental involvement.[3]

---

1. A preference-based explanation for the existence of systematic differences in public school quality is problematic as long as it remains divorced from an economic model of the local public finance and urban sector within which schools operate. In the absence of horizontal differentiation among schools, as long as all parents would prefer better schools to worse schools (even if the intensity of that preference differs), all parents would in fact choose the best available public school for their children because no tuition is charged in public schools to select among some parents who may value quality more than others. It is only when heterogeneous preference models are embedded into local public finance and urban models that less extreme heterogeneity can play a constructive role in identifying causes for public school quality differences. See, for example, Epple and Sieg (1999). Information-based explanations for differences in attitudes toward public school quality, however, are most plausible as stand-alone explanations for quality differences that are temporary rather than systematically present for long periods. While it may well be the case that reforms need to take account of the fact that information may be processed differently by different families, it becomes problematic to assume that some parents are consistently misinformed about which schools are good and which not when these differences persist over long periods.

2. Even when public schools are open for enrollment from outside the district, the better public schools are typically permitted to claim capacity constraints to prevent entry into the school from outside the district. It is noteworthy, for instance, that the Milwaukee school-choice program is actually one that allows choice by inner-city parents of suburban public schools and offers financial incentives for those schools to accept students from outside. In the end, however, the program became a private school choice plan because no suburban school agreed to accept children eligible in the program.

3. Empirical studies suggest that this correlation between nonpecuniary inputs and household income as well as the value of such nonpecuniary inputs into production is significant. One standard assumption is that child ability is (imperfectly) correlated with household income, thus providing a nonpecuniary input to high-income schools. Teacher quality, while perhaps not costing more due to state collective bargaining agreements,

An economic model that does not rely on preference or information differences in explaining large interdistrict variances in public school quality must therefore explicitly include empirically relevant levels of household income inequality and a housing market with uneven distributions of housing quality across districts, and it must allow for household mobility across districts. In addition, the model must contain some empirically relevant mechanism for funding public schools as well as a private school market that can account for observed levels of private school attendance. Each of these features is incorporated in this paper's underlying model.

The Structural Model

The underlying structural model accurately replicates a number of stylized features of public schools and local public finance.[4] It begins with a continuum of households N where each household is endowed with one house, a child with a given ability, an income level and preferences over private consumption, neighborhood and house quality, and school quality consumed by the household's child. The main features of the model can then be summarized:

—Preferences of all households are assumed to be identical.[5] But incomes, house endowments, and abilities differ across households (with income imperfectly correlated with child ability). The total number of different household types is 1,500.

—Houses are divided exogenously into neighborhoods. All houses in a neighborhood share the same quality and neighborhood characteristics,

---

tends to be higher in high-income districts; Loeb and Page (2000). And parental involvement and monitoring of public schools is significantly correlated with parental income; McMillan (1999).

4. Nechyba (1997a, 1997b, 1999, 2000, 2003).

5. The functional form of the utility function is $u(d,h,c,s) = k_{dh}c^\alpha s^\beta$, where d indicates school district, h indicates house type or neighborhood, c indicates private consumption, and s indicates school quality. The parameters α and β are calibrated so as to replicate spending levels per pupil in the data as those emerging from majority-rule voting. Any choice of utility function such as this necessarily introduces implicit assumptions about behavioral elasticities, with Cobb-Douglas forms such as this being no exception. As elasticities change, so will the magnitudes of the simulation results in tables such as those presented in this paper. In making benchmark functional form assumptions, Cobb-Douglas functional forms represent typical starting points, and therefore they feature prominently on both the preference and the technology sides of this model.

and collections of neighborhoods form school districts. There are three school districts—high-, middle-, and low-income—each with five neighborhoods. House-quality distributions potentially overlap across jurisdictions. The model takes the housing stock as given rather than explaining its evolution over time.

—Schools produce educational quality by combining per pupil spending with peer inputs.[6] All schools, public and private, face the same production technology. Per pupil spending levels are determined through majority-rule voting in public schools and through competitive price setting in private schools. The peer input contributed to a school by a household includes a component related to household income (proxying for nonpecuniary inputs) and a separate component related to child ability.

—Private schools have two competitive advantages over public schools: they can set a level of per pupil spending (which is equal to tuition) that reflects the desire of parents more closely, and they can select from student applicants. This gives rise to the effect that private schools seek to "cream-skim" from public schools by choosing only households of high student quality. At the same time, public schools have the advantage that they are free to anyone living within the district boundaries.[7]

The strategy in the line of research from which this paper draws is to begin by assuming there are neither efficiency gains from increased com-

---

6. The school production function is $s = f(x,q) = x^\rho q^{(1-\rho)}$ where x is per pupil spending and q is average peer inputs in the school (with a minimum of \$5,000 per pupil expenditure assumed to be necessary for a school to open). Although the studies of school production function are engaged in a debate over the degree to which financial resources (per pupil spending) matter for outcomes like test scores and graduation rates—see, for example, Hanushek (1999) and Krueger (1999)—this debate is not immediately relevant to the approach taken here because the approach here defines school quality more broadly in terms of parental perceptions of school quality. While spending may or may not matter for narrower school outcomes, there exists ample evidence that parents place importance on school spending. In the context of this structural model, a lack of spending in the production function would result in equal spending in all schools—and would furthermore give such an advantage to private schools that public schools could not survive.

7. In practice, the main advantage that is important for private schools is the ability to set peer inputs. Note that the specification of the private school sector implicitly assumes a perfectly elastic supply of private schools— that is, if a private school of particular characteristics is demanded and can make positive (or zero) profits, it will be supplied. The private school market modeled here therefore represents a long-run market, with short-run effects likely to include fewer private school market changes than predicted by the model.

Table 1. Housing Quality Parameters in the Model, by School District Income Level

District income level	Housing quality				
	1	*2*	*3*	*4*	*5*
Low (1)	0.820	0.882	0.930	0.978	1.021
Medium (2)	0.872	0.930	1.002	1.032	1.085
High (3)	0.930	0.950	1.063	1.182	1.267

Note: These values represent k_{dh} values in the utility functions $u(d,h,c,s) = k_{dh}c^\alpha s^\beta$ discussed in footnote 5. They were first reported in Nechyba (2003b) and are discussed in more detail there.

petition nor any private school advantages in school production.[8] While these assumptions can easily be relaxed, this paper documents the relative importance of general equilibrium effects in the absence of such factors. In other work I have demonstrated that an introduction of such effects, while changing the *absolute* predictions, does little to alter the *relative* importance of the general equilibrium effects.[9]

Using Data to Inform the Model

The data used to calibrate the model are from the New Jersey suburbs of New York City. School districts are divided into high-, middle-, and low-income districts in such a way as to have roughly equal population in each of the three categories. Average characteristics of districts falling into these categories are used to represent the stylized high-, middle-, and low-income districts in the model.[10]

In calibrating the model, the following stylized features are matched by the calibration algorithm:

—House and neighborhood quality parameters are set so as to replicate the distribution of house prices observed in the data. This calibration method implicitly incorporates the impact of local externalities and public amenities into the house quality parameters of the model. Table 1 provides the calibrated house quality parameters for each of the house types in the model.

—The income distribution is set to approximate the empirical distribu-

8. Hoxby (2000) finds evidence for a competitive effect on public school productivity, and Neal (1997) documents higher productivity in Catholic schools for at least some populations.

9. Nechyba (2003a, forthcoming).

10. A complete description of the data sources is given in Nechyba (2003c).

tion observed in the data. The child ability distribution is set so as to produce a .4 correlation with household income, suggested as an upper bound.[11]

—Household utility weights placed on private consumption and school quality are set so as to replicate the correct levels of public school spending set through majority-rule voting.

—A household's peer quality is determined by an equal weighting of the household's income with the child's ability level (in a Cobb-Douglas process). Sensitivity analysis that varies the relative weights on child ability and household income shows that the relative magnitudes of general equilibrium effects are largely unaffected by this weighting.

—The school production function is assumed to have constant returns to scale but requires a minimum of $5,000 per pupil in expenditures.[12] The weights placed on per pupil spending and peer quality inputs are set so as to replicate the levels of private school attendance observed.[13] The model implicitly assumes that peer contributions to school production are such that mixing of different peer-quality students results in higher overall school quality than separating peers.

—Finally, the benchmark model uses the New Jersey school financing formula; the later simulations introduce new public school financing methods holding fixed the structural parameters calibrated with the New Jersey formula and New Jersey data. Table 2 provides some key features of the data and compares them to the replicated results from the benchmark equilibrium. Most of the features in the data are replicated well by the calibrated structural model, with the level of private school attendance in district 3 being one notable exception, in part because the model does not include household incomes above $200,000. Such households would always choose private schools in the model, and their inclusion

---

11. Solon (1992); Zimmerman (1992).

12. The minimum expenditure requirement has two justifications: First, it is likely that states indeed require an implicit minimum spending level even when funding is purely local. Second, the computational algorithm to determine the equilibrium of the model becomes significantly more efficient if extremely low out-of-equilibrium spending levels are ruled out.

13. This determines precisely the relative weight that households in the model place on spending versus peers. If too much weight is placed on spending, private schools do not have a sufficient competitive advantage to be able to survive; if too much weight is placed on peer quality, private schools have too much of an advantage, thus not allowing the model to accurately replicate observed levels of public school attendance.

would eliminate half the difference between the actual and the predicted private school attendance rates in district 3. Given that these households (were they included explicitly) would not be on the margin of either moving or changing schools under different policies, the results of the simulations would be largely unaffected by expanding the model to include such households.

Economic Forces Driving the Equilibrium

Having determined the structural parameters to be used in policy simulations, it is now worthwhile to briefly explore with some stylized examples how general equilibrium forces unfold in the model.[14] In order to focus on the link between public schools and residential housing markets, the first row of table 3 therefore begins by simulating the distribution of households and housing prices when all households choose private schools and no public schools exist.[15] The purpose is not to discuss this as a serious policy alternative but rather to determine where households would live and what prices they would pay for housing when there are no price distortions that arise from the coupling of public schools with residential location. The results suggest that a substantial amount of residential income segregation exists simply because of differences in housing quality among districts.[16]

The second and third rows of the table then report results from the other extreme: no private schools are permitted and only public schools operate (funded locally in row 2 and funded centrally in row 3). Thus, while no bundling between school and residential location choices exists in row 1, the bundling is complete in rows 2 and 3. This bundling— whether accomplished through a locally or a centrally financed system—

14. This subsection draws heavily on the discussion in Nechyba (2002).

15. It should be noted that there always exists such an equilibrium (without public schools) in the model. This is because households are assumed to choose their political support for public schools after selecting whether to attend a private or a public school. In the absence of public schools, all households choose private schools. Given that they choose private schools, they will show no support at the ballot box for public schools.

16. Note, however, that because the model does not address the question of how housing quality stocks arose in the first place, this does not mean that the first row of table 3 illustrates the level of segregation there would have been if no public school distortions had ever entered into the construction of housing. Rather, it simply demonstrates expected segregation levels in the absence of public school distortions *given* current housing quality in different districts.

Table 2. New Jersey Benchmark Equilibrium and Actual Data, by School District Income Level

	District income level					
	Low (1)		Medium (2)		High (3)	
Categories[a]	Model	Actual	Model	Actual	Model	Actual
Property values (dollars)[b]	117,412	157,248	205,629	192,867	292,484	271,315
Average income (dollars)	31,120	30,639	46,216	45,248	65,863	67,312
Public school per pupil spending (dollars)	6,652	6,702	7,910	7,841	8,621	8,448
Funding raised locally (percent)	52	52	77	77	87	0.87
Peer inputs	0.2684	...	0.4701	...	0.6521	...
Public school quality	0.4322	...	0.6178	...	0.7803	...
Students attending private schools (percent)	20	21	23	23	13	20

a. See text for definitions of terms.
b. Property values are converted from annual flows (calculated in the computational model) using a 5.5 percent discount rate.

Table 3. School Financing and Average Income and Property Value Assumptions, by Income of School District[a]
Dollars

Private schools allowed	Public school financing	Average income			Average property value		
		Low (1)	Medium (2)	High (3)	Low (1)	Medium (2)	High (3)
Yes	None	25,700	50,175	67,325	158,327	227,189	266,474
No	Local property tax	17,628	39,647	85,925	101,683	204,075	392,402
	State income tax	19,875	42,250	81,075	102,086	220,725	387,549
Yes	Local property tax	29,725	50,262	63,212	123,224	211,729	294,825
	State income tax	29,891	51,309	67,325	118,486	226,345	316,308

Note: Values in this table are derived from portions of table 3 in Nechyba (2003a) and table 3 in Nechyba (2003c), with property values converted from annualized flows using a 5.5 percent discount rate. This table also appears in Nechyba (2002).

introduces substantial distortions in housing prices. In poor districts, houses are depressed as they capture the low school quality (see table 4), while in rich districts they are inflated because of the high quality of the schools. This then introduces substantial increases of segregation beyond what one would expect from interdistrict housing differences alone (see row 1). The precise method of financing public schools is thus quite secondary to the bundling of public schools with residential location and urban housing markets.

Finally, rows 4 and 5 of table 3 introduce the combination of a public and private system—again for both locally and centrally financed public schools. The difference between rows 2 and 3 on the one hand and rows 4 and 5 on the other is striking: not only does the introduction of private schools into a publicly financed system lessen income segregation, it actually causes income segregation in the model to become less than it would be simply due to housing quality differences between districts. When private schools are allowed, demand for housing in district 1 rises as households attending private schools seek to take advantage of low housing prices that are (for them) not linked to poor public schools. Similarly, demand for housing in district 3 declines as some households who would pay high housing prices when housing is bundled with public schools now "unbundle" their choices by choosing private schools in the poor district where housing is cheap. This raises the price of housing in poor districts relative to rich districts, but not to the point where it would be if housing were not connected to public school access (as in row 1). Thus the new equilibrium provides incentives to middle- and high-income households to reside in poor districts while sending their children to private schools. Table 4 provides additional school-related information for each of these simulations.

While public finance institutions thus matter for such outcomes as public school quality differences across districts, the link between residential housing and public school access matters just as much if not more. Even under full financial resource equalization through centralized school financing, substantial interjurisdictional differences in public school quality remain, and they remain precisely because equalization takes place within an urban environment in which other economic forces are at work. Therefore, both public finance institutions and urban housing markets, as well as the interaction of public and private school markets, ultimately are key to an analysis of urban school policy. And not

Table 4. Public and Private School Quality and Attendance under Assumptions of School Financing Method and Income of School District

Private schools allowed	Public school financing	Public school quality			Students attending private school (percent)		
		Low income (1)	Medium income (2)	High income (3)	Low income (1)	Medium income (2)	High income (3)
Yes	None	....	....	....	100	100	100
No	Local property tax	0.3239	0.6024	0.9521	0	0	0
	State income tax	0.3940	0.6244	0.9022	0	0	0
Yes	Local property tax	0.3674	0.6192	0.8183	30	20	10
	State income tax	0.4616	0.6316	0.6841	22.5	17.5	15

only do these matter independently, they are likely to interact in important ways. Public school financing institutions, for instance, can strengthen or weaken the connection of public school access to residential location, and they can cause growth or shrinkage in the private school market. It is to these interactions that I now turn for different types of state public finance policies.

School Finance Policies: Partial versus General Equilibrium

Each section that follows begins with a fully decentralized public school system financed solely through local property taxes determined within each district through majority-rule voting. It then considers the effect of different types of reforms under different assumptions about the responsiveness of households in the model. First, I report how the combination of public school spending, public school quality in each district, and average public and private school quality (in each district) changes when no economic response by households occurs. Second, I consider how these outcomes change when household residential location and schooling choices are held fixed but voting behavior adjusts. Finally, I report the full general equilibrium outcome when households fully adjust and prices are allowed to change to support the new equilibrium. Two points are emphasized throughout: first, in some cases the general equilibrium responses are significant. Second, when policies result in households switching to or away from private schools, it may be important to consider the impact of reforms not just on the public school sector but rather on the overall education sector (including private schools).

Centralization and Equalization of Public School Financing

This section begins by investigating the partial and general equilibrium effects of an extreme change in public school financing—from a purely decentralized system financed by property taxes to one in which the state fully equalizes expenditures across districts and funds expenditures through a state income tax. Table 5 shows three key outcomes under the different assumptions regarding the responsiveness of households in the model. For each outcome, the local property tax equilibrium is reported next to the results for the policy change to facilitate comparisons.

Table 5. School Spending and Quality under Decentralized or Centralized Taxation and Behavioral Assumptions, by District Income Level

District income level	Local property tax equilibrium	Centralized tax, equalized spending		
		No behavioral change[a]	Partial equilibrium voting[b]	Full general equilibrium
Public school per pupil spending (dollars)				
Low (1)	5,000	7,731	7,309	7,195
Medium (2)	7,326	7,731	7,309	7,195
High (3)	10,215	7,731	7,309	7,195
All[c]	7,731	7,731	7,309	7,195
Average public school quality				
Low (1)	0.3674	0.4618	0.4484	0.4616
Medium (2)	0.6192	0.6370	0.6184	0.6316
High (3)	0.8183	0.7070	0.6864	0.6841
All[c]	0.6204	0.6122	0.5943	0.5960
Average school quality (including private schools)				
Low (1)	0.5421	0.6082	0.5989	0.5755
Medium (2)	0.6853	0.6995	0.6847	0.6904
High (3)	0.8314	0.7313	0.7127	0.7267
All[c]	0.6863	0.6797	0.6654	0.6642

a. This column assumes that the state income tax rate is set so as to keep average public school spending equal to what it is under decentralization.

b. This column assumes that voters approve a state income tax rate used to fund all public schools equally, but no household behavior changes are permitted.

c. This row calculates average statewide values. For public school figures, this is a weighted average of the remainder of the column where the weights are the fraction within each district that attend public schools. For overall school figures (the last set of columns), it is simply an average of the previous values in the columns.

First, consider the impact on spending. The simulation results labeled "No behavioral change" assume that the state government is able to maintain the pre-reform average spending in public schools but now spreads that spending equally across districts. The "Partial equilibrium voting" column, however, assumes that, holding voters fixed at their pre-reform location, equalized state spending has to be approved through majority-rule voting. This effect by itself lowers spending by approximately 6 percent because of the well-known effect caused by the skewedness of the income distribution. Under decentralized voting the median voter in each district is pivotal, while under statewide voting the median state voter determines the outcome. In a stylized Tiebout model this implies that average spending in the state is determined by *mean* state income under decentralization while it depends on *median* income under centralization.[17] So long as the median is lower than the mean (which is the case in real-world income distributions such as the one modeled in this exercise), this implies that majority rule will lead to lower average spending under centralization than under decentralization.

Finally, the third column, labeled "Full general equilibrium," shows an additional 1.5 percent drop in average spending in public schools when the full general equilibrium effects unfold. This additional decrease in spending is due to a reduction in overall private school attendance as public school finances are centralized, thus leading to an increase in public school attendance and a decline in per pupil spending. This increase in private school attendance under centralization is counterintuitive in the sense that most would expect the decrease in local choice from centralization to lead to an increase rather than a decrease in private school attendance. However, the conventional intuition is incomplete because it does not consider two effects that may in fact lead to a decrease in private school attendance as financing of public schools is equalized.[18] First, a *direct* effect occurs in the poor district where public school quality improves as a result of centralization and thus leads to switching away from private schools. Second, an *indirect* effect (which is twice the magnitude of the direct effect in the model presented here) unfolds through general equilibrium adjustments in housing prices. As the cost of housing rises in poor districts (because of higher prices due to better public schools and because of the decoupling of tax burdens from location choice), households that previously chose private schools in part because the choice allowed them to consume cheap housing in poor districts now

---

17. Under a stylized Tiebout model, residents segregate into districts based on their type, and districts are therefore homogeneous. Thus within each district all households agree on the spending level and each household consumes its most preferred spending level. When decentralized spending levels are then averaged across the state, the average state spending level is simply the average of the most preferred spending levels by households. But in a state election, households disagree on the best spending level, and the median household in the state is pivotal (assuming no exit from or entry into the private school sector).

18. This is demonstrated more fully in Nechyba (2003a).

have less incentive to continue in the private sector. These two effects combine in the model to result in an increase in public school attendance under centralization, and thus a decline in per pupil spending.[19]

The second part of table 5 reports the impact on perceived public school quality. Here, the differences between models that assume no behavioral change and those that fully incorporate all general equilibrium effects are not dramatic. In all cases, centralization leads to a narrowing of public school quality differences across districts, primarily because of equalization of spending. As peer compositions within public schools change in the general equilibrium, little additional change takes place. The increase in public school quality in districts 1 and 2 between the partial equilibrium and the full general equilibrium is 2–3 percent and is due solely to an increase in peer quality in these schools as children previously in private schools in district 1 switch to public schools because of the general equilibrium effects in the housing market. In the case of centralization of public school financing, the main effects therefore seem clustered around what happens to public school spending. And because of the decline in public school spending, overall public school quality (averaged across districts) declines by about 4 percent despite the increase in peer quality within the public schools.

The last part of table 5 tells a somewhat different story. This differs from the previous results in that we now include in the average district school quality figures the role of private schools within each district. First, note that, while public school quality in district 1 rises by 22 percent in the full general equilibrium model, overall school quality in district 1 rises by only 6 percent because private school attendance falls from 30 percent to 22.5 percent—and this increase is half what it would be if the full set of behavioral changes implied by the general equilibrium model had not been considered. Overall school quality for all children in

---

19. The model would predict an increase in private school attendance under centralization if centralization also led to a decline in public school efficiency (as is sometimes argued). In fact the model, combined with empirical results in the literature, suggests that it may indeed be likely that public school spending becomes less efficient the more spending is centralized and equalized. More precisely, radical centralization and equalization of public school spending seems to be correlated with higher private school attendance (as, for example, in California). The model of this paper suggests this could only happen if an additional effect was falling public school productivity.

the state declines by an amount roughly similar to the decline in public school quality, but the distribution of the decline is different when private schools are included. In particular, the ratio of public school quality in district 3 to that in district 1 declines by 50 percent (from 2.23 to 1.48), with this decline being disproportionately due to an increase in public school quality in district 1. The ratio of *overall* school quality in district 3 to that in district 1, however, falls by only 21 percent (from 1.53 to 1.26), but with this decline being disproportionately due to a decrease in overall school quality in district 3 (with only a small increase in district 1).

Thus, when viewed through the lens of only the public school system, centralization leads to a substantial narrowing of interdistrict quality differences primarily because schools get better in poor districts. However, when viewed through the lens of the combined public and private school system, the narrowing of interdistrict average school quality occurs primarily because of a reduction in school quality in the rich districts.

State Grants-in-Aid

The extremes of full decentralization and full centralization modeled in the previous sections are rarely found in school systems in the United States. Rather, most states have designed complicated formulas for determining state aid. This results in hybrid systems of partial local funding (typically through the property tax) combined with some state funding (typically through state income or sales taxes). This section therefore provides some examples of state grant programs to investigate how partial and general equilibrium effects may affect an analysis of such hybrid systems. In particular, it begins with a comparison of state block grants (of $3,000 per pupil) to all school districts with a state matching grant program that requires roughly the same level of state funding. (The latter simulations match local spending by 40 cents for every dollar of local spending.) It then proceeds to an analysis of more targeted state aid, again simulating both block and matching grants. It is well understood that block and matching aid have rather different built-in incentives, with the block grants giving rise to an income effect while matching aid adds a substitution effect because it changes the relative price of funding local schools. In addition, however, these programs have general equilibrium effects that have not typically been treated in policy analysis. In each case, the results are presented in tables 6 and 7 in a format similar to that used in table 5.

STATEWIDE GRANTS. The top half of table 6 provides simulation results for the introduction of a $3,000 per pupil state block grant to all districts. The first column in each subsection (labeled "No behavior change") simply assumes districts will spend an additional $3,000 per pupil with no change in voter or household behavior. Naturally, a large increase in public school (and overall school) quality would then take place. The second column in each subsection (labeled "Partial equilibrium voting") assumes voters now vote on local taxes knowing that the state will provide an additional grant funded by income tax, but no additional household behavior changes are allowed. In district 1, per pupil spending then falls back to its original level while it changes slightly in the other districts. As a result, overall public school quality rises slightly. Finally, the third column in each subsection (labeled "Full general equilibrium") includes household behavior changes, which include most notably a small shift out of private schools and into public schools (private school enrollment in districts 1 and 3 drops by 2.5 percentage points) accompanied by small changes in house prices that cause additional marginal adjustments in household location choices. The full general equilibrium effect on public school quality is marginal, with the exception of district 3, where the small switch of households with high peer quality to public schools causes a significant increase in public school quality. Overall school quality changes similarly to show a small overall gain in school quality from the state block grant program. The interdistrict variance in both public and overall school quality, however, increases.

Marginal changes under block grants turn into much more significant changes under a matching grant program that results (in full equilibrium) in the same level of state spending as a $3,000 block grant. Again, the initial column simply assumes that local taxes remain constant under the block grant, but because of the substitution effect arising from the change in the relative price of public school spending, the "naïve" initial estimates of spending increases are essentially correct for districts 2 and 3. Only in district 1 does public school spending not rise as much when political adjustments by voters are taken into account (primarily because the constraint of a minimum spending level of $5,000 was initially binding on district 1). Thus the partial equilibrium political adjustment pre-

Table 6. School Spending and Quality under Two Grants-in-Aid Assumptions, by District Income Level

District income level	$3,000 Universal block grant				Equivalently funded matching grant			
	Local property tax equilibrium	No behavioral change[a]	Partial equilibrium voting[b]	Full general equilibrium	Local property tax equilibrium	No behavioral change[c]	Partial equilibrium voting[b]	Full general equilibrium
Public school per pupil spending (dollars)								
Low (1)	5,000	8,000	5,000	5,000	5,000	7,000	5,824	5,373
Medium (2)	7,326	10,326	7,281	7,267	7,326	10,256	10,386	10,062
High (3)	10,215	13,215	10,861	10,545	10,215	14,301	14,421	14,042
All[d]	7,731	10,731	7,958	7,834	7,731	10,823	10,569	9,944
Average public school quality								
Low (1)	0.3674	0.4704	0.3674	0.3781	0.5421	0.6142	0.5421	0.5384
Medium (2)	0.6192	0.7415	0.6172	0.6042	0.6853	0.7831	0.6837	0.6756
High (3)	0.8183	0.9368	0.8451	0.9056	0.8314	0.9309	0.8556	0.9098
All[d]	0.6204	0.7357	0.6298	0.6511	0.6863	0.7761	0.6938	0.7079
Average school quality (including private schools)								
Low (1)	0.3674	0.4383	0.3980	0.3992	0.5421	0.5917	0.5635	0.4821
Medium (2)	0.6192	0.7388	0.7437	0.7575	0.6853	0.7810	0.7849	0.7880
High (3)	0.8183	0.9765	0.9808	1.0951	0.8314	0.9738	0.9809	1.0934
All[d]	0.6204	0.7419	0.7317	0.7601	0.6863	0.7822	0.7764	0.7878

a. Assumes that any state block grant to the district simply raises total spending in the district by the amount of the block grant.
b. Assumes that voters approve a new local property tax rate after learning of the state aid program.
c. Assumes that local property taxes remain unchanged as the matching program is introduced and that the matched funds are simply spent on local public schools.
d. Calculates average statewide values. For public school figures, this is a weighted average of the remainder of the column where the weights are the fraction within each district that attend public schools.
For overall school figures (the last set of columns), it is simply an average of the previous values in the columns.

dicts substantial increases in public school quality, especially in districts 2 and 3. Finally, the full-equilibrium adjustment results in additional large changes. With public school quality increasing in all districts, substantial switching from private schools into public schools takes place, as well as migration of previous private-school-attending households from poor districts to wealthier districts as house prices adjust to reflect changes in public schools.[20] However, the decline in private school attendance in district 1 does not result in a large influx of high-peer-quality households into district 1 public schools because more than two-thirds of those leaving the private schools in district 1 migrate to other districts to use public schools there. Thus the full equilibrium simulations suggest small additional increases in public school quality in districts 1 and 2 and large increases in district 3. Overall school quality (which incorporates the impact of the disappearance of good private schools) actually drops by 12 percent in district 1 (even though public school quality rises by almost 9 percent), while it increases by over 30 percent in district 3.

The primary showing of table 6, then, is that universal state aid programs that are not targeted to struggling districts may result in some overall improvements in school quality but may simultaneously cause significantly larger inequities across districts. A $3,000 block grant improves public school quality by barely 3 percent in district 1 but by over 10 percent in district 3. Similarly, overall school quality (including that provided by private schools) declines slightly in district 1 while increasing by over 9 percent in district 3. For matching grants the results are even more dramatic. Partial equilibrium results that do not incorporate the general equilibrium household adjustments in residential location and private school choice tend to understate these effects.

TARGETED STATE AID. Grants specifically targeted to poor public school districts, those represented by district 1 in the model, are examined in table 7. The top part of the table reports results from a $7,000 per pupil block grant to district 1 public schools. The lower part focuses on results from an equally funded matching grant targeted only to district 1 with the aim of achieving the same level of spending in district 1 public schools as would emerge from the $7,000 targeted bock grant. Districts 2 and 3 remain funded solely through local property taxes.

---

20. Private school attendance drops by over 50 percent in district 1, from 30 percent to 12.5 percent, In districts 2 and 3, it drops by 50 percent.

Table 7. School Spending and Quality under Grants Targeted to Low-Income Districts and Behavioral Assumptions, by District Income Level

District income level	Local property tax equilibrium	$7,000 Block grant to district 1			Equivalent matching grant (match = 1.98)			
		No behavioral change[a]	Partial equilibrium voting[b]	Full general equilibrium	Local property tax equilibrium	No behavioral change[c]	Partial equilibrium voting[b]	Full general equilibrium
Public school per pupil spending (dollars)								
Low (1)	5,000	12,000	7,000	7,000	5,000	9,938	7,824	7,021
Medium (2)	7,326	7,326	7,326	8,496	7,326	7,326	7,326	8,461
High (3)	10,215	10,215	10,215	11,211	10,215	10,215	10,215	9,324
All[d]	7,731	9,773	8,314	9,026	7,731	9,171	8,555	8,277
Average public school quality								
Low (1)	0.3674	0.5817	0.4383	0.4457	0.3674	0.5269	0.4647	0.4721
Medium (2)	0.6192	0.6192	0.6192	0.6883	0.6192	0.6192	0.6192	0.6423
High (3)	0.8183	0.8183	0.8183	0.9369	0.8183	0.8183	0.8183	0.7855
All[d]	0.6204	0.6829	0.6411	0.7047	0.6204	0.6669	0.6488	0.6380
Average school quality (including private schools)								
Low (1)	0.5421	0.6758	0.5647	0.5704	0.5421	0.6537	0.6102	0.5578
Medium (2)	0.6853	0.6763	0.6763	0.7350	0.6853	0.6853	0.6853	0.6997
High (3)	0.8314	0.8319	0.8319	0.9416	0.8314	0.8314	0.8314	0.7855
All[d]	0.6863	0.7280	0.6910	0.7490	0.6863	0.7235	0.7090	0.6810

a. Assumes that any state block grant to the district simply raises total spending in the district by the amount of the block grant.
b. Assumes that voters approve a new local property tax rate after learning of the state aid program.
c. Assumes that local property taxes remain unchanged as the matching program is introduced and that the matched funds are simply spent on local public schools.
d. Calculates average statewide values. For public school figures, this is a weighted average of the remainder of the column where the weights are the fraction within each district that attend public schools. For overall school figures (the last set of columns), it is simply an average of the previous values in the columns.

Column 1 in each subsection again assumes no adjustment by voters or households. It is noteworthy that even under this "naïve" assumption—implying an increase of fully $7,000 (under the targeted block grant) in per pupil spending in district 1 with no change in spending in other districts—public school quality in district 1 would still not have risen to the level of public school quality in districts 2 and 3 (which spend considerably less). The calibrated production function of the model gives a substantial role to spending in public schools, but there is a limit to how much spending alone can accomplish. Furthermore, the political adjustment (holding all other household behavior fixed) implies that spending from heavily funded state programs targeted at poor districts will rise considerably less than dollar for dollar.

Since programs modeled in table 7 are strictly targeted to only the poor district, one might initially think that a partial equilibrium analysis may in fact not fall far short of a more general equilibrium approach. This, however, does not seem to be the case. In fact, a series of general equilibrium effects is set off by the introduction of such targeted grant programs, causing the effects of these programs to spill over into private school markets, housing markets, and public schools in other districts. Specifically, with schools improving substantially in district 1 under the partial equilibrium assumptions, and with property taxes falling as states pay for public schools, depressed housing prices rise in that district. This causes marginal households attending private schools (previously residing in district 1 to take advantage of low housing prices to send their children to private schools) to emigrate to other districts, often switching to their public schools and replacing residents that value schooling less.[21] Substantial declines in private school attendance then occur, particularly in district 1 but also in districts 2 and 3, as public schools there improve both through more spending (because of a larger political constituency for schools) and a better public school peer group. Despite the state block grant targeted solely at district 1, the general equilibrium model predicts increases in per pupil public school spending of 10 to 16 percent in the other districts. This spending increase is accompanied by an increase in public school peer quality within districts 2 and 3 (from households that

---

21. Private school attendance falls from 30 percent to 22.5 percent in district 1, from 20 percent to 15 percent in district 2, and from 10 percent to 7.5 percent in district 3.

previously attended private schools in district 1), pushing public school quality in those districts up by 12 to 15 percent. Public school quality in district 1, however, is virtually unchanged from its partial equilibrium level as only a few households switch from private schools in district 1 to the public school in that district.

Compared to results for a universal $3,000 block grant analyzed in table 6, the targeted $7,000 block grant in fact achieves universally preferable outcomes in terms of school quality (while requiring significantly less state funding), This is not the case under a partial equilibrium model where only district 1 experiences higher public and overall school quality under the larger targeted program than under the smaller universal grants. However, when the full general equilibrium effects are taken into account, both public and overall school quality levels are substantially higher in *all* districts under the targeted program. The significantly larger general equilibrium effects for the targeted program arise precisely because the program is targeted and thus causes larger relative price changes than does a nontargeted program.

An additional surprising result appears when targeted block grants are compared to targeted matching grants that result in the same level of public school spending in district 1. Because matching grants continue to require local property tax effort, general equilibrium increases in housing prices in district 1 are more muted, thus setting off smaller overall general equilibrium effects. While private school attendance also falls by similar magnitudes, the decline is different because it involves significantly less migration between districts than what arises under a targeted block grant. Average public school and overall school quality then do not change nearly as much as under a targeted block grant aimed at achieving the same increase in public school spending in district 1.

Thus while partial equilibrium adjustments in public school quality are more dramatic under a matching formula, general equilibrium adjustments are significantly larger under block grants. Overall, then, it seems that extending the analysis of school finance reforms from a partial to a general equilibrium context becomes more important the more targeted the aid programs and the more they contain block rather than matching elements.

STATE-FUNDED VOUCHERS. A final set of school reforms that is gaining increasing attention encompasses the state funding of private school vouchers or other state-funded choice programs.[22] Table 8 focuses on private school vouchers funded by state income taxes. For this set of school finance policies the general equilibrium effects are more immediately apparent and have been explored in more detail elsewhere.[23] This section simply illustrates the impact of two types of vouchers, both set at $2,500 per pupil. The first type is unrestricted with any household eligible, while the second is restricted to only those households residing in poor districts.[24] For purposes of the analysis that follows, a voucher is defined as a state subsidy of $2,500 or the full private school tuition (whichever is lower) for households choosing to send their child to a private school.

The first two columns under each subsection of table 8 differ slightly from those in the previous tables while the rest of the table follows a similar format. In particular, columns labeled "Little behavioral change" allow private schools to adjust tuition levels (and thus spending levels) in response to the introduction of the voucher, but no adjustment on the part of households or voters is allowed. Columns labeled "No migration equilibrium" allow for both the adjustment of political choices by households and the formation of new private schools to meet any additional demand by households seeking to switch from public to private schools in response to the voucher. However, no migration is permitted under this set of simulations. Finally, columns labeled "Full general equilibrium" report simulations that allow for all household choices to change, including most importantly the choice of residential location.

The difference between a partial and a general equilibrium model is perhaps starkest for the case of private school vouchers. Since no additional state money is provided to public schools, no change in public school spending occurs under the first column in both voucher scenarios. With households permitted to switch to private schools in the second column (labeled "No migration equilibrium"), the potential for a change in per pupil spending in public schools emerges as those households that switch to private schools are assumed to no longer support taxes going to public schools. However, only in district 1 do any households switch to

---

22. Although this is not explicitly explored here, publicly funded charter schools—to the extent that they do not base admission on residential location—would have general equilibrium effects similar to those reported here for private school vouchers.

23. Nechyba (1999, 2000, 2002, 2003a, c).

24. The latter type of voucher (targeted to districts) is one that has been proposed at the national level by the Bush administration and has been passed at the state level in Florida.

Table 8. School Spending and Quality under Universal and Targeted Private School Vouchers and Three Behavioral Assumptions, by District Income Level

District income level	Local property tax equilibrium	$2,500 voucher				$2,500 voucher to district 1		
		No behavioral change[a]	No migration equilibrium[b]	Full general equilibrium[c]	Local property tax equilibrium	No behavioral change[a]	No migration equilibrium[b]	Full general equilibrium[c]
Public school per pupil spending (dollars)								
Low (1)	5,000	5,000	5,000	5,000	5,000	5,000	5,000	5,000
Medium (2)	7,326	7,326	7,326	7,645	7,326	7,326	7,326	6,346
High (3)	10,215	10,215	10,215	9,555	10,215	10,215	10,215	8,333
All	7,731	7,731	7,731	8,012	7,731	7,731	7,731	7,115
Average public school quality								
Low (1)	0.3674	0.3674	0.3522	0.3393	0.3674	0.3674	0.3522	0.3247
Medium (2)	0.6192	0.6192	0.6192	0.4930	0.6192	0.6192	0.6192	0.4435
High (3)	0.8183	0.8183	0.8183	0.7299	0.8183	0.8183	0.8183	0.6503
All	0.6204	0.6204	0.6160	0.5739	0.6204	0.6204	0.6160	0.5271
Average school quality (including private schools)								
Low (1)	0.5421	0.5481	0.5623	0.6318	0.5421	0.5481	0.5623	0.6137
Medium (2)	0.6853	0.6963	0.6963	0.6187	0.6853	0.6963	0.6963	0.5973
High (3)	0.8314	0.8452	0.8452	0.7396	0.8314	0.8452	0.8452	0.6794
All	0.6863	0.6965	0.7013	0.6634	0.6863	0.6965	0.7013	0.6368

a. The only behavioral change permitted under these simulations is for existing private schools to alter their tuition level in response to the voucher.
b. Households can choose to switch to private schools and vote differently in the political process, new private schools can form, and existing private schools can alter their tuition policies.
c. All households and private school choices can change in response to the changed economic environment.

private schools. Because public schools in district 1 are already spending the minimum per pupil ($5,000), no further erosion in public school spending is possible.[25] Public school quality, however, falls slightly in district 1 as higher-peer-quality families exit the public schools. At the same time, overall school quality increases in district 1 as the average quality of new private schools is greater than that in public school s. Similar increases in overall school quality occur in districts 2 and 3 even though no household switches to private schools because existing private schools raise their spending slightly in response to the introduction of vouchers.[26] Since only households in district 1 switch from public to private schools as a result of a voucher universally available in all districts, results are identical for the partial equilibrium simulations when vouchers are targeted only to district 1.

While partial equilibrium effects are therefore small, the general equilibrium effects reported in the last column of each subsection in table 8 are large and driven almost solely by migration effects and housing price adjustments. Given the depressed housing prices in district 1 (and the similarly inflated housing prices in district 3), the model does not predict large increases in private school attendance unless households interested in switching from public to private schools are able to move in order to take advantage of lower housing prices when making the switch. Thus marginal households in districts 2 and 3 previously were willing to pay inflated housing prices to gain access to good public schools but are now more easily able to afford private school tuition. As a result, there is no reason for them to continue to pay relatively high housing prices when more housing of the same quality is available in district 1 at lower prices. Private school attendance in district 1 therefore increases dramatically (from 30 percent to 62.5 percent under the universal voucher and from 30 percent to 70 percent under the targeted voucher), primarily because

25. In models where local public school spending is not at its minimum level, private school vouchers could actually have the effect of raising per pupil public school spending despite a decline in political support for public schools because the existing public school budget is spread over fewer school children when many in the district attend private schools. In effect, the exit of some families into the private market makes per pupil spending cheaper, therefore acting like a matching grant for voters who continue to send their children to public school.

26. The increase in spending in existing private schools is predicted to be small because the $2,500 voucher only gives rise to a small income effect for households that already choose private schools.

households of high peer quality leave public schools in districts 2 and 3 to reside in district 1 to use the voucher. Increases in private school attendance in districts 2 and 3 are more modest.[27]

One of the more notable findings from this line of research is that the feared negative impact of vouchers on public schools is strongest not in districts where most private school vouchers are used (district 1) but rather in districts from which those who switch from public to private school originate. Their loss in districts 2 and 3 causes decreases in public school peer quality as well as declining political support for public schools (in district 3). While public school quality thus falls by 8 percent in district 1 under universal vouchers, it falls by 26 percent in district 2 and by 12 percent in district 3. Even more dramatically, under a voucher targeted solely to district 1, public school quality falls by 13 percent in district 1—a modest effect compared to declines of 40 percent and 26 percent in districts 2 and 3. The impact on district 2 is particularly large because residents of district 2 can more easily find appropriate housing choices in district 1 as they switch to private schools than can residents of district 3 (because the house-quality distribution of district 1 overlaps more with that of district 2 than with that of district 3.) Migration and general equilibrium price effects then cause cream-skimming by private schools to affect disproportionately public schools in districts other than those in which the vouchers are used, particularly middle-income districts. And, as in the previous section, these general equilibrium effects are stronger when the policy is targeted.

Although it is certainly the case that the impact of private school vouchers on public schools is of independent importance, the last column of table 8—reporting results for overall school quality (including private schools)—is nevertheless striking. Because of the disproportionate use of vouchers in district 1, average school quality in district 1 actually surpasses average school quality in district 2 and comes remarkably close to that of district 3. Given the results for public school quality, this clearly masks an enormous heterogeneity in school quality within the poor district between private and public schools. Nevertheless, if good private schools, and the high-peer-quality households that choose them, have

---

27. Under both types of vouchers, private school attendance increases to 40 percent in district 2. In district 3, private school attendance rises from 10 to 12.5 percent under the universal voucher but does not rise under the targeted voucher.

independent positive effects (which are not modeled) on communities, the last column of the table may hold other important lessons for urban policymakers.

Although these results are striking, the importance of general equilibrium effects in general, and in the case of vouchers in particular, should not be that surprising. Local policymakers have long been aware of the close connection between residential housing markets, local school quality, and local tax rates. Each of the policies analyzed has altered this connection in some way and has given rise to general equilibrium effects that are often absent from policy analysis. For vouchers these effects are particularly large in comparison to partial equilibrium effects because vouchers most directly affect the key reason identified earlier for why public schools can be so different in equilibrium. This reason was found in the bundling of residential housing and school choices, a bundling that arises because of residence-based admission to local public schools. Vouchers, more than any other policy, unbundle this connection by making it easier for households to choose housing and school quality separately. If the bundling is important (as I argue it must be), unbundling must be important as well. The same forces play a similar but less dramatic role for the other types of school finance reforms analyzed in this paper.

Finally, it is noteworthy that overall (public and private) school quality is shown to decline with private school vouchers. This is a direct result of two assumptions in the model: first, the model assumes no competitive gains from increased competition. As noted earlier, if such an effect were included in the model, the general equilibrium effects emphasized in this paper remain, while overall school quality would improve (as would public school quality in each district if the competitive effect is sufficiently large).[28] Second, the role of peer inputs into the school production model is specified in such a way as to cause average school quality to increase (all else being equal) the more households with different peer quality mix within schools. Because private schools seek to skim high-peer-quality households from public schools, an increase in private school attendance implies less mixing of household types within schools. Again, it is shown elsewhere that the general equilibrium effects emphasized here do not change if this model of peer inputs into school produc-

28. See Nechyba (2003c).

tion is altered to make mixing less efficient, but overall school quality would then increase with higher private school attendance.[29]

Perceived and Real Limits of the Analysis

Although the computational approach used in this paper provides a powerful engine for analyzing questions of the kind tackled here, the approach has inherent limits. Any structural model that attempts to merge all of the relevant economic forces for urban school policy must by definition make explicit assumptions that are almost certainly only crude approximations of complex real-world processes. While, in the words of one commentator on this work, the engine that drives the analysis can be "intoxicating" by providing explicit numerical estimates for policy alternatives, it is thus not appropriate to interpret the results too literally. The advantage of the approach is that it provides a single, internally consistent method for comparing policies and tracing partial and general equilibrium effects, and it therefore provides a useful guide for thinking about the *relative* quantitative importance of different real-world economic forces. At the same time, the assumptions made in the process of modeling complex forces are tenuous enough to recommend caution in interpreting results as firm absolute predictions.

Some Common Concerns and Misunderstandings

Some of the caution arises from technical details such as implicit elasticities embedded in functional form assumptions of preferences and production. The empirical literature has often not provided a firm sense of what these elasticities should be, and the approach therefore takes standard functional forms as a starting point. Sensitivity analysis suggests that the relative magnitudes of general and partial equilibrium results are unlikely to change dramatically as these implicit assumptions are changed. Similarly, concerns may arise from the assumption that housing stocks are taken as given in the model and do not change as general equilibrium effects cause migration of some households within and across districts. In other work I have argued that, while such concerns are cer-

29. Nechyba (2003c).

tainly valid, the assumption actually tends to understate the kinds of general equilibrium effects highlighted in most of this paper.[30] Thus as housing stocks are more flexibly modeled, general equilibrium effects are likely to become more rather than less important.

The same is true for a concern that non-school-related externalities from migration are not explicitly modeled as migration takes place. Some commentators, for instance, have mistakenly argued that the model assumes too great a willingness of households to seek lower housing costs because the model does not take into account such factors as the characteristics of neighbors, other neighborhood amenities, and so forth. Since housing prices are used to calibrate benchmark housing and neighborhood quality levels, all such factors *are* taken into account in the initial benchmark model because all such factors would indeed be capitalized into prices. While it is true that the model then holds non-school-related neighborhood externalities fixed as migration occurs, any movement of high-income households into low-income areas would tend to raise non-school-related neighborhood quality, increasing rather than decreasing the migration effects highlighted in many of the simulations. Thus, to the extent that policies like private school vouchers cause high-income households in the model to move to low-income districts, the model understates rather than overstates the willingness of households to move. It is only in simulations where migration occurs from poor to rich areas that the exclusion of changes in neighborhood externalities would bias the general equilibrium results upward.

Finally, many of the results reported here highlight general equilibrium effects that include migration of households between districts as well as switching behavior from public to private schools or vice versa. Such effects would not emerge if households generally faced high moving costs, and concerns may arise that general equilibrium effects in the model depend too much on the assumption of an absence of such costs. I view such concerns as very valid in the short run but largely unimportant in the long run for urban economies in the United States. American households move often, typically for reasons other than schools. Such moves occur because of job-related changes or because changes in family size or income dictate a discrete change in housing consumption. The appropriate interpretation of the mobility behavior observed in this paper

---

30. Nechyba (1999, 2000, 2003c).

is one that emphasizes that as families move for a variety of reasons, the economic environment in which they make their new housing decision matters. School policy changes that environment, and thus alters the way in which housing and schooling decisions are simultaneously made as families find themselves moving for reasons that may have little to do with schooling. Given the frequency with which American families move, the "long run" in which these general equilibrium effects become important may then not be very long at all.

Some Effects That Are Not Modeled but Might Be Important

Other concerns may arise from the fact that certain possible effects that are sometimes claimed but are not firmly established empirically are excluded from this analysis. For instance, the simulations reported here do not include a "competitive productivity effect" in public schools resulting from increased private or public school competition. In other work, I have shown that the presence and *relative* size of the general equilibrium effects highlighted in this paper are not affected by the inclusion of such a competitive effect, although the *absolute* value of school quality predictions does depend on it.[31] Thus, in simulations of private school vouchers, for instance, public and overall school quality may well improve with vouchers if competition causes productivity gains in public schools. But the simulations reported in this paper do not show such an improvement because the competitive effect is not modeled. Similarly, it is sometimes argued that decentralized school finance results in better use of local information and thus greater school productivity than does centralized finance. Again, while this may certainly be the case, the effect is not modeled here and may therefore affect the *absolute* value of some of the outcome variables even as the *relative* importance of partial and general equilibrium effects remains roughly the same.

Two additional features of the real world that are not modeled should add to one's skepticism of the immediate applicability of the absolute predictions of the model to contemporary urban settings. First, the model currently does not include any heterogeneity in household preferences. In some sense, this is in part a strength of the current approach because it keeps out of the analysis any unnecessary appeal to preference hetero-

31. Nechyba (2002, 2003c).

geneity in explaining heterogeneous outcomes within the public school sector. At the same time, however, measurable characteristics such as religious preferences of households are important determinants of school choices made by households. In fact, when religious heterogeneity is added to the model used in this paper, structural estimates demonstrate that this heterogeneity carries considerable explanatory power.[32] Second, it is difficult to ultimately provide true predictions of the impact of school policies in urban settings unless not just income heterogeneity but also racial heterogeneity is modeled explicitly. The inclusion of race in the model used in this paper, however, remains a project for future research.

Conclusions

The approach taken in this paper has allowed for an explicit comparison of partial and general equilibrium effects from school finance policy reforms in a single, internally consistent framework that can successfully replicate important features of the data under current school finance policies. On a number of occasions the approach has led to the conclusion that general equilibrium effects may alter conclusions drawn from a partial equilibrium analysis in surprising and large ways. This implies that school finance policy cannot easily be analyzed without explicitly taking the link to housing markets and private school markets into account. Furthermore, when analyzing the politics of school reform, it may be the case that policy change (or lack thereof) arises not so much because of the impact of such change on schools but rather because of the implied general equilibrium effects on housing values and thus household wealth distributions. In the case of vouchers, for instance, high-income residents in good school districts could suffer substantial capital losses while low-income residents in poor school districts might experience capital gains.

32. Ferreyra (2002).

Comments

Eric A. Hanushek: Public and professional debate about the best way to fund schools have been going on for a very long time, but their intensity has increased enormously over the past three decades. Yet this debate remains resistant to careful and thorough analysis. The paper by Thomas Nechyba provides a clear statement of the value of systematic analysis of important policy issues. This paper, which provides an overview of a series of papers by Nechyba, is a dramatic departure from most previous discussions. It provides specific insights into the likely outcomes of a number of policies currently being discussed. But more important, it develops a structure for thinking about the entire funding matter. I am a great fan of this line of research, and I think it has provided considerable clarity to an area clouded in slogans, emotions, and vested interests.

This powerful analysis introduces economic theory into policy evaluation. In some areas such as regulatory policy or monetary and fiscal policy, economic analysis is common. Such is not the case when it comes to schools and their finance. Moreover, while Nechyba describes this work as "applied theory," he has now developed a machine that goes beyond theory and gets close to the details of actual policy proposals.

The central theme of this line of research is that school finance cannot be analyzed in isolation from other choices and behavior. In various other subjects of interest, partial equilibrium analysis gives very satisfactory answers. This is not true for school finance, where general equilibrium effects almost certainly dominate. This line of research, which is clearly presented in the paper, shows the importance of considering the outcomes for schools of individual behavior.

Nechyba identifies the key interactions among household location, school finance policies, and school outcomes. Public schooling that is linked to the residence of a family implies that location and schools are a joint decision. This jointness implies that policies that affect people's evaluation of the finance and quality of schools can change their evaluation of a particular residential location, and families are likely to respond to policy changes by adjusting their location. A theme that weaves throughout the analysis is that the role of private schooling has been misunderstood. Private schooling allows some families to break the link between household location and the schools that their children attend. Thus, for example, we find that there is less income segregation by jurisdictions when private school alternatives are available. This general equilibrium finding contrasts sharply with the common public view and the typical policy debates that suggest private schools are a segregating influence.

Who is surprised by these results? For the most part, economists who study public finance and urban location are not. Although many of these people have not spent much time thinking about the institutional details and the general equilibrium effects that might be expected, with a little thought they would likely come up with the overall conclusions that Nechyba reaches. Of course, they would not have a good sense of the magnitude of any effects, but that is also where Nechyba cautions us to be careful. The magnitudes are a direct function of some key parameters that are not fully analyzed or known.

The group that would be surprised most completely by this analysis is today's decisionmakers on school finance—the state courts, the state legislatures, and the state education departments. School finance issues have been near the top of the policy agenda for at least the past three decades. This represents the confluence of two different streams of thinking. First, growing out the 1960s with the concerns about poverty and equity, a series of lawsuits directly attacked the common mode of school finance. The beginning was the California suit, *Serrano* v. *Priest*, which argued that it was a violation of the Fourteenth Amendment of the U.S. Constitution to make "the quality of one's school based on the wealth of neighbors." With the common use of local property taxes to fund schools, jurisdictions with larger tax bases could more easily fund their schools. Although the U.S. Supreme Court declared in 1974 that this local funding did not violate the Constitution, these suits have entered a majority of state courts under the separate state constitutions. Second, in part propelled by the report, *A Nation at Risk*, policymakers became very concerned with the quality of the schools. This concern, which has continued for the two decades since release of the report, appears to dovetail neatly with the issues of providing funding for schools.

As a result, issues of funding have been debated intensely in all states. The debates in courts and legislatures take a very simple view. People are stuck in their current jurisdictions. The rich take advantage of their wealth and superior purchasing power to buy better schools, while the poor are relegated to underfunded schools. The debates virtually never acknowledge that households might generally be choosing both locations and schools. Nor do they consider the possibility that these decisions would change with different funding arrangements and that these changes might yield a variety of capital gains and losses for homeowners. As a result, virtually everybody in the center of these debates would be surprised by the thinking and the analysis in Nechyba's work.

Another element of Nechyba's analytical framework deserves note. His modeling incorporates decisions to attend private schools and includes the educational outcomes observed in private schools. In most debates, students choosing the private schools are written out of the discussion.

This work extends Nechyba's previous analyses of school finance. Simply comparing the modeling advances reported here with what was possible just a few years ago shows the remarkable strides of this effort. My only plea is that he speed up the development of this work, and in that spirit I want to suggest some areas for development.

There are some issues on which Nechyba is at the mercy of other researchers. Specifically, he must build the behavior in his model on parameters and models that he gets from other sources. In some key areas, the other research does not help him out very much. His modeling stresses the role of peers in developing the quality of schools. The direct modeling of peers, however, has not been very precise on the strength and form of any such relationships. Part of this is explicable, because the identification and estimation of peer effects is notoriously difficult.[33] But Nechyba also extends the view of peer influences in what I believe to be productive ways. The empirical studies on peers concentrate almost

33. Hanushek and others (2003).

exclusively on individual peer interactions in the classroom. This view ignores the larger political economy issues surrounding how parents interact with schools to improve schools' performance, set their agenda, and the like. Thus while his specifications depend on the quantitative and qualitative interaction of peers in determining school quality, he does not get much guidance from existing research.

A second area where existing research is not very helpful is the determinants of private school attendance. Research on private schools has focused almost exclusive attention on their quality and not on the determinants of attendance rates.[34] A central innovation in the current generation of modeling by Nechyba is the inclusion of private schools as an important component of the behavior. This extension of previous work is nontrivial from a modeling perspective, but it greatly enriches the models. Indeed, the adjustment on the private school margin is one of the significant aspects of the policy changes he considers. Yet, at least over the past thirty years, the overall rate of private school attendance has been virtually constant at 11 to 12 percent. It has been constant in the face of significant centralization of school funding at the state level (largely as a result of earlier school finance cases). It has also been constant in the face of a more than doubling of the real spending per pupil on public schools. These kinds of changes would lead to noticeable private school adjustment in Nechyba's model, but one does not see them in the data. This suggests that even though the introduction of private schooling is, in my opinion, a great stride forward, more thought has to be given to the form and extent of behavioral reactions in that area.

There are obviously complex forces at work in the private school market. For example, while the overall rate of attendance has been constant, the character of private schools has changed considerably. There has been a dramatic decrease in Catholic school attendance, for instance, but this has been offset by increases in attendance at other religious schools. Some of the complicated influences on overall attendance may indeed be masking some of the changes on which Nechyba focuses his modeling efforts.

There are two clear areas of extension that I would like to see Nechyba pursue. The first is consideration of commercial and industrial property. His current modeling has only residential property in the prop-

---

34. Neal (1998).

erty tax base. This approach greatly simplifies both the modeling and policy discussion, because property-wealthy districts tend also to be income-wealthy districts, and everything tends to move together. However, the reality differs from the modeling in important ways. For example, New York City is a property-wealthy school district that has very large concentrations of poor people. This pattern varies by state; New Jersey has more property-poor central cities than most, so that property tax base and income of residents are more positively correlated. The distinction between the wealth of the community (tax base) and the income of the residents has been blurred, perhaps intentionally at times, in much of the actual debate on school finance. It would be very useful if Nechyba could extend his work to capture the differences between the taxable property and the income and wealth of the residents. This wish is, of course, easier for a discussant to call for than for a researcher to carry out. It greatly complicates some of the adjustments that must be accounted for in the model, and not a lot of research would indicate how commercial and industrial locations might themselves adjust.

Nechyba's current housing prices of course capture a variety of locational advantages that exist in his basic data. Thus other elements of the property tax base are implicitly included. The difficulty comes in policy discussions that treat household income and tax base as being close to synonymous.

The second major consideration that seems crucial is the inclusion of race. Constraints on housing location that go with race are undoubtedly more real and important than those on income.[35] If true, this implies that a specific subgroup may in fact have less opportunity to adjust to optimal locations. Additionally, my own work points to the importance of peer groups in terms of race (higher black concentrations hurt black students). Thus it would be important to bring these elements into the analysis. Nechyba of course recognizes this, so my mentioning it is more along the line of trying to help him set his future research agenda.

The final issue that I cannot help but underscore is the interpretation of the equilibrium outcomes of this modeling effort. Nechyba builds his analysis on the idea of perceptions and behavior of parents. He stops short of making welfare comparisons on the basis of any improved or deteriorating school quality. This corresponds to my view of the current

35. Hanushek, Kain, and Rivkin (2002).

structure of schools. There is little evidence that spending on schools is a good index of school quality, even if parents might tend to use that index. Thus his model predicts behavior of parents based on their preferences, but it does not provide guidance on the educational quality issues that weave around the school finance debates. Current court cases and legislative actions are propelled by both equity and quality issues, but they have been unable to describe any quality changes that might result from policy changes. Nechyba recognizes this clearly.

The overall judgment: this is an exceptionally clear and important line of research. Nechyba has taken the analysis to new heights, and we can only hope that he continues rapidly with this development.

Susanna Loeb: In "Public School Finance and Urban School Policy," Thomas Nechyba summarizes his research using computational models to estimate the impact of policies on schooling and residential location decisions. Perhaps because of the fixed costs of developing sufficiently complex and accurate models, computational models are rarely used for educational policy analysis, even though they have the potential to greatly enrich our understanding of policy dynamics and our ability to predict the impact of policy choices. Nechyba's work stands out because it applies such models to estimate conditions under a variety of policy alternatives. His framework assumes that families' utility is a function of house quality, private consumption, and school quality, which is itself a function of per pupil spending and average peer inputs. Housing, both quality and quantity, is fixed. Using data on suburban New Jersey districts, he chooses the parameters of the utility function and the school quality function so that the sorting of families into districts and into public or private schools most accurately matches the sorting in the data. Three points are worth noting. First, understanding general equilibrium effects is central to understanding the impact of education policy. Second, there is a wide variety of potential general equilibrium effects worth considering when one attempts to predict the impact of education finance reforms. Finally, there are reasons to be cautious about using the estimates from these models to predict the impact of specific policy changes, especially in urban areas.

Nechyba's work demonstrates the importance of understanding general equilibrium effects if we are to predict the impact of education finance reforms. For example, the models show that a shift from local to state funding decreases income segregation slightly when private schooling is not an option for families, but increases income segregation when private schooling is an option. Private schooling decreases in low-income communities and increases in high-income communities as a result of the change in finance, which increases segregation.

General equilibrium effects are evident in empirical studies as well. For example, while the Tennessee Star experiment showed positive effects on student learning of reducing class size, especially in the early grades, large-scale reduction in California increased the demand for teachers and resulted in a new sorting of teachers across schools.[36] The re-sorting of teachers reduced teacher quality in some schools enough to reverse the potentially positive impact of smaller classes.[37] The example of class size points more generally to a concern that while experiments have become the standard in education research, the prevalence of general equilibrium effects may make experiments poor predictors of the impacts of large-scale policy changes. Certainly it is agreed that the small-scale voucher demonstrations are unlikely to force public schools to respond to market pressures in the same way that a larger reform might. Similarly, private schools that open in response to a large-scale voucher program may differ from those already in place or those that respond to a small-scale experiment. In Cleveland, for example, the secular private schools that did open in response to demand were unable to survive; only Catholic schools remained to serve voucher students.[38] Thus an understanding of general equilibrium effects is essential for predicting the impact of education reforms: the reduction in class size in 15,000 districts will not have the same result as the reduction in one district or one classroom; vouchers for 10 will not have the same result as vouchers for 10,000 or 10 million; and an increase in spending in one school will not have the same impact as an overall increase. By allowing families to move and choose their private school and by allowing housing prices to change, Nechyba introduces general equilibrium considerations into the assessment of education policy and demonstrates their importance.

There are many possible general equilibrium effects worth considering. Nechyba's paper focuses on three of them: capitalization or changes

---

36. Mosteller (1995); Bohrnstedt and Stecher (1999).
37. Jepsen and Rivkin (2002).
38. Carnoy (2001).

in property values, cross-district mobility, and the choice of public or private school. Studies provide evidence that housing prices change in response to education policy. Jeffrey Guilfoyle, for example, found substantial capitalization as a result of the 1994 Michigan school finance reform.[39] Randall Reback, looking at the introduction of open enrollment in Minnesota, found that increased property values in net sending districts (probably those with previously lesser-quality schools) was enough that if property tax rates did not change, the change in property tax revenues would compensate for the loss in students.[40]

However, while the evidence on capitalization is substantial, the evidence of the responsiveness of private schooling decisions to school finance reform is less clear. Thomas Downes and David Schoeman did find some change in private school enrollment after the implementation of Proposition 13 in California, which dramatically altered the state's school finance system.[41] Yet the exodus to private schools has not been substantial.[42] As an indication that the model may not capture the true responsiveness of the public/private choice, table 2 shows that the model does a good job of replicating most of the distributions in the data. It somewhat underestimates property values in low-income districts and overestimates them in high-income districts, but the differences are small. The difference between predicted and actual private school enrollment in high-income districts, however, is significant. Specification checks show that if private schooling were fixed at the actual levels, the predictions of the model would not change. But the lack of consistency with the data when this element is not fixed may indicate problems with the underlying assumptions. There are a number of reasons that the responsiveness of private schooling may not be great. The supply side of the private school market, in particular, may limit this responsiveness. The model currently assumes perfectly elastic private schooling, but this is unlikely to be realistic. The charter school movement demonstrates the difficulty of scaling up successful programs. New private schools will differ from private schools already in operation.

It is worth considering whether there are indirect effects other than those considered by Nechyba that may significantly bias policy predic-

39. Guilfoyle (1998).
40. Reback (2002).
41. Downes and Schoeman (1998).
42. Sonstelie, Brunner, and Ardon (2000).

tions if ignored. There probably are. For example, when constrained by school finance policies in the purchase of education through taxes, districts may respond by encouraging increased private donations.[43] Alternatively, districts may reduce public spending in other agencies, such as county or city parks and recreation departments, to substitute for education spending.[44] Housing quality may adjust; even parents' contribution to education in the home may change. Political support for education (demand) also may be influenced by the structure of the finance reform. In the case of the implementation of a voucher program, for example, voter support for public schooling may shift if part of voters' willingness to pay for public education in the current system stems from a desire to support shared institutions (public schools with teams and concerts) in the community.

A priori, it is difficult to know which of the many possible responses are important for accurately predicting policy effects. The computational models are complex enough that it is difficult to incorporate all possible responses into a single model. Here, there is a role for empirical research that uses policy changes to estimate the magnitude of various possible responses and to identify those indirect mechanisms most likely to affect final outcomes. This empirical work alone would not accomplish what Nechyba's work does. Empirical studies do not predict, prior to implementation, the effect of policies in different communities and under different conditions. Computational general equilibrium models can incorporate characteristics, such as housing stocks and income distributions, to simulate how effects of policy may vary. We, however, do need to know which general equilibrium effects to incorporate.

When using Nechyba's model to predict the absolute or relative impact of school finance policy, especially in urban environments, there are reasons to be cautious. The first reason stems from my previous discussion. The models only incorporate some indirect effects. They may be missing influential mechanisms. Second, the effects that it does incorporate, particularly the choice of private or public school, may not be as responsive as the model assumes. This is important, given that many of the policy dynamics described in the paper appear dependent on the public-private school mechanism. Finally, this model assumes multiple dis-

---

43. Brunner and Sonstelie (1996).
44. Cullen and Loeb (2002).

tricts and smoothly functioning social choice mechanisms. These assumptions may be more applicable to suburban areas, such as the New Jersey region where the data come from, than to true urban areas, where race, patronage, politics, and central leadership can play far greater roles in determining policy effects than the Tiebout mechanisms captured by the model. Clearly race plays a significant role in families' residential location decisions, even in suburban areas.[45] These cautions do not imply that the simulations are not worthwhile, but that it is essential to assess the sensitivity of the models to underlying assumptions. Varying the structural framework of the models is likely to take substantial effort. Yet it may be worth the effort to see whether other mechanisms may be key to understanding policy dynamics. Other specification checks, such as varying the details of the policies analyzed and varying the data, may not require as much work. Even slightly different policies may have different effects. For example, Nechyba's finding that targeted block grants are more effective than targeted matching grants may not apply if the grant size is smaller so that the block grant does not exceed the minimum allowed spending level. Different data, with different income distributions and different housing stocks, may also lead to alternative conclusions. This is clearly too large an agenda for a single researcher. Nechyba's work can serve as an example for the expanded use of computable general equilibrium models in education policy research.

45. Lankford and Wyckoff (2000); Barrow (forthcoming).

References

Barrow, Lisa. Forthcoming. "School Choice through Relocation: Evidence from the Washington, D.C. Area." *Journal of Public Economics.*

Bayer, Patrick. 1999. "An Empirical Analysis of the Equilibrium in the Education Market." Ph.D. dissertation. Stanford University.

Black, Sandra E. 1999. "Do Better Schools Matter? Parental Valuation of Elementary Education." *Quarterly Journal of Economics* 114 (2): 577–99.

Bohrnstedt, George W., and Brian M. Stecher, eds. 1999. *Class Size Reduction in California: Early Evaluation Findings, 1996–1998.* Palo Alto, California, American Institutes for Research.

Brunner, Eric, and Jon Sonstelie. 1996. "Coping with Serrano: Voluntary Contributions to California's Local Public Schools." *Proceedings of the Eighty-Ninth Annual Conference on Taxation:* 372–81.

Carnoy, Martin. 2001. "School Vouchers: Examining the Evidence." Washington, D.C., Economic Policy Institute.

Cullen, Julie, and Susanna Loeb. 2002. "Fiscal Substitution in the Context of School Finance Equalization." Working Paper. Stanford University.

Downes, Thomas, and David Schoeman. 1998. "School Finance Reform and Private School Enrollment Evidence from California." *Journal of Urban Economics* 43 (3): 418–43.

Epple, Dennis, and Holger Sieg. 1999. "Estimating Equilibrium Models of Local Jurisdictions." *Journal of Political Economy* 107 (4): 645–81.

Epple, Dennis, Thomas Romer, and Holger Sieg. 2001. "Interjurisdictional Sorting and Majority Rule: An Empirical Analysis." *Econometrica* 69 (6): 1437–65.

Ferreyra, Maria. 2002. "Estimating a General Equilibrium Model with Multiple Jurisdictions and Private Schools." Working Paper. Carnegie Mellon University.

Guilfoyle, Jeffrey R. 1998. "The Effect of Property Taxes and School Spending on House Prices: Evidence from Michigan's Proposal A." Michigan Department of Treasury (February).

Hanushek, Eric. 1999. "Some Findings from an Independent Investigation of the Tennessee STAR Experiment and from Other Investigations of Class Size Effects." In *Earning and Learning: How Schools Matter*, edited by Susan E. Mayer and Paul E. Peterson. Brookings.

Hanushek, Eric A., John F. Kain, and Steve G. Rivkin. 2002. "New Evidence about Brown v. Board of Education: The Complex Effects of School Racial Composition on Achievement." Working Paper 8741. Cambridge, Mass.: National Bureau of Economic Research (January).

Hanushek, Eric A., and others. 2003. "Does Peer Ability Affect Student Achievement?" *Journal of Applied Econometrics.*

Hoxby, Caroline M. 1994. "Do Private Schools Provide Competition for Public Schools?" Working Paper 4978. Cambridge, Mass.: National Bureau of Economic Research.

————. 2000. "Does Competition among Public Schools Benefit Students and Taxpayers?" *American Economic Review* 90 (5): 1209–38.

Jepsen, Christopher, and Steven Rivkin. 2002. *Class Size Reduction, Teacher Quality, and Academic Achievement in California Public Elementary Schools.* San Francisco: Public Policy Institute of California.

Krueger, Alan. 1999. "Experimental Estimates of Education Production Functions." *Quarterly Journal of Economics* 114 (2): 497–532.

Lankford, Hamilton, and James Wyckoff. 2000. "The Effect of School Choice and Residential Location on the Racial Segregation of K-12 Students." Working Paper. State University of New York at Albany.

Loeb, Susanna, and Marianne Page. 2000. "Examining the Link between Teacher Wages and Student Outcomes: The Importance of Alternative Labor Market Opportunities and Non-Pecuniary Variation." *Review of Economics and Statistics* 82 (3): 393–408.

McMillan, Robert. 1999. "Parental Involvement and Competition: An Empirical Analysis of the Determinants of Public School Quality." Working Paper. Stanford University.

Mosteller, Frederick. 1995. "The Tennessee Study of Class Size in the Early School Grades." *Future of Children* 5 (Summer-Fall): 113–27.

Neal, Derek. 1997. "The Effect of Catholic Secondary Schooling on Educational Achievement." *Journal of Labor Economics* 15 (1): 98–123.

————. 1998. "What Have We Learned about the Benefits of Private Schooling?" *Federal Reserve Bank of New York Economic Policy Review* 4 (March): 79–86.

Nechyba, Thomas. 1997a. "Existence of Equilibrium and Stratification in Local and Hierarchical Tiebout Economies with Property Taxes and Voting." *Economic Theory* 10 (2): 277–304.

————. 1997b. "Local Property and State Income Taxes: The Role of Interjurisdictional Competition and Collusion." *Journal of Political Economy* 105 (2): 351–84.

————. 1999. "School Finance Induced Migration Patterns: The Impact of Private School Vouchers." *Journal of Public Economic Theory* 1 (1): 5–50.

————. 2000. "Mobility, Targeting and Private-School Vouchers." *American Economic Review* 90 (March): 130–46.

————. 2002. "Prospects for Achieving Equity or Adequacy in Education: The Limits of State Aid in General Equilibrium." Working Paper. Duke University.

————. 2003a. "School Finance, Spatial Segregation and the Nature of Communities." *Journal of Urban Economics,* 54: 61–88.

————. 2003b. "Centralization, Fiscal Federalism and Private School Attendance." *International Economic Review* 44 (1): 179–204.

————. 2003c. "Introducing School Choice into Multi-District Public School Systems." In *The Economics of School Choice*, edited by Caroline Hoxby. University of Chicago Press, 145–94.

Nechyba, Thomas, and Robert Strauss. 1998. "Community Choice and Local Public Services: A Discrete Choice Approach." *Regional Science and Urban Economics* 28 (1): 51–74.

Oates, Wallace. 1969. "The Effects of Property Taxes and Local Public Spending on Property Values: An Empirical Study of Tax Capitalization and the Tiebout Hypothesis." *Journal of Political Economy* 77 (6): 957–71.

Solon, Gary. 1992. "Intergenerational Income Mobility in the United States." *American Economic Review* 82 (June): 393–409.

Zimmerman, David. 1992. "Regression toward Mediocrity in Economic Stature." *American Economic Review* 82 (June): 409–29.

BRIAN A. JACOB
John F. Kennedy School of Government, Harvard University

STEVEN D. LEVITT
University of Chicago and American Bar Foundation

Catching Cheating Teachers: The Results of an Unusual Experiment in Implementing Theory

EDUCATIONAL REFORM is a critical issue in urban areas. Most large urban school districts in the United States suffer from low test scores, high dropout rates, and frequent teacher turnover. Poor performance of city schools induces flight to the suburbs by affluent families with children, eroding the urban tax base. In response to these concerns, the past decade has seen an increasing emphasis on high-stakes testing. While there is evidence such testing has been associated with impressive gains in test scores in some instances, critics have argued that these gains are artificially induced by "teaching to the test."[1] Indeed, much of the observed test score gain has been shown to be test-specific, not generalizing to other standardized tests that seemingly measure the same skills.[2] Even more ominous is the possibility that the emphasis on high-stakes testing induces cheating on the part of students, teachers, and administrators.

We have developed a method for detecting cheating by teachers and administrators on standardized tests.[3] The basic idea underlying the

We would like to thank Marisa de la Torre, Arne Duncan, John Easton, and Jessie Qualls of the Chicago Public Schools for their extensive cooperation on this project. Phil Cook, William Gale, Austan Goolsbee, Janet Pack, and Bruce Sacerdote provided valuable comments on the paper. This paper was completed while the second author was a Fellow of the Center for Advanced Study in the Behavioral Sciences, Stanford, California.

1. For testing and gains, see Jacob (2002); Grissmer and others (2000).
2. Jacob (2002); Klein and others (2000).
3. Jacob and Levitt (forthcoming).

method (which is described in greater detail later) is that cheating classrooms will systematically differ from other classrooms along a number of dimensions. For instance, students in cheating classrooms are likely to experience unusually large test score gains in the year of the cheating, followed by unusually small gains or even declines in the following year when the boost attributable to cheating disappears. Just as important as test score fluctuations as an indicator of cheating, however, are telltale patterns of suspicious answer strings—identical blocks of answers for many students in a classroom or cases where students are unable to answer easy questions correctly but do exceptionally well on the most difficult questions. We have concluded that cheating occurs in 3 to 5 percent of elementary school classrooms each year in the Chicago Public Schools (CPS).

Most academic theories, regardless of their inherent merit, fail to influence policy or do so only indirectly and with a long lag. In this paper we report the results of a rare counterexample to this familiar pattern involving collaboration between the CPS and the authors. At the invitation of Arne Duncan, CEO of the Chicago Public Schools, we were granted the opportunity to work with the CPS administration to design and implement auditing and retesting procedures using the tools we developed. With our cheating detection algorithm, we selected roughly 120 classrooms to be retested on the spring 2002 Iowa Test of Basic Skills (ITBS) that was administered to students in the third to eighth grades. The classrooms retested included not only instances suspected of cheating, but also those that had achieved large gains but were not suspected of cheating, as well as a randomly selected control group. As a consequence, the implementation also allowed a prospective test of the validity of the tools we developed.

The results of the retesting provided strong support for the effectiveness of the cheating-detection algorithm. Classrooms suspected of cheating experienced large declines in test scores when retested under controlled conditions. Classrooms not suspected previously of cheating maintained almost all of their gains on the retest. The results of the retests were used to launch investigations of twenty-nine classrooms. While these investigations have not yet been completed, it is expected that disciplinary action will be brought against a substantial number of teachers, test administrators, and principals.

Finally, the data generated by the auditing experiment provided a unique opportunity for evaluating and improving the techniques for detecting cheating. The cheating algorithm was developed without access to multiple observations for the same classrooms. By observing two sets of results from the same classrooms (one from the original test and a second from the retest), we are able for the first time to directly evaluate the predictive power of the various elements of the algorithm. The results suggest improvements to the ad hoc functional form assumptions used in the original research, and also suggest that some of our indicators are much better predictors than are others. By changing the weights used in the algorithm, we should be able substantially to improve the predictive value of the model in future implementations.

In the remainder of the paper we first present background information on teacher cheating and the detection methods. The next section outlines the design and implementation of the retesting procedure. We then report the results of the retests. The final section shows how the data from the retests were used to analyze the predictive value of the various components of the algorithm and identifies a number of possible improvements to the methods.

Teacher Cheating and Its Detection

The emphasis placed on standardized tests in elementary and secondary education has been steadily increasing over the past decade. The recent federal reauthorization of the Elementary and Secondary Education Act (ESEA), which requires states to test students in third through eighth grade each year and to judge the performance of schools based on student achievement scores, is just one prominent example of this trend. Before the passage of that law, every state in the country except Iowa already administered statewide assessment tests to students in elementary and secondary school. Twenty-four states required students to pass an exit examination to graduate from high school. California recently put into place a policy providing for merit pay bonuses of as much as $25,000 for each teacher in schools with large test score gains.

Critics of high-stakes testing argue that linking incentives to performance on standardized tests will lead teachers to minimize other teaching skills or topics not directly tested on the accountability exam.[4] Studies of districts that have implemented such policies provide mixed evidence, suggesting some improvements in student performance along with indications of increased teaching to the test and shifts away from teaching subjects that were not tested.[5]

A more sinister behavioral distortion is outright cheating on the part of teachers, administrators, and principals, such as erasing student answers and filling in the correct response or telling students the answers.[6] While the idea of elementary school teachers manipulating student answer sheets may seem far-fetched, cheating scandals have appeared in many places, including California, Massachusetts, New York, Texas, and Great Britain.[7] We have provided the first systematic analysis of teacher cheating.[8] We argued that cheating classrooms are likely to share three characteristics: unusually large test score gains for students in the class the year the cheating occurs, unusually small gains the following year for those same students, and distinctive patterns of "suspicious" answer strings.

The first two characteristics relating to test scores are straightforward. Large increases are expected in cheating classrooms because raising test scores is the very reason for the cheating. Unlike gains associated with true learning, however, one expects no persistence in the artificial test score gains due to cheating. Thus if the children in cheating classrooms this year are not in cheating classes next year, one expects the full magnitude of the cheating-related gain to evaporate.

---

4. Holmstrom and Milgrom (1991).

5. See, for example, Deere and Strayer (2001); Grissmer and others (2000); Heubert and Hauser (1999); Jacob (2001, 2002); Klein and others (2000); Richards and Sheu (1992); Smith and Mickelson (2000); Tepper (2001).

6. As a shorthand, we refer to this behavior simply as teacher cheating, although in using this terminology we are by no means excluding cheating by administrators and principals.

7. For California see Meredith May, "State Fears Cheating by Teachers," *San Francisco Chronicle*, October 4, 2000, p. A1. For Massachusetts, Jon Marcus, "Faking the Grade," *Boston Magazine,* February, 2000. For New York, Loughran and Comiskey (1999). For Texas, Claudia Kolker, "Texas Offers Hard Lessons on School Accountability," *Los Angeles Times*, April 14, 1999, p. 1. For Great Britain, Tony Tysome, "Cheating Purge: Inspectors Out," *Times Higher Education Supplement*, August 19, 1994, p. 1.

8. Jacob and Levitt (forthcoming). In contrast, there is a well-developed literature analyzing student cheating: Aiken (1991); Angoff (1974); Frary, Tideman, and Watts (1977); van der Linden and Sotaridona (2002).

Establishing what factors signify suspicious answer strings is more complicated. Teachers may cheat in a variety of ways. The crudest, most readily detected cheating involves changing answers in a block of consecutive questions so that they are identical for many or all students in a classroom. From the teacher's perspective, this is the quickest and easiest way to alter test forms. A slightly more sophisticated type of cheating involves changing the answers to nonconsecutive questions to avoid conspicuous blocks of identical answers. An even cleverer teacher may change a few answers for each student, but be careful not to change the same questions across students.

We use four separate measures of suspicious strings to detect these varieties of cheating.[9] All four of our indicators are based on deviations by students from the patterns of answers one would expect the students themselves to generate. Thus the first step in analyzing suspicious strings is to estimate the probability each child would give a particular answer on each question. This estimation is done using a multinomial logit framework with past test scores, demographics, and socioeconomic characteristics as explanatory variables. Past test scores, particularly on tests of the same subject, are very powerful predictors of the student answers on a current test.

The first suspicious-string indicator is a measure of how likely it is that, by chance, the single most unusual block of identical answers given by any set of students in the class on any consecutive set of questions would have arisen. This cheating indicator is likely to capture effectively the most naive form of cheating but may not adequately identify more sophisticated types, which are addressed by our second and third measures. The second indicator measures the overall extent of correlation across student answers in a classroom. A high degree of correlation may indicate cheating, since the cheating is likely to take the form of changing haphazardly incorrect answers to shared correct answers. The third indicator captures the cross-question variation in student correlations. If a classroom produces a few questions in which the correlation in student answers is very high but the degree of correlation across students in the classroom on other questions is unremarkable, this suggests intervention on the part of the teacher on the questions for which answers are highly

---

9. For the formal mathematical derivation of how each of the cheating indicators is constructed, see Jacob and Levitt (forthcoming).

correlated. The fourth and final indicator of a suspicious string measures the extent to which students in a classroom get the easy questions wrong and the hard questions correct. In other words, by comparing the responses given by a particular student to those of all other students who got the same number of correct answers on that test, we are able to construct an index of dissimilarity in the answers each student gives.

To construct an overall summary statistic measuring the degree of suspiciousness of a classroom's answers, we rank the classes from least to most suspicious within subject and grade on each of the four measures. We then take the sum of squared ranks as our summary statistic. By squaring these ranks, greater emphasis is put on variations in rank in the right-hand tail (that is, the most suspicious part) of the distribution. A parallel statistic is constructed for the two test-score-gain measures corresponding to a given year's gain and the following year's gain for students in the class.

Although skepticism about the ability of these indicators to identify cheating might seem warranted, we present a range of evidence supporting the argument that these measures have predictive power empirically.[10] For instance, among classrooms that have large test score gains this year, children in classrooms that have suspicious answer strings do much worse on standardized tests the following year. This suggests that big test score gains that are not accompanied by suspicious answer strings represent real learning (which partially persists to the following year), whereas large test score gains accompanied by suspicious strings are likely due to cheating. Second, there tend to be strong correlations across subjects within a classroom and within classrooms over time in the incidence of our cheating indicators. That result is consistent with a subset of teachers who tend to cheat repeatedly. Third, the apparent cheating is highly correlated with certain incentives. For example, cheating is more likely to occur in poorly achieving schools that face the risk of being put on probation, and when social promotion is ended, cheating increases in the affected grades.

Perhaps the most convincing evidence of the usefulness of the cheating indicators, however, is visual. In figure 1 the horizontal axis reflects how suspicious the answer strings are in a classroom and the vertical axis is the probability that students in a classroom experience an unusually

10. Jacob and Levitt (forthcoming).

Figure 1. The Relationship between Unusual Test Scores and Suspicious Answer Strings

Probability of large
test score fluctuation

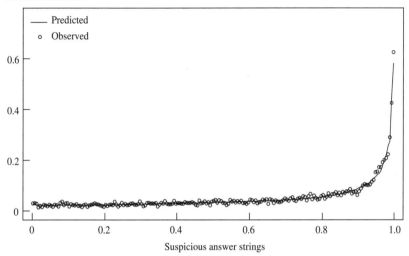

Suspicious answer strings

Notes: The measure of suspicious answer strings on the horizontal axis is measured in terms of the classroom's rank within its grade, subject, and year, with 0 representing the least suspicious classroom and 1 representing the most suspicious classroom. The 95th percentile is the cutoff for both the suspicious answer strings and test score fluctuation measures. The results are not sensitive to the cutoff used. The observed points represent averages from 200 equally spaced cells along the x-axis. The predicted line is based on a probit model estimated with seventh order polynomials in the suspicious string measure.

large test score gain in the current year followed by an unexpectedly small increase (or even a decline) in the following year.[11] Up to roughly the 90th percentile on suspicious strings and even higher, there is little or no relationship between the frequency of large test score fluctuations and suspicious strings in this subset of the data. Based on these data, if one were to predict what the pattern in the rest of the data would likely be, a continued flat line might be a reasonable conjecture. In actuality, however, there is a dramatic spike in the frequency of large test score fluctuations for classrooms that have very suspicious answers, as evidenced in the right-hand tail of figure 1.

Our interpretation of this striking pattern is that the enormous increase in unexpected test score fluctuations in the right-hand side of the figure

11. More precisely, to qualify as having large test score fluctuations in this figure, a classroom must be in the top 5 percent of classrooms with respect to the magnitude of the current year's increase relative to the following year's decrease.

reflects the fact that teacher cheating increases the likelihood of suspicious strings and of large test score increases. In a previous study we formally demonstrated that under carefully articulated assumptions, the area beneath the curve in the right-hand tail of figure 1 measures the overall incidence of teacher cheating. Empirically, our findings imply that as many as 5 percent of the classrooms in the CPS show evidence of cheating on the ITBS in any given year.

Using the Cheating Detection Algorithm in 2002 ITBS Testing

Each spring, 100,000 CPS students take the ITBS test. The results of this test determine which schools will be placed on academic probation or reconstituted, which students will be required to attend summer school and potentially be retained (third, sixth, and eighth grade only), and which students are eligible to apply to the most sought-after test-based magnet high schools in the CPS system (seventh grade).

The accountability department of CPS conducts retests of the ITBS in about 100 classrooms annually to achieve quality assurance. The retests, which use a different version of the exam, occur three to four weeks after the initial testing. Specially trained staff in the accountability office administer the retests. Unlike the initial round of testing, which is subject to relatively lax oversight and control and potentially affords various school staff members access to the test booklets, the retest answer sheets are closely guarded. Until the past few years, classrooms were randomly selected for retests.[12] Since then, retests have been focused on those classrooms achieving the largest test score gains relative to the previous year. Formal investigations have been undertaken when major discrepancies arise between the official testing and the retesting, but punishment is rare. We are aware of only one instance in the last decade in which disciplinary actions have been taken in CPS as a consequence of teacher cheating on ITBS.

In spring 2002 Arne Duncan, CEO of the CPS, having read our earlier work on teacher cheating, invited us to work with the staff of CPS in selecting the classrooms to be retested. The only real constraint on the

---

12. The exception to this rule was that if credible accusations of cheating were made about a classroom, that classroom would be retested with certainty.

implementation of the audits was that budget limitations restricted the total number of classrooms audited to no more than 120; our earlier research on cheating estimated that roughly 200 classrooms cheated each year in CPS. Thus the budget constraint meant that we were able to audit only a small fraction of the suspected cheaters.

Selecting individual classrooms with the goal of *prospectively* identifying cheating raised an important issue because the original method to detect cheating we developed in earlier work relies heavily on the availability of the following year's test scores (to determine whether large test score gains in the current year are purely transitory as would be suspected with cheating).[13] In selecting classrooms to retest, however, the next year's test scores did not, of course, exist. As a consequence, the choice of classes to audit could depend only on test scores from the current and previous years, as well as suspicious answer strings from the current year.

Table 1 outlines the structure of the design we developed. Classrooms to be audited were divided into five categories. The first group exhibited both unusually large test score gains and highly suspicious patterns of answer strings. These classrooms were judged to be the most likely to have experience cheating. A second group had very suspicious patterns of answer strings but did not have unusually large test score gains. Those patterns are consistent with a bad teacher who has failed to teach the students adequately and has attempted to cover up this fact by cheating. Thus these classrooms were suspected of high rates of cheating. A third category of classrooms encompassed those for which anonymous allegations of cheating had been made to CPS officials. There were only four of these, none of which would have otherwise made the cutoff for inclusion in our first two groups of suspected cheaters.

The remaining two categories of classrooms audited were not suspected of cheating; they served as control groups. One category included classrooms with large test score gains but with answer string patterns that did not point to cheating. These classrooms were judged likely to have good teachers capable of generating big test score gains without resorting to devious means.[14] As such, they provided an important comparison with the suspected cheaters with large gains. A fifth and final set had classrooms

13. Jacob and Levitt (forthcoming).
14. Alternatively, these classes may have had cheating, but of a form that our methods failed to detect.

Table 1. Design of the 2002 Sample of Classrooms to Be Audited[a]

Category of classroom	Comments	Did the classroom have suspicious patterns of answer strings on spring 2002 ITBS?	Did the students in the classroom achieve unusually high test score gains between 2001 and 2002 ITBS?	Prediction about how test scores will change between spring 2002 ITBS and audit test	Number of classrooms audited
Suspected cheaters					
Most likely cheaters	Look suspicious on both dimensions	Yes	Yes	Big decline in test scores when audited	51
Bad teachers suspected of cheating	Even though they cheat, test score gains not that great because teach students so little	Yes	No	Big decline in test scores when audited	21
Anonymous tips	Complaints to CPS	Varies	Varies	Big decline in test scores if complaint is legitimate	4
Control groups					
Good teachers	Big gains, but no suspicion of cheating	No	Yes	Little change between original test and audit	17
Randomly selected rooms	Control group	No	No	Little change between original test and audit	24

a. Not all classrooms were administered both reading and mathematics tests. In particular, to conserve resources, each classroom in the randomly selected control group was given only one portion of the test (either reading, or one of the three sections of mathematics). For the other classrooms, either the entire test was administered, just reading, or all three sections of the mathematics exam.

that were randomly chosen from all remaining classrooms. These classrooms were also unlikely to have high rates of cheating.

With the exception of those attributed to anonymous tips and the classrooms that were randomly chosen, we did not employ a rigid cutoff rule for allocating classrooms into the various categories. To be assigned to the first or second category, a classroom generally needed to be in the top few percent of those with suspicious answer strings on at least one subject test. For the first category the classroom also typically had to be in the top few percent on test score gains. In cases where multiple subject tests had elevated levels of suspicious strings, the cutoffs were sometimes relaxed. In addition, some classrooms that appeared suspicious but otherwise would not have made it into categories one or two, were included because other classrooms in the same school did qualify and we were interested in isolating schoolwide instances of cheating.

Dividing classrooms to be audited in this manner provides two benefits. First, the presence of two control groups (the randomly selected classrooms and the rooms that showed large achievement gains but did not have suspicious answer strings) allows a stronger test of the hypothesis that other classrooms are cheating. In the absence of these control groups, one might argue that large declines in the retest scores relative to the initial test in classrooms suspected of cheating are due to reduced effort on the part of students on the retest.[15] By isolating a set of classrooms that made large gains in achievement but did not appear to cheat, we are able to determine the extent to which declines in scores among the high-achieving suspected cheaters may simply be the consequence of reversion to mean. Second, including the control groups allows us to more effectively test how various components of our model are working in identifying cheating after it has occurred. The cost of the retest structure with the inclusion of a control group meant that we were able to retest fewer classrooms suspected of cheating. Of the 117 retested, 76 were suspected of cheating (51 with suspicious strings and large test score gains, 21 with suspicious strings but no large gains in scores, and 4 identified by anonymous tips). Again, there were many more classrooms

15. Indeed, when administering the retest, the proctors are told to emphasize that the outcome of the retest will not affect the students in any way. These retests are not used to determine summer school or magnet school eligibility and are not recorded in a student's master file.

that looked equally suspicious or nearly so but were not retested because of the budget constraints.[16]

In some cases, classrooms were retested on only the mathematics or the reading tests, not both.[17] In particular, those that were suspected of cheating on only the mathematics test were generally not retested on reading. Classes for which there were anonymous tips were retested only on reading. Finally, in the randomly selected control group, either the mathematics or the reading test was administered, but not both. In the results presented in the next section, we report test score comparisons only for those subjects on which retesting took place.

Results of the Retests

The basic results of the retests are shown in table 2. For most of the categories of classrooms we defined, six average test score gains are presented (three each for mathematics and reading).[18] For the randomly selected classrooms, there were so few data that we lumped together mathematics and reading. For the classes identified by anonymous tips, audits took place only on reading tests, so we do not report mathematics scores. In all cases the test score gains are reported in terms of standard score units, the preferred metric of the CPS. A typical student gains approximately fifteen standard score units in an academic year.

The first three columns show the results on the reading test (and the combined reading and mathematics test results for the randomly selected classrooms). Column 1 presents test scores between the spring 2001 and spring 2002 ITBS (the actual test, not the retest). For all classrooms in

16. Aware of the overall resource constraints, we provided an initial list of classrooms to CPS that had 68, 36, and 25 classrooms in categories 1, 2, and 4 respectively. Had resources been unlimited, more suspected classrooms could have been identified. Within each category, classrooms on our list were not ordered by degree of suspicion. The choice of which schools to retest from our list was made by CPS staff. In response to resistance on the part of principals at heavily targeted schools, a limited number of classrooms were retested at any one school. In a few cases, principals and parents simply refused to allow the retests to be carried out.

17. The mathematics portion of the ITBS has three sections. Every class retested on mathematics was given all three sections of the exam, even if the classroom was suspected of cheating on only one or two sections of the initial test.

18. When we talk about test score gains, we are referring to the change in test scores for a given student on tests taken at different times.

Table 2. Results for Spring 2002 ITBS and 2002 Audit Test[a]
Standard score units

Category of classroom	Reading gains			Mathematics gains		
	Spring 2001 to spring 2002	Spring 2002 and 2002 retest	Spring 2001 and 2002 retest	Spring 2001 to spring 2002	Spring 2002 and 2002 retest	Spring 2001 and 2002 retest
All classrooms in CPS	14.3	...	...	16.9	...	...
Most likely cheaters (N = 36 on math, N = 39 on reading)	28.8	-16.2	12.6	30.0	-10.7	19.3
Bad teachers suspected of cheating (N = 16 on math, N = 20 on reading)	16.6	-8.8	7.8	17.3	-10.5	6.8
Anonymous tips (N = 0 on math, N = 4 on reading)	26.2	-6.8	19.4	...	...	...
Good teachers (N = 17 on math, N = 17 on reading)	20.6	0.5	21.1	28.8	-3.3	25.5
Randomly selected classrooms (N = 24 overall, but only one test per classroom)	14.5	-2.3	12.2	14.5	-2.3	12.2

a. Because of limited data, mathematics and reading results for the randomly selected classrooms are combined. Only data for the first two columns are available for all CPS classrooms because audits were performed only on a subset of classrooms.

CPS (those that are retested and those that are not), the average gain on the reading test was 14.3 standard score points. Classrooms identified in advance as most suspicious achieved gains almost twice as large; that is, students in these classes tested roughly two grade equivalents higher than they had in tests in 2001. The control group of good teachers achieved gains that were large (20.6) but not as great as those of the suspected cheaters. Bad teachers suspected of cheating had test score gains slightly above the average CPS classroom. The scores of the randomly selected classes were in line with the scores of the CPS average, as would be expected.

Column 2 shows how the reading test scores changed between the spring 2002 test and the spring 2002 retest conducted a few weeks later. The results are striking. The most likely cheaters saw a decline of 16.2 standard score points, or more than a full grade equivalent. The bad teachers suspected of cheating saw declines of 8.8 standard score points. The classes identified by anonymous tips lost 6.8 points. In stark contrast the classrooms with good teachers actually registered small *increases* on the audit test relative to the original.[19] The randomly selected classrooms lost 2.3 points, or only one-seventh as much as the most likely cheaters. The fact that the two control groups (those with good teachers and the randomly selected classes) saw only small declines suggests that the impact of decreased effort by students on the retest is likely to be minimal. The much larger decline in scores on the audit test for the suspected cheaters is consistent with the hypothesis that their initial reading scores were inflated by cheating.

Column 3 shows the gain in test scores between the spring 2001 ITBS and the spring 2002 retest and thus represents an estimate of the "true" gain in test scores, once the 2002 cheating is eliminated (the figures in column 3 are simply the sums of those in columns 1 and 2).[20] The largest "true" gains, as would be expected, are in the classrooms identified as having good teachers. The classes most likely cheating that scored so high on the initial test look merely average in terms of "true" gains, sug-

19. As noted earlier, mathematics and reading scores are lumped together for the randomly selected classrooms, so the decline of 2.3 reported in column 2 would be applicable here as well.

20. This statement is subject to the caveat that effort might have been weaker on the retest and that the spring 2001 scores might themselves be inflated by cheating that occurred in the previous year.

gesting that all of their apparent success is attributable to cheating. For the bad-teacher category, once the cheating is stripped away, the reading performance is truly dismal: gains of just 7.8 standard score points, or little more than half a grade equivalent in a year. Classrooms identified through anonymous tips experienced some declines on the retest but continued to score well above average.

Columns 4 through 6 show results parallel to those in the first three columns, but for the mathematics tests. The results are generally similar to those for reading, but less stark.[21] The good teachers have baseline mathematics gains commensurate with those of the most likely cheaters (column 4), which was not true in reading. The results of the audit tests in column 5 once again show large declines for the two categories of classrooms suspected of cheating (declines of more than 10 standard score points in each case). The classrooms with good teachers also show a small decline in mathematics scores on the retest (3.3 points), unlike on the reading retest, where they gained. Finally, in column 6 a notable difference between the results for reading and mathematics is that the classrooms considered most likely to be cheating showed above average "true" gains in mathematics, which was not the case for reading. This result is likely due to the fact that the modified algorithm used for predicting cheaters relies in part on large test score gains and thus is biased toward identifying classrooms that have large real gains. (In contrast, the retrospective algorithm used to assess teacher cheating in our earlier published work is specifically designed to be neutral in this regard; without access to the next year's test scores, however, this neutrality is lost). In other words, the false positives generated by the prospective algorithm are likely to be concentrated among classrooms with large true gains.[22]

---

21. A partial explanation for why the results on the mathematics test are less stark than those for reading is that the mathematics test is made up of three parts, unlike the reading test, which is in one self-contained section. When the retests were conducted, classrooms suspected of cheating on any of the three mathematics sections were retested on the entire test. Thus, included in the mathematics results are some classes where there was strong evidence of cheating on one part of the exam but not on another part. Even when the results are further disaggregated, identifying particular sections of the exam where classes were judged beforehand as likely to have cheated, the results are not as clean as for the reading test.

22. Alternatively, it could just be that good teachers are also more likely to cheat. We are skeptical of this hypothesis since using our retrospective measure, we have found cheating to be concentrated in the lowest-achieving schools and classrooms; Jacob and Levitt (forthcoming).

Figure 2. Cumulative Distribution of Change in Reading Test Scores between Initial Test and Retest, by Audit Category

Cumulative percentage
of classrooms

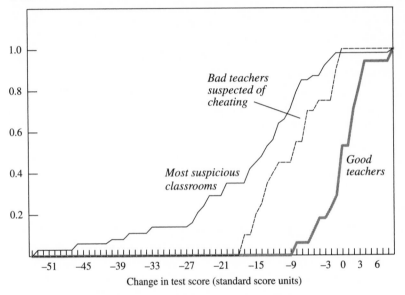

Change in test score (standard score units)

Figures 2 and 3 show the cumulative distribution of changes in reading and mathematics test scores between the initial spring 2002 test and the retest for classrooms in different categories. These figures highlight the stark differences between the classes predicted to be cheating and those identified as having good teachers. The vertical axis is the cumulative percentage of classrooms with a test score change between the initial test and the audit that is less than the value measured on the horizontal axis. Three cumulative distributions are plotted in each figure, corresponding to the classrooms previously considered most suspicious—those with bad teachers suspected of cheating—and those with good teachers. The striking feature of the figure is how little overlap there is between the distributions of the cheating and the good teachers.

In figure 2 the worst outcome for the most suspicious classrooms was a decline of 54 points (roughly three grade equivalents). Many classes in this category experienced very large losses. The bad teachers suspected of cheating are not represented by a long left tail like the most suspicious cheaters, but have a high concentration of cases in which there are dou-

Figure 3. Cumulative Distribution of Change in Mathematics Test Scores between Initial Test and Retest, by Audit Category

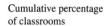

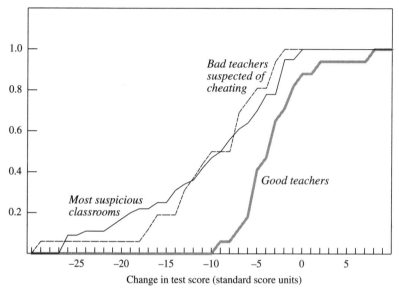

Change in test score (standard score units)

ble-digit losses. In contrast, the single biggest test score decline experienced by a good-teacher classroom on reading is 7 standard points (as indicated by the cumulative distribution rising above zero at that point for the good-teacher curve). More than 80 percent of the most suspicious classrooms experienced losses greater than that, and almost 60 percent of classrooms with bad teachers saw bigger declines. About one-third of the good-teacher classrooms experienced test score gains, whereas virtually none of the suspected cheating classrooms did.

The results shown in figure 3 are similar. The primary differences between the two figures are, first, that the distribution of outcomes for the most suspicious teachers and the bad teachers suspected of cheating are almost identical on the mathematics test and, second, the gap between the good teachers and the suspected cheaters is not quite as pronounced. Figures 2 and 3 demonstrate that the differences in means presented in table 2 are not driven by a few outliers, but rather represent systematic differences throughout the entire distribution. One implication of these findings is that our methods not only provide a means of identifying potential cheating classrooms, but also that they are at least as successful in identifying classrooms with good teachers whose students' gains are legitimate and who are possibly deserving of rewards and of analysis as exemplifying the best instructional practices.[23]

Thus far we have focused exclusively on the classroom as the unit of analysis. Another question of interest is the extent to which cheating tends to be clustered in particular schools, and if so, why?[24] Unfortunately, the way in which the audits were conducted limits the amount of light we are able to shed on answers to this question. The CPS officials who determined which classrooms to audit intentionally tried to avoid retesting large numbers of classes in particular schools because such an action could elicit negative reactions. There are at least two schools, however, in which the audits provided systematic evidence of centralized cheating likely to have been perpetrated by school administrators. These cases are currently under investigation by CPS. More generally, however, it appears that most cheating incidents are consistent with cheating by teachers rather than by administrators.

Using the Retests to Evaluate and Improve Cheating Detection

This paper has so far focused on evaluating how effective the methods previously developed were in identifying prospective cheaters. The retest also provides a unique opportunity for refining the cheating detection algorithm. In developing the algorithm we made a number of relatively arbitrary functional form and weighting assumptions, which can be tested using the data generated by the retests.

Our measure of how suspicious a classroom's answer strings are is based on an average of that class's rank on each of the four indicators

---

23. Some caution, however, must be exercised in discussing "good" teachers. Our findings suggest that classrooms with large gains in test scores that do not have suspicious patterns of answer strings can maintain their gains on retests. Whether the large test score gains are the result of artificially low test scores in the previous year (due perhaps to a bad teacher or adverse test conditions in that year) is not something we have explored.

24. Possible explanations include cheating by central administration, explicit collusion by corrupt teachers (teachers generally do not proctor their own students during the exam, so cooperation of other teachers aids in cheating), a school environment or culture that encourages cheating, or systematic differences in incentives among schools (for example, because schools performing badly are threatened with probation and reconstitution).

discussed earlier. The indicators have been given equal weight in the algorithm. Moreover, although greater weight is given to variation in the right-hand tail of the distribution of each measure, the weighting function (squaring the ranks) used was chosen somewhat arbitrarily. Using the results of the retest, we are able to test the validity of these assumptions by estimating regressions of the form

$$Change\_in\_test\_score_{cs} = Suspicious\_string\_measures_{cs}'\Gamma + \gamma_s + \theta_g,$$

where the left-hand-side variable is the change in test score between the initial spring 2002 test and the audit for a given classroom c on subject s. The primary right-hand-side variables are the suspicious string measures, which will be entered in a variety of ways to test the predictive ability of alternative functional form and weighting assumptions. The unit of observation in the regression is a classroom-subject test. Subject- and grade-fixed effects are included in all specifications. The four subject tests (reading comprehension and three mathematics tests) are pooled together and estimated jointly. In some cases we also include the gain between the spring 2001 and spring 2002 ITBS tests as a control for possible mean reversion on the retest. The suspiciousness of a classroom's answers on other subject tests on the same exams is also sometimes included as a covariate in the model. The standard errors are clustered at the classroom level to account for within-classroom correlation across different exams.

It is important to note that the sample of classrooms for which we have retest data (and thus can estimate the equation) is a highly selective one in which extreme values of suspicious answer strings are greatly overrepresented. On the one hand, this is desirable because the parameters are being identified from the part of the distribution that has many cheaters. On the other hand, it is possible that the inference from this select sample will be misleading if applied out of sample to the whole set of classrooms. When thinking about how to improve our algorithm's prospective ability to identify cheaters, that latter (potentially misleading) exercise is precisely what we have in mind. So some caution is warranted.

The first column of table 3 presents the results using the overall measure of suspicious strings that we developed in our initial paper. To aid in interpretation, we use a simple framework in which two indicator vari-

Table 3. Suspicious Answer Strings and Score Declines on the 2002 Retest[a]

Standard score units

Measures of suspicious answer strings	1	2	3	4	5	6	7	8
Overall measures (omitted category is 1–89th percentile)								
Class is in 99th percentile on overall measure	−14.2	...	−6.0	−5.5	−11.9	...	−5.6	−5.1
	(1.6)		(2.6)	(2.6)	(1.6)		(2.5)	(2.5)
Class is in 90th–98th percentile on overall measure	−4.3	...	−1.4	−1.0	−3.6	...	−1.3	−0.8
	(0.9)		(1.4)	(1.4)	(1.0)		(1.3)	(1.3)
Number of individual measures on which class is in 99th percentile (omitted category is zero)								
Four	...	−21.1	−14.9	−12.4	...	−18.0	−12.2	−9.3
		(2.3)	(3.5)	(3.3)		(2.0)	(3.4)	(3.0)
Three	...	−11.3	−7.6	−6.0	...	−9.0	−5.5	−3.7
		(2.2)	(2.6)	(2.5)		(2.1)	(2.5)	(2.5)
Two	...	−8.1	−5.2	−4.5	...	−6.5	−3.8	−3.0
		(2.2)	(2.2)	(2.1)		(2.0)	(2.0)	(2.0)
One	...	−4.3	−2.4	−2.3	...	−3.7	−1.9	−1.8
		(1.2)	(1.4)	(1.3)		(1.3)	(1.4)	(1.4)
Number of individual measures on which class is in 90th–98th percentile (omitted category is zero)								
Four	...	−8.7	−4.1	−2.5	...	−7.6	−3.2	−1.4
		(2.1)	(3.3)	(3.4)		(2.1)	(3.1)	(3.1)
Three	...	−4.1	−1.8	−0.7	...	−3.2	−1.1	0.3
		(1.2)	(1.7)	(1.6)		(1.2)	(1.8)	(1.7)
Two	...	−5.4	−3.9	−3.0	...	−5.1	−3.7	−2.6
		(1.4)	(1.8)	(1.7)		(1.4)	(1.7)	(1.6)
One	...	−4.6	−3.9	−3.0	...	−4.8	−4.2	−3.0
		(1.1)	(1.2)	(1.2)		(1.0)	(1.1)	(1.1)
Average number of categories in 99th percentile on *other* subjects	...	...	...	−1.3	...	...	...	−1.5
				(0.6)				(0.6)
Average number of categories in 90th–98th percentile on other subjects	...	...	...	−0.8	...	...	...	−1.0
				(0.5)				(0.6)
Test score gain, spring 2001 to spring 2002	...	...	...	...	−.24	−.22	−.21	−.22
					(.06)	(.06)	(.06)	(.05)
Summary statistic								
R^2	.462	.518	.530		.512	.559	.569	.582

a. The dependent variable is the change in the mean standard score between the spring 2002 ITBS and the retest for students taking both exams. The sample is the classrooms that were retested in spring 2002. The unit of observation is a classroom subject. Sample size is 316. Grade-fixed effects and subject-fixed effects are included in all regressions. Standard errors are in parantheses and are clustered to take into account correlation within classrooms across different subject tests.

ables correspond to whether a classroom is in the 99th percentile on this measure or between the 90th and 99th percentiles. We have experimented with a fuller parameterization, but this sparse specification appears to capture the relevant variation adequately. Classrooms in the 99th percentile on the overall measure of suspicious strings on average lose 14.2 standard score points (about one grade equivalent) on the retest relative to the omitted category (classes below the 90th percentile). This result is statistically highly significant. Classes in the 90th to 98th percentiles lose only one-third as much, although the result is still statistically significant.[25] Thus there appears to be a sharp discontinuity occurring in the last 1 percent of the distribution. In the sample used to estimate this regression, we can explain almost half of the variation in the retest results using these two variables alone.

Column 2 adopts a different functional form for the measure of suspicious answer strings. Rather than aggregating over the four indicators, we count the number of individual indicators for which a classroom is in the 99th percentile, or alternatively, the 90th percentile. Relative to the first column, the second column emphasizes classrooms that look extreme on particular measures (although possibly not extreme at all on others) relative to classrooms that are somewhat elevated on all four measures. Being in the 99th percentile on all four measures individually—an extreme outcome—is associated with a decline of 21.1 points on the retest relative to the omitted category, which is below the 90th percentile on all four measures. Although there is a large difference between being in the 99th percentile on all four measures rather than on three of four (−21.1 compared to −11.3), the marginal impact of an extra indicator above the 99th percentile is about 4 standard score points otherwise. Having one test score above the 90th percentile (but below the 99th) is associated with as great a decline in test scores as having one test above the 99th percentile, but there is no incremental impact of having two or three measures above the 90th percentile. The explanatory power of the specification is substantially higher than that of the first column, although this is in part due to the greater degrees of freedom in the model.

25. If one allows the impact of the 90th to 94th percentile to differ from the 95th to 98th, one cannot deny that the coefficients are identical on those two variables. Indeed, the point estimate on the 90th to 94th percentiles is slightly larger than that on the 95th to 98th.

Further evidence of the usefulness of including the additional detail provided by the model in column 2 is presented in column 3, which nests the models of the preceding two specifications. The coefficients on the aggregate measure in the first two rows fall to less than half their previous magnitude, and only for the 99th percentile variable is the estimate statistically different from zero. In contrast, the indicator variables for the separate measures continue to enter strongly and with a pattern similar to the one before. The R^2 of the nested model in column 3 is only slightly higher than that of column 2. These results suggest that our initial approach to aggregating the information in the original paper (along the lines of column 1) is less effective in predicting outcomes than the alternative presented in column 2.

When the suspiciousness of answer strings on other parts of the exam is added to the specification (column 4), the results are not greatly affected. Observing suspicious answers on the remainder of the test is predictive of greater test declines on the audit, although the magnitude of the effect is relatively small. Even having all four indicators above the 99th percentile on all three of the other subject tests (compared to none of the indicators above the 90th percentile on any of the other subjects) is associated with only a 5 point test score decline on the audit. Thus, while pooling information across subject areas is somewhat useful in identifying cheating, it is much less potent than the information contained in the answer strings to the actual subject test.

Columns 5 to 8 replicate the specifications of the first four columns, but with the baseline test score gain from spring 2001 to spring 2002 included as a regressor. In most cases the results are somewhat attenuated by the inclusion of this variable, which enters significantly negative with a coefficient of roughly –.20. The general conclusions, however, are unaltered.[26]

The specifications in table 3 give equal treatment to each of the four suspicious string measures. Table 4 relaxes that constraint, allowing separate coefficients on each of the measures. Columns 1 and 3 include only indicator variables for being in the 99th percentile on the different measures; columns 2 and 4 also include dummies for the 90th to 98th per-

---

26. We are guarded in our interpretation of this coefficient and these specifications in general, however, because in results not presented in the table we obtain a coefficient close to zero on this mean reversion variable when we limit the sample to classrooms not suspected of cheating (that is, good teachers and randomly selected controls).

Table 4. Performance of the Individual Suspicious String Indicators in Predicting Score Declines on the Retest[a]

Standard score units

Cheating indicator	1	2	3	4
Hard questions right, easy questions wrong				
99th percentile	−9.6	−10.4	−8.7	−9.5
	(2.0)	(2.0)	(1.7)	(1.7)
90th–98th percentile	. . .	−3.6	. . .	−3.1
		(1.2)		(1.2)
Identical answer blocks				
99th percentile	−3.0	−3.9	−1.2	−1.9
	(1.8)	(1.9)	(1.8)	(2.0)
90th–98th percentile	. . .	−2.5	. . .	−1.7
		(1.1)		(1.0)
High overall correlation across students				
99th percentile	−5.3	−5.7	−4.4	−4.9
	(2.2)	(2.4)	(1.9)	(2.1)
90th–98th percentile	. . .	−1.8	. . .	−1.6
		(1.0)		(1.0)
High variance in correlation across questions				
99th percentile	−1.8	−0.8	−2.4	−1.7
	(2.5)	(2.6)	(2.3)	(2.4)
90th–98th percentile	. . .	0.6	. . .	0.3
		(1.1)		(1.1)
Test score gain, spring 2001 to spring 2002	. . .	. . .	−.23	−.20
			(.06)	(.06)
Summary statistic				
R^2	.482	.524	.529	.558

a. The dependent variable is the change in the mean standard score between the spring 2002 ITBS and the retest, for students taking both exams. The sample is the classrooms that were retested in spring 2002. The unit of observation is a classroom subject. Sample size is 316. Grade-fixed effects and subject-fixed effects are included in all regressions. Standard errors are in parentheses and are clustered to take into account correlation within classrooms across different subject tests.

centiles. The final two columns allow for mean reversion. The striking result is that being in the 99th percentile on our measure of students getting the hard questions right but the easy questions wrong is much more effective in predicting score declines on the retest than are the other three measures. The implied decline of roughly 10 standard score points associated with being above this threshold is about the same magnitude as being in the 99th percentile on all three of the other measures. The second most effective cheating indicator is a high degree of overall correlation across student answers. Perhaps surprisingly, identical blocks of answers, which are so visually persuasive, are not particularly good predictors of declines on the retest. This measure is only borderline statistically significant, and one cannot reject equality of coefficients between being in the 99th percentile and the 90th to 98th percentiles. A large variance in the extent of correlation across questions on the test is the worst predictor among the four measures. None of the coefficients on this indicator are statistically significant and all of the point estimates are small in magnitude.

The results of table 4 suggest that our initial formulation of the suspicious string measures, which used equal weights for all four indicators, would be improved by placing greater emphasis on the measure reflecting students' getting the hard questions right and the easy ones wrong, and by deemphasizing or eliminating altogether the measure of variance across questions.

Conclusions

This paper summarizes the results of a unique policy implementation that allowed a test of tools for predicting and detecting cheating that we had developed. The results of retests generally support the validity of these tools for identifying teacher cheating. Classrooms selected as likely cheaters experienced dramatic declines in scores on retests, whereas classes identified as having good teachers and the randomly selected classrooms experienced little or no decline. In addition, the availability of the retest data provided a direct test of the methods developed, yielding important improvements in the functional form and weighting assumptions underlying the algorithm, which should make the algorithm even more effective in future applications.

On a more practical level, the implementation demonstrated the value of these tools to school districts interested in catching cheaters or deterring future cheating. Out of almost 7,000 potential classrooms, our methods isolated approximately 70 suspicious classrooms that were retested (as well as many more equally suspicious classrooms that were not retested because of budget constraints). Of these 70, almost all experienced substantial declines on the retest, which indicated cheating. In 29 classrooms the declines in test scores were particularly great (more than one grade-equivalent on average across the subjects retested). CPS staff undertook further investigation of these 29 classrooms, including analysis of erasure patterns and on-site investigations. Although disciplinary actions are still in progress at the time of this writing, there is every indication that for the first time in recent history, a substantial number of cheating teachers will be disciplined for their actions. If punishment is indeed handed out, then estimating the deterrent effect of this punishment on cheating on next year's test will be a potentially interesting subject for exploration.

Although our primary focus has been on the negative outcome of cheating, the positive aspect of this algorithm also deserves emphasis. Using these tools, we were able to identify a set of classrooms that made extraordinary test score gains without any indication of cheating. Without our tools, distinguishing between cheaters and outstanding teachers posed a difficult task. Consequently, identifying outstanding teachers was a tricky endeavor. With our algorithm, however, we can be almost certain that classrooms that do not have suspicious answer strings were not cheating (at least not in ways that lead to test score declines on retests), allowing for a system of rewards that will not inadvertently be directed toward cheaters.

Explicit cheating of the type we identify is not likely to be a serious enough problem by itself to call into question high-stakes testing, both because it is relatively rare (only 1 to 2 percent of classrooms on any given exam) and likely to become much less prevalent with the introduction of proper safeguards such as the cheating detection techniques we have developed. However, our work on cheating highlights the nearly unlimited capacity of human beings to distort behavior in response to incentives. The sort of cheating we catch is just one of many potential behavioral responses to high-stakes testing. Other responses, like teaching to the test and cheating in a subtler manner, such as giving the students extra time, are presumably also present but are harder to measure. Ultimately, the aim of public policy should be to design rules and incentives that provide the most favorable trade-off between the real benefits of high-stakes testing and the real costs associated with behavioral distortions aimed at artificially gaming the standard.

Comments

Philip J. Cook: W. C. Fields, acting in the movie *You Can't Cheat an Honest Man*, opines, "If a thing is worth winning, it's worth cheating for."[27] As school systems across the country have raised the stakes associated with standardized testing, cheating on these tests has become a tempting option for some teachers and administrators. The investigation for the Chicago Public Schools by Brian Jacob and Steven Levitt has documented cheating by 5 percent or more of the teachers.[28] Their article in this volume describes the system they developed for detecting cheating, based partly on an analysis of patterns of test answers, and provides persuasive validation of that system.

W. C. Fields would not have been surprised by the recent wave of corporate scandals involving accounting manipulations that have the effect of faking profitability, to the great profit of the cheaters. It is also unsurprising that Asian students seeking entrance to American universities would be tempted to fake command of the English language: apparently large numbers of them in recent years have taken advantage of web sites based in China and Korea that posted illegally obtained questions and answers to the verbal part of the Graduate Record Examinations.[29] But it is troubling (to those less cynical than W. C. Fields) that teachers, for whom truthfulness is a professional norm, could succumb to the tempta-

27. Quoted in Kleiman (2002).
28. Jacob and Levitt (2001).
29. Russell Contreras, "Inquiry Uncovers Possible Cheating on GRE in Asia," Associated Press, August (www.irps.ucsd.edu/irps/innews/ap080702).

tion to cheat, especially when the stakes for the individual teachers themselves do not appear that high.

What are the stakes? In the Chicago Public Schools, the superintendent decreed that beginning in 1996 poor performance on the test could result in penalties for both individual students and for entire schools.[30] Students are required to meet minimum standards on the mathematics and reading tests to be promoted from third, sixth, and eighth grades. Schools must have at least 15 percent of their students score above national norms on the reading exam or be placed on probation. Schools placed on probation are threatened with being reconstituted by the central administration if they exhibit insufficient progress in subsequent years. Unlike a number of state systems, Chicago chose not to institute cash bonuses to teachers in schools that did well on the standardized tests.

From the perspective of an individual teacher in Chicago, the incentive to cheat appears dilute. The direct threats are to the individual students (who may be held back) or to entire schools. The performance by any one teacher's students is just a part of the average performance by which her school is judged, and it would be an unusual circumstance that changing some answers for one class would make much difference in the likelihood that her school would end up on probation.[31]

But perhaps that is not the whole story. It would be useful to better understand the incentives to Chicago teachers. One possibility is that teachers *do* have a personal stake in test results, which would be true, for example, if principals would evaluate teachers on the basis of their students' test performance. That would presumably be of greatest concern to new teachers who have not yet received tenure, and suggests that new teachers would be more likely to cheat than established teachers. Another possibility is that teachers cheat out of sympathy for students who would otherwise be held back, which suggests that teachers will be more likely to change the test answers for those students who are likely to fail. These speculations are testable with the Jacob-Levitt data.

Deterrence

Jacob and Levitt have provided the Chicago Public Schools with a tool to help deter future cheating. Their results have triggered an investigation

---

30. Jacob and Levitt (2001).

31. School administrators have a more direct incentive to encourage or implement cheating, but it appears that most of the "action" in Chicago involved teachers.

by the administration, with penalties likely for several teachers. But if these events are perceived as unique, and unlikely to be repeated, they will have little deterrent value. Is it feasible to construct an ongoing deterrence-based system incorporating the Jacob-Levitt indicators?

To be effective, a deterrence-based system would necessarily include the threat of sanctions for individual teachers. If it is to be accepted by the teachers and their union, it seems essential that it be viewed as fair and reliable. Cost is also a consideration.

Social psychologists thirty years ago demonstrated that the perceived "fairness" of a surveillance system affects the propensity to follow the rules.[32] Perceived fairness may require among other things a degree of transparency. The indicators proposed by Jacob and Levitt, while valid, are difficult to understand and may be hard to sell to the teachers as part of an ongoing system. Even if, as seems likely, the indicators would be used only as the basis for deciding which classrooms required further investigation, that investigation would itself be viewed as punitive by the teachers, and thus would be subject to fairness concerns.

An example of a more transparent indicator is average classroom score on the standardized test relative to expected score (based on past performance of the students). Instances in which a class exceeded expectations by a wide margin would be considered suspect. While Jacob and Levitt have demonstrated that this approach by itself creates more false positives and false negatives than a system that incorporates their indicators, that loss of precision may be a price worth paying.

To economize, investigations could be limited to those classes where the cheating, if it in fact occurred, would likely have made a difference with respect to incurring any of the contingent penalties. That limitation would not affect the deterrent value of this auditing approach.

Prevention

Any deterrence-based system, unless entirely effective, is likely to erode teacher morale. And even if rare, news stories of teachers caught cheating will be costly to the reputation of the school system. Other things equal (including effectiveness and cost), a prevention-oriented system may be preferable.

---

32. See, for example, Friedland, Thibaut, and Walker (1973).

North Carolina, one of the leaders in high-stakes testing, provides a model. North Carolina public schools are evaluated on the basis of standardized tests, with a more extensive set of contingencies than in the Chicago system. Schools that perform poorly are threatened with intervention by the state. Schools that perform well are rewarded by public recognition, and the teachers in those schools receive cash bonuses of as much as $1,500.[33] The North Carolina Department of Public Instruction anticipated that teachers and school administrators might be tempted to cheat or at least find ways to game the system, so it instituted an extensive set of procedural requirements.[34] The end-of-year test is taken under the supervision of the students' regular teacher, who is observed by a proctor; the proctor must be an adult and is ordinarily not a colleague. Teachers are not allowed to talk to the students during the test, or even to distribute candy or other favors that might serve to improve their mood. Three versions of the test are distributed so that the students cannot copy from each other so easily. Teachers edit the answer sheets for errors in name and other identifiers, but only at a set time and place together with other teachers—otherwise the test sheets are locked up. Teachers cannot have the test booklets with them when editing. The entire school system must take the test on the same day. Attendance must be at least 99 percent (with the denominator carefully defined) for the school to qualify for any honors. And so forth.

Such requirements are a nuisance and might be viewed by some teachers as an insult to their integrity. But they are inexpensive and probably very effective in preventing individual teachers from cheating.[35]

At a more basic level, prevention can be built into the system of contingencies. Helen Ladd observes that "balance must be found so financial awards are large enough to change behavior, but not so large that they induce outright cheating."[36] It is not just the size of the awards that matters, however, but also the contingency system. If cheating is most likely to be a temptation for individual teachers, then perhaps diluting the individual incentive to cheat by tying consequences to the performance of the

---

33. Ladd and Zelli (2002).

34. These requirements were related to me by Elizabeth Camden Cook, an experienced eighth-grade teacher in the Durham, North Carolina, Public Schools.

35. There may still be room in this system for administrators to cheat, so it does not entirely negate the usefulness of an occasional audit.

36. Ladd (1996, p. 14).

school rather than the classroom would be useful—as has been done in North Carolina, the Chicago Public Schools, and elsewhere. Whether that system will also reduce useful efforts to improve student performance depends on the locus of relevant decisionmaking within the school. To the extent that the relevant features of the instructional process are set by the school or district (for example, choice of texts, pacing, student tracking), then placing the contingency at the school level is entirely appropriate.

Honest Cheating

George Washington Plunkett of Tamany Hall famously distinguished between "dishonest graft" and "honest graft."[37] By today's standard, that might be the distinction between outright bribes as opposed to (legal) influence-buying through campaign contributions. The distinction can usefully be appropriated for high-stakes testing, which can lead to "dishonest cheating" (of the sort documented by Jacob and Levitt) but also "honest cheating." More precisely, "dishonest cheating" means to change the relationship between the performance score and the "true" level of student accomplishment in some way not permitted by the rules. "Honest cheating" means to change the relationship between the score and the true level of accomplishment in some way that is permitted, but defeats the purpose of the system.

"Teaching to the test" is a phrase that suggests some of the most obvious forms of honest cheating. For example, if the purpose of high-stakes testing is to make schools more productive in educating children to read, write, and figure, but the test score is heavily influenced by the students' ability to manage multiple-choice tests effectively, then much instructional time will be devoted to developing test-taking skills at the cost of instruction in substance. Likewise, history, science, physical education, and any other subject that is unmeasured by the test, and therefore outside the ambit of reward and punishment, will be neglected, even if it is generally acknowledged to be important.[38] Furthermore, the type of average or summary score used to rate a school may create an incentive for distributing resources inappropriately; in Chicago, for example, if a school is struggling to avoid probation, the school administration may be

---

37. See the discussion in Robert D. Behn, "Cheating—Honest & Dishonest," *New Public Innovator* (May–June, 1998), pp. 18–19.
38. Ladd (1996, p. 12).

tempted to focus instructional resources on the most able students to ensure that at least 15 percent reach the national norm.

An ounce or two of prevention may be sufficient to reduce dishonest cheating to some minimal, acceptable level. But there are no cheap remedies available for honest cheating except to do away with high-stakes testing.

Bruce Sacerdote: This is a very exciting and unusual paper that illustrates both how people respond to incentives and how statistical tools can be used to solve real-world problems. The paper is a continuation of Brian Jacob and Steve Levitt's earlier work on the problem of detecting teacher cheating on standardized tests given to secondary school students. In the earlier paper the authors developed several measures of suspicious patterns of answers at the classroom level, and they showed that suspicious patterns were strongly correlated with student test score gains that were not sustained the following year. For the current paper the authors were permitted to choose certain classrooms for auditing and retesting to better ascertain the extent to which suspicious answer patterns were caused by cheating teachers. Below I present several reasons social scientists and policymakers will care about these results and then discuss some implications of the work that the authors did not highlight but might have.

The paper is incredibly interesting for several reasons. First, the use of high-stakes testing is becoming increasingly common and important in public schools. This paper highlights at least one of the potential distortions in behavior from such testing. If students' grade promotion or graduation is tied to their test performance, they will have a strong incentive to cheat, or a teacher might cheat on the students' behalf. Similarly, if jobs and salaries for teachers are tied to aggregate test performance (either at the school or classroom level), the teacher is also given a strong incentive to cheat. Current testing conditions are often far from rigorous. For example, teachers may have access to the answer sheets long after the students have completed the test. And in the case of the Iowa Test of Basic Skills used in the Chicago Public School system, questions are often reused every few years. This practice can allow teachers to give their students some of the actual test questions ahead of time. Jacob and Levitt demonstrate that a number of teachers do take advantage of the lax testing conditions.

Clearly policymakers could respond to this problem by increasing the chance that cheating teachers get caught, and the paper provides a nice set of tools to detect certain forms of cheating. Policymakers could also make it more difficult or time-consuming to cheat with simple steps such as not allowing teachers to proctor their own exams. Cheating of the kind and frequency examined in the paper does not necessarily demonstrate that high-stakes testing is not a viable policy, particularly given that school administrators have a number of low-cost options they could use to reduce cheating. The next interesting direction in this research program will be to see how teacher behavior in Chicago changes following the investigations described in the paper. An interesting question will be whether teachers can substitute more sophisticated cheating strategies that are harder to detect.

One broader message of the paper is that incentives matter and that human beings are inventive in finding ways to game a system. And we should be aware that teachers or police or clergy members are subject to the same economic forces that explain many aspects of human behavior in general. A second broad message is that microdata often contain a great deal of information in the covariance of data items across individual people. In this case the authors show that much can be learned from the extent to which students answers are correlated within a classroom. For example, unusual and large blocks of identical answers from within a classroom may indicate that students cheated from each other or that a teacher filled in portions of the answer sheets. By sifting through the within-classroom correlations of answers, the authors are able to make inferences about student and teacher behavior.

One of my favorite aspects of the paper is the experimental design used for the audit. Rather than have one treatment (suspected cheaters) and one control group, the audit design has three different groups of suspected cheaters and two control groups. Within the suspected cheaters are classrooms with suspicious answer strings and unusual gains in scores, classrooms with suspicious answer strings and normal gains, and classrooms for which there were anonymous accusations of cheating. The retesting of this third group is particularly important for validating the paper's methodology. All three groups of suspected classrooms (including those selected because of anonymous tips that cheating was occurring) experience significant declines in scores on the retest (audit); the control groups do not. Suspected cheaters experience large declines on the retest even when they are identified through tips rather than by statistical tools. Given these results, one can be fairly confident that the authors' methodology is indeed picking up cheating.

The authors did not discuss what happened in cities that tried to detect cheating through methods other than statistical analysis, but I found reading about such attempts very informative. Gary, Indiana, uncovered a major teacher cheating scandal early in 2002; New York City conducted a similar investigation in 1999. The investigation in New York City was started when a high school that was in danger of being closed because of poor test scores suddenly experienced large score gains. Investigators interviewed a host of witnesses, including students and teacher's aides, and found actual cheat sheets that students had been handed. These instances demonstrate that statistical sophistication is not a precondition to being able to catch cheaters.

However, some of the New York classrooms accused of cheating retained their large improvements in scores, and it is possible that some of the teachers who were reassigned or dismissed were simply those who had succeeded in improving their students' test-taking ability. This possibility illustrates the danger and irony of using score improvements alone to determine who gets investigated, and it speaks further to the value of the current paper.

Do cheaters prosper? Based on the retest, students in cheating classrooms still experience average test score increases, even after one removes their ill-gotten gains from cheating. In fact, on the mathematics retest, students in cheating classrooms had better annual gains than the average student in the Chicago public schools. On the initial test in 2002 the most likely cheaters experienced an annual gain of 30.0 points on the mathematics test versus the systemwide average gain of 16.9 points. On the retest the most likely cheaters still racked up a gain of 19.3 points, though this gain is probably not statistically significantly greater than the 16.9 average gain. This may indicate that the most aggressively cheating teachers are not necessarily short-changing their students in the classroom. In fact, if the teacher is highly motivated, she might use multiple ways to try to increase scores, including both approved and disapproved methods.

Overall the paper makes large contributions on various levels. First, it gives school administrators and researchers tools for detecting cheating. Second, it shows one of the potential pitfalls of tying teachers' jobs or students' promotions to standardized tests. With regard to this point, the evidence suggests that schools are currently doing little to prevent teachers from cheating. Therefore low-cost increases in deterrence may cause large reductions in the frequency and extent of cheating. Third, the paper is an inspiration to other researchers who want to do policy-oriented work that has some near-term impact on the world. The paper shows that collaborative efforts between researchers and practitioners can be highly productive. Finally, it reminds us that people respond to incentives in very rational ways and that social science can tell us a great deal about some aspects of human behavior.

References

Angoff, William H. 1974. "The Development of Statistical Indices for Detecting Cheaters." *Journal of the American Statistical Association* 69 (345): 44–49.

Cizek, Gregory J. 1999. *Cheating on Tests: How to Do It, Detect It and Prevent It.* Lawrence Erlbaum Associates.

Deere, Donald, and Wayne Strayer. 2001. "Putting Schools to the Test: School Accountability, Incentives and Behavior." Working Paper 0113. Department of Economics, Texas A&M University.

Frary, Robert B., T. Nicolaus Tideman, and Thomas Morton Watts. 1977. "Indices of Cheating on Multiple-Choice Tests." *Journal of Educational Statistics* 2 (4): 235–56.

Friedland, Nehemia, John Thibaut, and W. Laurens Walker. 1973. "Some Determinants of the Violation of Rules." *Journal of Applied Social Psychology* 3 (2): 103–18.

Grissmer, David W., and others. 2000. *Improving Student Achievement: What NAEP Test Scores Tell Us.* MR-924-EDU. Santa Monica: RAND Corporation.

Heubert, Jay P., and Robert M. Hauser, eds. 1999. *High Stakes: Testing for Tracking, Promotion and Graduation.* National Academy Press.

Holmstrom, Bengt, and Paul Milgrom. 1991. "Multitask Principal-Agent Analyses: Incentive Contracts, Asset Ownership and Job Design." *Journal of Law, Economics and Organization* 7 (Spring): 24-51.

Jacob, Brian A. 2001. "Getting Tough? The Impact of Mandatory High School Graduation Exams on Student Outcomes." *Educational Evaluation and Policy Analysis* 23 (2): 99–121.

———. 2002. "The Impact of Test-Based Accountability in Schools: Evidence from Chicago." Unpublished manuscript. John F. Kennedy School of Government, Harvard University.

Jacob, Brian A., and Steven D. Levitt. Forthcoming. "Rotten Apples: An Estimation of the Prevalence and Predictors of Teacher Cheating." *Quarterly Journal of Economics.*

Kleiman, Mark A. R. 2002. "Dukenfield's Law of Incentive Management." Department of Policy Studies, University of California at Los Angeles.

Klein, Stephen P., and others. 2000. "What Do Test Scores in Texas Tell Us?" Santa Monica: RAND.

Ladd, Helen F., ed. 1996. "Introduction." In *Holding Schools Accountable: Performance-Based Reform in Education*, edited by Helen F. Ladd, 1–21. Brookings.

Ladd, Helen F., and Arnaldo Zelli. 2002. "School Based Accountability in North Carolina: The Responses of School Principals." *Educational Administration Quarterly* 38 (October): 494–529.

Loughran, Regina, and Thomas Comiskey. 1999. "Cheating the Children: Educator Misconduct on Standardized Tests." Report of the City of New York Special Commisioner of Investigation for the New York City School District (December).

Richards, Craig E., and Tian Ming Sheu. 1992. "The South Carolina School Incentive Reward Program: A Policy Analysis." *Economics of Education Review* 11 (1): 71–86.

Smith, Stephen S., and Roslyn A. Mickelson. 2000. "All that Glitters Is Not Gold: School Reform in Charlotte-Mecklenburg." *Educational Evaluation and Policy Analysis* 22 (2): 101–27.

Tepper, Robin Leslie. 2001. *The Influence of High-Stakes Testing on Instructional Practice in Chicago.* Seattle: American Educational Research Association.

Van der Linden, Wim, and Leonardo Sotaridona. 2002. "A Statistical Test for Detecting Answer Copying on Multiple-Choice Tests." University of Twente, Netherlands.

BENGTE EVENSON
Illinois State University

WILLIAM C. WHEATON
Massachusetts Institute of Technology

Local Variation in Land Use Regulations

IN THE UNITED STATES, land use regulation is the responsibility of more than 18,000 local governments, mostly cities and towns. While the legal authority for such regulation lies with state governments in virtually all parts of the county, such power has been legislatively delegated to local government for almost half a century. This delegation of authority has its origins in the idea that such regulation is designed largely to manage situations where local property owners adversely affect one another through their development decisions or other actions. These externalities need some mechanism for dispute resolution—and such a role for land use regulation received early economic justification by Ronald Coase.[1] He argued that with the imperfect assignment of property rights, public intervention might be needed in place of private bargaining. The powers that local governments have acquired over the years now are quite broad. In a nutshell towns can

—regulate the part of their open land that is developed for a range of uses (commercial, industrial, residential); and

We wish to thank the employees of the Massachusetts Executive Office of Environmental Affairs (EOEA) and various regional planning agencies, especially Allen Bishop and Jane Pfister, who were very helpful in obtaining and interpreting these data. Buildout data were provided by the EOEA and are part of a statewide buildout project completed between 1999 and 2002 with the assistance of the commonwealth's thirteen regional planning agencies. Source data were supplied by the Executive Office of Environmental Affairs, MassGIS. We also wish to thank Sarah Williams at MIT, who was instrumental in helping to prepare the data for analysis.
    1. Coase (1960).

—regulate the intensity of each use that occurs on that land (density or floor-area ratio, or FAR).

Recently it has been recognized that such broad land use controls might have impacts on the wider metropolitan economy. Clearly, if many towns choose to zone out industrial development, the economic growth of the metropolitan economy as a whole could be endangered. Likewise, if all towns set strict maximum density limits, the provision of housing for low- or moderate-income families will be difficult. Such limits also would make housing in general more expensive. Finally, if towns choose to provide extensive greenbelts or open spaces, the region as a whole becomes more spread out, with resulting increases in travel distances, times, and congestion.

The specter of such problems has led a few economists to develop simple positive (as opposed to normative) models of how and why towns decide on such regulations. Generally, they do so to increase the well-being of their own residents—without regard to broader consequences. Bruce Hamilton speculates about the objectives of towns in the setting aside of land into open space.[2] Michelle J. White, Edwin S. Mills and Wallace E. Oates, and William Wheaton discuss how minimum-lot-size (MLS) zoning results from the desire of town residents to avoid the tax burden of providing services to residents with below-town-average income.[3] William Fischel and Rodney A. Erickson and Michael J. Wasylenko discuss the complicated trade-off that towns make when considering how much commercial development to permit within their boundaries.[4]

Empirically, there has been little study of zoning regulations. In large measure this reflects the difficulty of obtaining consistent information across so many local jurisdictions. Generally, local jurisdictions are not required to report systematically their zoning categories, area so zoned, and buildouts or density. In terms of process, there also are usually no systematic data on how many zoning or variance applications each town receives, what the average process time is, or what proportion are disapproved and later appealed. With little data, the few theories that have been advanced have never been carefully tested.

2. Hamilton (1978).
3. White (1975); Mills and Oates (1975); Wheaton (1993).
4. Fischel (1975); Erickson and Wasylenko (1980).

This research paper has two objectives. First, we describe a unique database created in the State of Massachusetts in 1999. This database used satellite technology to document the exact nature of all open land in each of the state's 351 cities and towns. The database then geo-recorded the zoning ordinances for each jurisdiction to ascertain how this open land was zoned. The data can be used to document the proportion of open land that is zoned for residential or commercial use as well as the build-out that is allowed there.

With these data, our second objective is to establish a series of stylized facts about how towns zone. Which towns zone for the largest lot sizes? What is the income elasticity of demand for open space? What kinds of jurisdictions are most strict about commercial use? Our conclusions are:

—Existing town density and development are crucial determinants of zoned density and allowed development; thus zoning seems to follow the current market.

—Future commercial development is permitted primarily in higher-density, lower-income cities and towns.

—Town income is strongly related to the extent that towns allow development at all. Higher town income leads to significantly more land set aside in protected categories and less zoned for either commercial or residential use.

—There appears to be no significant impact of town income on the density of future development, either residential or commercial.

In the next section we review what has been written in the economics studies about community zoning, both theoretically and empirically. Then we describe the data collected in the 1999 study and those covariates also used in our study. The next section presents statistics and a series of reduced-form equations that analyze the determinants of how much land in each use towns allow, and what buildout can occur on that land. We then draw some conclusions and present a list of suggestions for future research.

Previous Studies

Previous studies have generally covered minimum lot sizes, provision of open space, commercial development, and housing outcomes.

Minimum Lot Sizes

By far the greatest number of studies on land use regulations relates to the almost universal practice of towns' creating residential zones with minimum-lot-size (MLS) regulations. At one level it has been argued that such regulation internalizes an externality between property owners: by expanding one's own lot, greater green space is created for all abutters. Recent evidence confirms that individual lot prices vary significantly with the characteristics of adjoining ones.[5] In addition, such regulations provide insurance for current owners that later development will be of a predictable density. There is also considerable evidence that residents are quite willing to pay for such insurance controls.[6] In these studies MLS zoning appears to be an efficiency-enhancing tool to help control traditional Coasian externalities.

Almost thirty years ago economists began to realize that MLS zoning also had a significant impact on the distribution of households by income across towns. With property tax financing local services, sorting across communities is not necessarily achieved.[7] In fact towns have a strong fiscal incentive to prevent any household that has below average housing demand from developing in a town. The tool that allows them to do this is MLS zoning. By insisting that newly developing land have lot sizes that are at least as large as those currently existing, towns can enhance their fiscal surplus. Papers by White and others in a well-known volume edited by Mills and Oates explored the consequences of such "discriminatory" zoning.[8]

While several later authors have qualified the conclusions of Mills and Oates—for example, Wheaton in 1993—the general practice of "fiscal zoning" is now widely accepted, and often highly criticized.[9] Again, because data were lacking, there has been little documentation of exactly how widespread MLS zoning is, how binding or strict the density limits are, or how cumbersome the permitting process is. In fact, there are virtually no empirical or theoretical studies on the nature and extent of this zoning.

5. Thorsnes (2000).
6. Speyrer (1989).
7. Tiebout (1956).
8. Mills and Oates (1975).
9. Haar and Kayden (1989).

Provision of Open Space

Another aspect of local land use regulation is the provision of open space by either local jurisdictions or regional governments. Open space can be acquired through direct public purchase, from donations by private parties in exchange for tax advantages, or obtained de facto by limiting development on wetlands, certain types of soil, public water frontage, and so forth. When land is acquired through this last channel, public or environmental goals must be clear before the regulatory power of government can override landowner rights.

Economists have viewed open space as a legitimate public good. At the same time, however, widespread provision of open space can alter the supply of land to urban development and thus potentially drive up housing prices. This trade-off was carefully studied empirically in the case of the California Coastal Commission's regulation.[10] Jan K. Brueckner also developed a theoretical model to explain how limiting land under development might work within a competitive system of cities, each gaining a public good but in so doing paying a price through the higher land values caused by a greater scarcity of accessible urban land.[11]

Bengte Evenson and William Wheaton have been the first to combine a theoretical model explaining the incentives of towns competing for housing demand within a market to regulate land use with empirical evidence.[12] Each town is assumed to trade off the cost of regulation with the dual benefits of a newly created public good and an increase in house prices resulting from regulation.

Recently, there have also been a few studies of town demand for open space that attempt to characterize those types of towns that, through one means or another, have acquired open space. Laurie J. Bates and Rexford E. Santerre, estimating the demand for open space in Connecticut, find, for example, that private and public provision of land are not good substitutes.[13]

---

10. Dale-Johnson and Yim (1990).

11. Brueckner (1996).

12. Evenson and Wheaton (2002) use the same data presented here later, although with different sample selection criteria. Their predictions are retested under these new assumptions in this analysis.

13. Bates and Santerre (1994, 2001).

Commercial Development

The role that town regulations play in the development of commercial land has received even less attention than regulations limiting residential development. An early article by Fischel outlines the considerations that towns face in deciding whether to allow industrial or commercial development.[14] Generally such developments use far less in local services than they pay in property taxes: hence they provide the town with a net fiscal gain. At the same time, however, such uses can contribute to congestion, crowding, loss of rural character, and even environmental decay. Towns ultimately must weigh these costs against the fiscal gains.

Empirically, a study by Helen F. Ladd validated this view by showing that communities with a large historical fraction of commercial development face a lower "tax price" for their residents and as such tend to spend more on local services (all else equal).[15] A later study by Erickson and Wasylenko demonstrated that many towns in a particular metropolitan area effectively do zone out industrial or commercial development and that there is a distinct pattern to this practice—it is made up of wealthier towns with generally low property tax rates.[16] This would again be consistent with Fischel's view because such towns gain less property tax relief under the presumption that environmental valuation is income elastic.

Housing Outcomes

Although there has not been much research about the extent and character of zoning, there is a somewhat longer list of research studies about the presumed negative impacts of such regulation on the housing market. Edward L. Glaeser and Joseph Gyourko and Larry Ozanne and Thomas Thibodeau find evidence that house prices are higher in areas with greater regulation, while Christopher J. Mayer and C. Tsuriel Sommerville and Bengte Evenson conclude that housing supply is less elastic in markets with greater regulation.[17] Although suggestive, the studies on housing outcomes do suffer from the lack of any rigorously defined measure of local regulation. Unfortunately, we are not able to test the

14. Fischel (1975).
15. Ladd (1975).
16. Erickson and Wasylenko (1980).
17. Glaeser and Gyourko (2002); Ozanne and Thibodeau (1983); Mayer and Sommerville (2002); Evenson (2002).

hypotheses of these studies because they tend to use statistics summarizing the differences in land use regulation across metropolitan areas. Our data cover parts of only two metropolitan areas.

Zoning Statutes and the Zoning Process

Each state in the United States designs its zoning system differently. In Massachusetts, much emphasis is placed on the statutory plan that each city or town enacts, and the degree of administrative flexibility around that plan is somewhat limited. In effect, zoning in Massachusetts is relatively rigid and not simply an open bargaining session between developer and town planning board.

Each city or town must start by preparing a master plan that includes a land use category and density level for all areas of the community. Once prepared, this plan is adopted by either city council or full town meeting. Any changes require amending the plan, which again requires the full vote of either the city council or full town meeting. Furthermore, the process of amending a plan requires a substantial period of notification, the holding of hearings, and a period of grace afterward. It cannot be done expeditiously.

Within a plan, there are generally two provisions for administrative amendments. These are special permits and variances, both of which can be granted by the planning board after public hearings. Specially permitted uses can differ from that use that an area is zoned for, but must be carefully specified in advance in the plan, and must apply to all areas that are similarly zoned. Thus a town might specify light commerce as a special permit use in one-acre residential areas, but it must be such for all areas of the town so zoned. Hearings and public input are important in determining whether special permits are granted.

Variances are complete exemptions from whatever the zoning plan intends for a particular area. As in many states, the granting of variances requires that the developer conclusively demonstrate economic hardship if the variance is not granted. Judicial precedent generally requires that such hardship involve the full loss of value rather than simply diminished value.[18] In Massachusetts any aggrieved party may challenge a variance

18. Haar and Kayden (1989) contains a review of variance procedures.

that is granted by a planning board if he or she feels that full hardship was not demonstrated.

With such cumbersome procedures the only real way for cities or towns to create flexible zoning is to designate broad, mixed-use districts and get them accepted into the plan. This of course assumes that local residents will assent to such a designation that effectively puts development out of their control. In the downtowns of the larger cities in the commonwealth, such flexible mixed-use districts sometimes exist, but in most smaller cities or suburban towns, single-use zones with limited special permits tend to be the most common. In most Massachusetts towns, if an area is zoned one-acre residential, developers with commercial or higher density residential intentions need not apply. In this paper we take the view that the zoning plan of the town does reflect its intentions for the future.

Data

We merge data on both current land use and its regulation in Massachusetts cities and towns into a unique new data set. [19] All the data maps were created for use with Geographic Information Systems (GIS) software, which allows the researcher to link the graphical depiction with an underlying spreadsheet of data. Therefore, the data maps give actual land use and the regulation of land in Massachusetts in a format that can be transformed for analysis using a standard statistical package. To create our data set, we merged or intersected (or both) the maps and converted the resulting spreadsheets into a format used by the statistical program STATA. The ability to merge and intersect these data spatially means that they are incredibly precise relative to what little data have been available previously. For example, we are able to take a plot of land with a given land use designation and subdivide it into protected and unpro-

---

19. "These digital data represent the efforts of the Massachusetts Executive Office of Environmental Affairs [MAEOEA] and its agencies to compile or record information from the cited source materials. EOEA maintains an ongoing program to record and correct errors in these data that are brought to its attention. The agency makes no claims as to the absolute validity or reliability of these data or their fitness for any particular use. EOEA maintains records regarding all methods used to collect and process these digital data and will disclose this information upon request."

tected status, making it easy to identify parcels as small as Boston Common, Boston Garden, and the parkway between the east- and west-bound lanes of Commonwealth Avenue separately.

Current Land Use Data

Data on current land use were interpreted from aerial photographs of the state, taken in each town in 1999 by the Massachusetts Office of Geographic and Environmental Information (MASSGIS). Each photograph was taken from a height of approximately 15,000 feet, leading to a scale of 1:25,000 inches. Each parcel was assigned one of thirty-six current land use categories, making these data both detailed and complete. We collapsed these thirty-six categories into four general land use classifications for our analysis, so that all land in the state is categorized as either residential land (R_i), commercial and industrial land (C_i), open land (O_i), or other land (X_i).[20]

Data on Protected Land

A separate data set on protected land was also created by MASSGIS and is maintained at the local level. The maps combine federal and state landholding with local tax assessor maps and existing open space plans. For each protected parcel the level of protection is identified as protected in perpetuity, temporarily, on a limited basis, or not legally protected. Since this last is associated with land typically assumed to be unbuildable, such as school sports fields, we identify all land in this data set as protected.[21]

These data were intersected with the current land use data, and protected land from each of the relevant current land use categories was

20. Open space includes land used for intensive or extensive agriculture, forests and woody perennials, participation and recreation and open land (with the exception of lands covered by power lines or used for transportation purposes, which are included in the commercial-industrial category). All else, including cemeteries and land with unknown use, was included in an "other" category. Other land includes land that cannot be built on (for example, waste disposal sites, cemeteries, and beaches), land that is already developed with an alternative use (for example, racetracks, fairgrounds, and swimming pools), and a small amount of land whose use is categorized as unknown. The subscript i in each case is an index of the town, $i = 1,351$. See www.state.ma.us/mgis/lus.htm.

21. For the complete definitions of these protection levels, see www.state.ma.us/mgis/osp.htm.

aggregated into a fifth land classification (Z_i). Not surprisingly, the majority of the protected land comes out of the open land category, although the residential and commercial-industrial categories did contribute some protected land. However, this category does not include protected land from the "other" land use category since these lands cannot be built on. We ignore these lands, such as protected beaches along Cape Cod, because this paper is concerned with the regulatory division of buildable and unbuildable lands.

Zoning Data

Each town in Massachusetts was required to send digital zoning data to MASSGIS, which linked each map to the zoning bylaws to increase the detail and consistency of the data. These maps were submitted in June 2000, and the vast majority (97.5 percent) are current as of 1996.[22] Further, 84 percent are current as of 1999. Local zoning codes were collapsed into twenty-one primary use codes, which we then collapsed to match our four major land use categories.[23] These data were intersected with the current land use data (minus protected land). This allowed us to subdivide currently open land available for building into four categories: open land zoned for future residential use (OR_i), open land zoned for future commercial or industrial use (OC_i), open land protected (included in Z_i), and open land not currently zoned (OO_i).

Buildout Data

Data on possible future buildout were created by the Massachusetts Executive Office of Environmental Affairs in conjunction with the state's thirteen regional planning boards.[24] Planning board consultants worked with each of the towns in their region to create a series of uniform maps giving a detailed description of the maximum potential building that

22. Only two communities submitted maps dated before 1993. Monroe, an isolated town of 100 residents on less than 7,700 acres (of which 4,240 acres is state forest) is current as of only 1990. Tolland, a town of 400 residents on nearly 20,500 acres (nearly all of which is zoned residential-agricultural), is current as of only 1978.

23. For the complete definitions of the zoning categories see www.state.ma.us/mgis/zn.htm.

24. Under the EOEA definition, "buildout" is defined as the number of units that can be built on open land under current land use laws. This definition does not allow for demolition or density increases.

could take place in the state given current zoning laws, protection clauses, and geographic constraints.[25] These maps were then linked to spreadsheets that summarize the data in each series.

These summary buildout statistics should be relatively accurate because the series they were calculated from consists of five extremely detailed maps for each town. These background maps are described by the EOEA as follows:

> Map 1 allows communities to see how they have used the land within their municipal boundaries to date. It depicts, in varying colors, lands that have already been developed or protected as well as lands that are absolutely constrained to development. . . . [Map 2 shows the amount and location of land within a community that is available for future development.] . . . Hatched patterns indicate partial constraints to development, such as wetlands, the second 100-foot buffer zone under the Rivers Protection Act, or overlay districts, such as a water protection overlay district which limits impervious surface, bans underground storage tanks and requires that a special permit be issued for the storage of hazardous materials. . . . The third map in the buildout analysis series is intended to simplify the information seen on the first two maps. . . . Each buildout map series includes an aerial photo [map 4] of the community taken from approximately 15,000 feet above the ground. . . . [This map is] useful to examine the patterns of subdivisions, buildings, power lines, roads and other geographic features, such as recreational fields, water bodies, forests and farmlands, which are also readily apparent. The regional planning agencies (RPA) and consultants who completed the buildout analyses also used this map as a type of base map from which to derive new GIS layers and to check the accuracy of other maps produced for the buildout series. . . . [Map 5] shows a community's current zoning. . . . Essentially, it acts as a blueprint for a community's future development, showing how it has divided its land to accommodate varied development interests.[26]

Final Land Use Data Description

The five EOEA maps for each town were combined with the corresponding maps detailing current land use, zoning, and protection. The result is a data set in which land is catgorized into land that is currently in residential use, in commercial or industrial use, open, protected, or other

---

25. "Current" in this case describes data collected between 1999 and 2001, depending on the town.

26. For the EOEA's full description of each type of map and sample maps, see www.commpres.env.state.ma.us/community/cmty_main.asp?community ID=1#Absolute.

(unbuildable). Further, open land is subcategorized by zoning regulation; checked for geographic constraints that might impede building, such as wet soil or steep slopes; and divided by the relevant minimum lot size of floor-to-area ratio to determine the maximum possible number of new buildings. This allows for the calculation of the maximum potential increase in population, students, and water use in each town.

It is important to note that these latter are hypothetical measures of growth that depend on a strict interpretation of the current zoning code. These data describe a well-defined potential growth scenario: maximum growth under the current regulatory regime. However, they do not define either the growth that is necessarily expected or the timing of the growth. The maps were developed as a visual aid to guide future development plans both within and across towns, suggesting that neither desired nor expected eventual growth patterns in Massachusetts will match these data. Rather, the data describe a set of equilibrium outcomes for the local regulatory processes at a point in time. We are using a cross-sectional data set in the standard, static sense.

Demographic Data

The demographic data consist mainly of Census data collected from the Massachusetts state website. However, driving distance to Boston for each town was collected from Mapquest.com, a standard software for obtaining driving directions.[27]

As stated earlier, the data set contains at least portions of the data for all 351 towns in Massachusetts. Unfortunately, most of the buildout data are not available for three of the cities: Boston, Worcester, and Nantucket. We argue that dropping Boston and Worcester, two of the most populated cities in Massachusetts, from the analysis should not affect the results. These cities effectively have no land use decisions left to make. It is possible that a very small decision may be made, such as not to build housing on current golf courses. In addition, renovation and revitalization decisions are not included. However, for the land we determine to be subject to a regulatory decision, the assumption that no decision is left to be made is likely to be fairly accurate.

This view is supported by the data themselves, which show that sev-

---

27. We used the shortest driving distance regardless of road type.

eral other densely populated cities have no open land subject to a land use decision under the current regulatory regime. Chelsea, Everett, Somerville, Watertown, and Winthrop all have no land available for additional residential development. Another fifty-one towns have no land available for commercial or industrial development. Finally, Winthrop, one of the most densely populated towns, has no land available for residential, commercial, or industrial development. In addition several cities have included redevelopment in their analysis of commercial and industrial buildout. On average, these are relatively small, more densely populated towns that are geographically closer to Boston. We check for possible bias by dropping near-Boston communities from the sample and comparing the results.

Results

We begin by reviewing the notation used for measuring current and future allowed land use in each town i defined earlier.

Land Use Share Variables

R_i = acres of land currently used for residential purposes.

C_i = acres of land currently used for commercial or industrial purposes.

O_i = acres of land currently open. This is subdivided into acres of open land zoned for residential purposes (OR_i), acres of open land zoned for commercial or industrial purposes (OC_i), acres of open land protected (OZ_i, included in Z_i), and acres of open land not zoned (OO_i).

Z_i = acres of land currently protected.

Regulated Density Variables

FR_i = average zoned residential density for future building (maximum potential new residences divided by OR_i).

FC_i = average zoned commercial density for future building (maximum potential commercial or industrial square feet divided by OC_i).

ER_i = existing residential density (units in 2000 divided by R_i).

EC_i = existing commercial density measured as the proportion of currently built land used for commercial or industrial purposes ($C_i/(C_i+R_i)$).

Table 1. Summary Statistics for the Land Use Regulation Variables

Variable[a]	N	Mean	Standard deviation	Minimum	Maximum
R_i	351	2,643	1,947	70	14,376
C_i	351	584	732	0	8,162
Z_i	351	3,974	3,670	90	28,301
O_i	351	6,356	4,663	51	24,580
$\%R_i$	351	0.22	0.15	0.01	0.69
$\%C_i$	351	0.05	0.06	0	0.46
$\%Z_i$	351	0.25	0.13	0.02	0.72
$\%O_i$	351	0.40	0.18	0.03	0.87
OR_i	350	5,492	4,444	0	20,448
OC_i	350	797	1,880	0	19,271
OZ_i	350	3,811	3,605	56	26,784
OO_i	350	13	50	0	515
$\%OR_i$	350	0.51	0.19	0	0.96
$\%OC_i$	350	0.09	0.12	0	0.85
$\%OZ_i$	350	0.40	0.17	0.03	0.95
$\%OO_i$	350	0.002	0.01	0	0.12
FR_i	335	2.10	5.72	0.23	55.96
FC_i	302	0.36	0.55	0	4.64
ER_i	351	2.49	3.15	0.45	26.88
EC_i	351	0.16	0.10	0	0.61

a. See text for explanation of variables.

In the state as a whole, 18 percent of the land is used for housing, 4 percent is used for commercial or industrial buildings, 26 percent is protected, 43 percent is open, and about 8 percent is unbuildable. Of protected land, approximately 4 percent is federally owned, 34 percent is state owned, less than 1 percent is county owned, and 21 percent is municipality owned. The rest of protected land is, for example, owned privately or is an inholding within other protected lands.

Table 1 shows the summary statistics for the share of land use regulation variables. On average, the towns in Massachusetts use 22 percent of their land for housing, 5 percent for commercial and industrial uses; 25 percent is protected, and 40 percent is left open without protection.[28] Eight Boston suburbs (Arlington, Belmont, Malden, Marblehead, New-

28. This means that approximately 8 percent of land is in the "other" (unbuildable) category.

ton, Somerville, Swampscott, and Winchester) use over 60 percent of their land for housing, while four rural communities in mid- to western Massachusetts (Hawley, Monroe, Mount Washington, and New Salem) use less than 1.5 percent. Six cities (Boston, Cambridge, Chelsea, Everett, Lawrence, and Somerville) devote more than 25 percent of their land to commercial or industrial uses, while two rural communities (Gosnold Island and Mount Washington) allow no commercial or industrial uses in their towns.

In determining future allowable land use of open land ($O_i + Z_i$), towns, on average, devote 51 percent to housing, 9 percent to commercial and industrial uses; nearly 40 percent is protected, and less than 1 percent is left unzoned. However, these variables range widely. For example, Alford (in the western part of the state), Plympton (southern), and Richmond (western) zone over 90 percent of their open land for residences.[29] Conway and Templeton (mid-western) zone over 75 percent their open land for commercial and industrial uses. Several towns on the Cape (Provincetown, Truro, Wellfleet) protect more than 80 percent of their open land, as do several towns close to Boston (Belmont, Medford, Quincy, Stoneham, Wellesley). The towns that zone a high percentage of open land for housing (Alford, Plympton) also protect a low percentage, less than 4.5 percent of their land.

Summary statistics for the density regulation variables are shown in table 1. On average, towns allow only 2.1 residences an acre, as opposed to 2.5 residences an acre currently built. However, these are not statistically distinguishable. The future current commercial and industrial density is 0.36 acres allowed for building for each acre zoned commercial. We do not have a comparable measure of current commercial and industrial density, so we use the percentage of built land being used for commercial and industrial purposes as a proxy. On average, towns in Massachusetts are using nearly 16 percent of their built land for commercial and industrial buildings (and therefore just over 84 percent for housing). By comparison, towns in Massachusetts plan on using only about 14 percent (not statistically distinguishable) of their open land zoned for future building for commercial and industrial buildings.

We now proceed to examine some of the hypotheses from the literature. We divide the presentation of results according to the major strands

---

29. These residences may include agricultural land.

in the literature. However, the discussion of all four strands relies heavily on the bivariate correlations in table 2 as well as the multivariate linear regressions presented in tables 3 and 4. In both tables 3 and 4 the first set of columns describes the entire sample, while the second set describes only cities included in the Boston CMSA.[30] In table 3, columns 1 and 4 show the determinants of the percentage of open land zoned for residential use, columns 2 and 5 show the determinants of the percentage of open land zoned for commercial or industrial use, and columns 3 and 6 show the determinants of the percentage of open land protected from future building. In table 4, columns 1 and 3 show the determinants of maximum future residential density, and columns 2 and 4 show the determinants of future commercial and industrial density.

Does Zoning Follow the Market?

We first turn to analyzing the extent to which the zoning of future land use simply follows current land use patterns. The short answer is yes—in virtually every respect. If we examine current and zoned residential density, the bivariate correlation between FR_i and ER_i is, as expected, significant with a value of .74. In other words, towns with relatively high current housing densities tend to zone higher future densities. This relationship is shown graphically along with the 45° line in figure 1. Future residential density is, as foreshadowed by figure 1, significantly related to current residential density. In the multivariate regressions of table 4, this is reinforced with a very significant coefficient of 1.9.

The regression results from table 3 show that the extent of current residential development also predicts the extent of zoned future land for residential use. The greater the fraction of current land that is used for residential use $(1 - EC_i)$, the greater the amount of open land that is zoned for future residential development. In addition, towns with lower current residential density also zone a significantly higher proportion of open land for future housing. Specifically, if ER_i decreases by one house an acre, all things equal, then OR_i/O_i is expected to increase by 1.6 percentage points. This would imply a nearly 3 percent increase in the propor-

30. Unfortunately, we are not able to capture the entire CMSA because we do not have data for towns in Connecticut, Rhode Island, or Maine. Therefore, interactions between towns, such as those that are important in Evenson and Wheaton (2002), will not be fully accounted for and coefficient estimates may be biased.

Table 2. Bivariate Correlation Coefficients for the Land Use Regulation Variables

Variable[a]	$\%R_i$	$\%C_i$	$\%Z_i$	$\%O_i$	$\%OR_i$	$\%OC_i$	$\%OZ_i$	$\%OO_i$	FR_i	FC_i	ER_i	EC_i	O_i	O_i per capita	Income per capita 1999	Distance from Boston
$\%R_i$	1															
$\%C_i$	.6*	1														
$\%Z_i$	-.5*	-.5*	1													
$\%O_i$	-.7*	-.5*	-.1*	1												
$\%OR_i$	-.3*	-.3*	-.4*	.7*	1											
$\%OC_i$	.1	.3*	-.3*	0	-.5*	1										
$\%OZ_i$	.2*	.1	.7*	-.7*	-.8*	-.2*	1									
$\%OO_i$	.1	.1*	-.1*	-.1	-.1	.2*	-.1	1								
FR_i	.3*	.4*	-.1*	-.4*	-.3*	0	.3*	.1	1							
FC_i	.1*	.2*	0	-.2*	0	-.1*	-.1	0	.4*	1						
ER_i	.5*	.8*	-.3*	-.5*	-.3*	.2*	.2*	.1	.7*	.4*	1					
EC_i	.2*	.7*	-.3*	-.2*	-.2*	.3*	-.1	.1	.2*	.1	.5*	1				
O_i	-.7*	-.4*	.1	.7*	.4*	0	-.4*	-.1*	-.3*	-.1*	-.4*	-.2*	1			
O_i per capita	-.5*	-.3*	.3*	.4*	.1*	-.1	-.1	-.1	-.1*	-.1	-.2*	-.1*	.3*	1		
Income per capita 1999	.3*	-.1	0	-.3*	-.1*	-.2*	.3*	0	0	0	-.1*	-.3*	-.3*	-.1*	1	
Distance from Boston	-.7*	-.5*	.4*	.5*	.2*	-.1	-.1	-.1*	-.3*	-.2*	-.4*	-.2*	.5*	.5*	-.4*	1

*Significance at the 5 percent level of confidence.
a. See text for explanation of variables.

Table 3. Multivariate OLS Determinants of the Proportion of Open Land Zoned for Future Residential, Commercial/Industrial, and Protected Use[a]

	Full sample			Boston CMSA sample		
Variable[b]	OR_i/O_i	OC_i/O_i	OZ_i/O_i	OR_i/O_i	OC_i/O_i	OZ_i/O_i
ER_i	−0.016***	−0.0023	0.017***	−0.013**	−0.0046**	0.015***
	(0.0051)	(0.0025)	(0.004)	(0.0055)	(0.0021)	(0.004)
EC_i	−0.039	0.370***	−0.305***	0.00063	0.564***	−0.53***
	(0.112)	(0.093)	(0.10)	(0.13)	(0.083)	(0.13)
O_i	0.000012***	0.0000015	−0.000014***	0.0000080*	0.00000018	−0.0000077*
	(0.0000029)	(0.0000024)	(0.0000022)	(0.0000041)	(0.0000024)	(0.0000042)
O_i per capita	0.00023	−0.00022	0.0000034	0.024	0.0096	−0.033
	(0.0020)	(0.0013)	(0.0015)	(0.024)	(0.014)	(0.024)
Income per capita 1999	−0.0000023*	−0.000000002***	0.000004***	−0.0000020	−0.0000019***	0.0000039***
	(0.0000013)	(0.0000007)	(0.0000012)	(0.0000013)	(0.00000072)	(0.0000014)
Distance from Boston	−0.00038	−0.00054***	0.0010***	0.0020*	−0.00082	−0.0011
	(0.00036)	(0.00021)	(0.0003)	(0.0011)	(0.0007)	(0.0010)
Summary statistics						
Constant	0.562***	0.12***	0.307***	0.471***	0.094*	0.414***
	(0.067)	(0.04)	(0.059)	(0.084)	(0.053)	(0.080)
N	350	350	351	211	211	212
R^2	0.21	0.14	0.28	0.35	0.26	0.39

*Significant at the 10 percent level of confidence.
**Significant at the 5 percent level of confidence.
***Significant at the 1 percent level of confidence.
a. Standard errors are in parentheses.
b. See text for explanation of variables.

Table 4. Multivariate OLS Determinants of Future Residential and Commercial-Industrial Density[a]

Variable[b]	Full sample		Boston CMSA sample	
	FR_i	FC_i	FR_i	FC_i
ER_i	1.92***	0.083**	2.01***	0.090**
	(0.30)	(0.033)	(0.304)	(0.035)
EC_i	−7.36***	−1.15***	−6.45**	−1.33**
	(2.20)	(0.38)	(3.10)	(0.57)
O_i	0.000055**	0.0000094	0.000031	0.000012
	(0.000025)	(0.0000064)	(0.000044)	(0.000012)
O_i per capita	0.118***	−0.0058	1.50***	0.05
	(0.038)	(0.007)	(0.48)	(0.12)
Income per capita 1999	−0.00000087	−0.0000044	−0.000026	−0.000006
	(0.000027)	(0.0000043)	(0.000041)	(0.0000057)
Distance from Boston	−0.011*	−0.0016*	−0.071**	−0.0024
	(0.006)	(0.00082)	(0.031)	(0.0035)
Summary statistics				
Constant	−0.966	0.479*	0.74	0.53
	(1.072)	(0.250)	(2.08)	(0.37)
N	335	302	205	206
R^2	0.57	0.19	0.60	0.19

*Significant at the 10 percent level of confidence.
**Significant at the 5 percent level of confidence.
***Significant at the 1 percent level of confidence.
a. Standard errors are in parentheses.
b. See text for explanation of variables.

tion of open land devoted to future housing in the average town with a land use base that is 50 percent residential.

A similar story holds for commercial development. Towns with a higher proportion of currently built land that is used for commercial and industrial purposes tend to zone a significantly higher proportion of open land for future commercial and industrial building (figure 2). Specifically, if EC_i increases by 1 percentage point, all things equal, then OC_i/O_i is predicted to increase by 0.37 percentage point. This would be a 4 percent increase in the proportion of future commercial or industrial land in the average town where commercial use is nearly 9 percent.

The only seeming contradiction to this general pattern concerns future commercial and industrial density. Towns with a large share of current commercial use (a proxy for existing commercial density) tend to zone future commercial use at lower density (FAR) rather than a higher density as is the case with residential use.

Figure 1. Current Residential Density and Maximum Future Residential Density

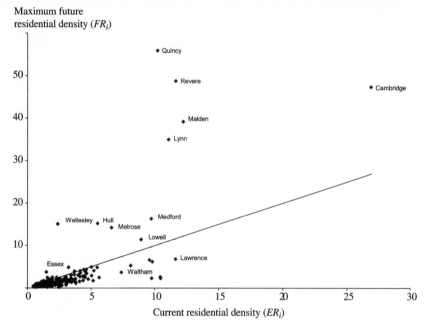

Columns 4 and 5 of table 3 and columns 3 and 4 of table 4 show that virtually all these results hold up when the sample is restricted to only those cities and towns within the greater Boston CMSA.

Is There Down-Zoning?

In table 4 the regression coefficient of 1.9 suggests that the down-zoning observed in figure 1 is actually outweighed by the up-zoning of the few very dense near-Boston suburbs. When only suburban towns are included in the sample (those located more than fifteen miles out from Boston), the coefficient drops to 0.7 as shown in table 5. This suggests that most towns in Massachusetts allow future residential building at only about 70 percent of their currently observable housing density. The more densely developed cities and towns near to Boston, however, seem to encourage redevelopment of their limited vacant land at higher-than-existing densities. Thus while down-zoning is somewhat present in the further out suburbs, its prevalence is actually quite limited and moderate.

Figure 2. Current Commercial-Industrial Share and Maximum Future Commercial-Industrial Density

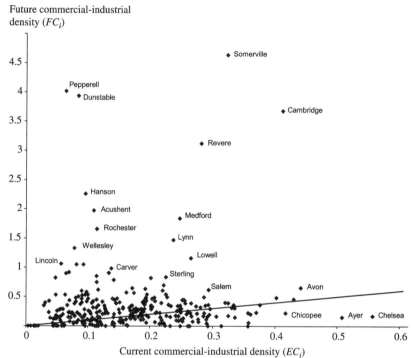

Future commercial-industrial density (FC_i)

Current commercial-industrial density (EC_i)

This explanation is further amplified in figure 3. As the few higher density cities and towns are truncated from the sample, and the graph blown up, the extent of down-zoning becomes apparent. The fitted bivariate regression line in both figures has a slope very close to the .70 of the multivariate regression in table 5.

It is interesting that there is substantial evidence of commercial down-zoning as well. To begin with, figure 2 suggests that most towns limit commercial development to have an average FAR of less than 0.5. This is despite the fact that many older towns in Massachusetts have existing commercial development that is much more dense. Next, there is little if any discernable slope in figure 2 between the extent of current commercial use and future commercial density. Finally, as shown in tables 3 and 4, towns with extensive existing commercial uses may zone more land for future such development, but they do so at lower FAR levels. Perhaps

Table 5. OLS Determinants of Future Residential Density Excluding Near–Boston Suburbs[a]

Variable[b]	Full sample (FR$_i$)	Boston CMSA sample (FR$_i$)
ER$_i$	0.60***	0.719***
	(0.119)	(0.157)
EC$_i$	–0.501	–1.53*
	(0.614)	(0.781)
O$_i$	–0.0000083	–0.000023**
	(0.0000094)	(0.00001)
O$_i$ per capita	0.005	0.2539*
	(0.010)	(0.1396)
Income per capita 1999	–0.0000064	–0.00000095
	(0.0000047)	(0.0000066)
Distance from Boston	–0.0002	–0.12*
	(0.0015)	(0.007)
Summary statistics		
Constant	0.037	0.588
	(0.295)	(0.419)
N	289	159
R^2	0.65	0.70

*Significant at the 10 percent level of confidence.
**Significant t the 5 percent level of confidence.
***Significant at the 1 percent level of confidence.
a. Standard errors are in parentheses.
b. See text for explanation of variables.

those with experience in commercial development believe that lower densities are needed to mitigate traffic, noise, or other externalities that may arise from such uses.[31]

Provision of Open Space Results

In their 2002 paper Evenson and Wheaton suggest that the proportion of land protected from development (OZ$_i$/O$_i$) should be negatively correlated with both the current residential density and the amount of open land per capita. The intuition for the former is that when homeowners have less land, they have less incentive to increase housing values by protecting open space. The intuition for the latter is that when there is more total open space, protecting a given proportion is more costly to each current resident. In addition, Evenson and Wheaton predict that towns with less open land will protect more land because they will be

31. A current future density of more than one denotes that the buildings are multiple stories.

Figure 3. Current Residential Density and Maximum Future Residential Density Enlargements

Maximum future residential
density (FR_i)

Panel A

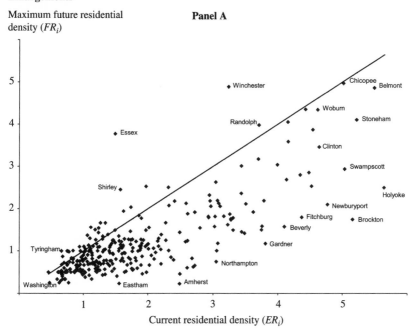

Current residential density (ER_i)

Maximum future residential
density (FR_i)

Panel B

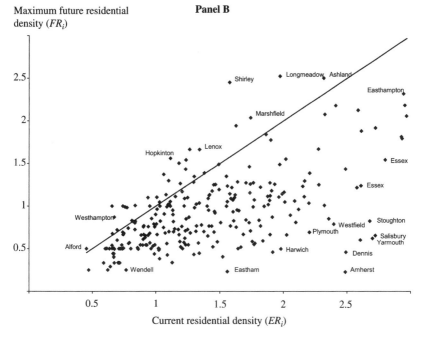

Current residential density (ER_i)

able to capitalize the effects of regulation into house prices more effectively than towns with more total open land.[32]

Only two of the three correlation coefficients are as expected. Towns with more open land tend to regulate less (r = –.42, significant). Towns in which regulating a given share is more costly because there is more open land per capita tend to regulate less (r = –0.05), as expected, but the correlation is insignificant. However, if protected land is limited to municipally owned protected land, this correlation actually becomes significant with a value of –.33. This matches Evenson and Wheaton's prediction. Contrary to Evenson and Wheaton's prediction, more densely populated areas, whose residents have less to gain from increased house prices because they are consuming less housing, tend to regulate more (r = .24, significant). This basic result (r = .48, significant) also holds if protected land is restricted to municipally owned land, as does the first result (r = –.60, significant).

32. For clarity, we quote Evenson and Wheaton's *Review of Predicted Results.* "The model generates three specific predictions about the relationship between town characteristics and land use regulation. These predictions are based on a theory which assumes all residents are the same, so the optimization problem each local government faces when determining land use is equivalent to that any individual currently residing in the town faces.

1) Towns with more open land available to future development for each current resident should choose to restrict less land from development. The intuition behind this is that towns with more current residents will be able to spread the costs of regulating a given amount of open land across residents, so that the cost each resident faces when determining the optimal amount of land use regulation is smaller.

2) Towns in which existing residential density is high should choose to restrict more land from development. The intuition behind this is that residents with lower land (housing) consumption should receive less of a benefit from the capital gains, assumed to be price times the units of land (housing) consumed, induced by regulating land use. If less housing is consumed the total benefit from the price of housing is lower.

3) Towns with more open land available to future development *ceteris paribus* should choose to restrict less of this land from development. There is no intuitive explanation for this result; it is simply a prediction of the model that smaller towns will be able to capitalize the effects of regulation into house prices more effectively than larger towns. It rests on the interaction between towns and the fact that smaller towns are able to increase house prices without decreasing the market-wide utility level of incoming residents (which would decrease the demand for housing and subsequently house prices in the town). This implies that smaller towns will receive a larger benefit from regulation, and so will choose to regulate more. By construction, our measure of the share of open land restricted is positively correlated to the amount of open land, so our analysis will be biased against finding this result. This is unfortunate given that this is the prediction that the model was conceived to generate in order to explain the result of several previous empirical papers." (p. 20)

These correlations are borne out in the multivariate regression analysis, shown in columns 3 and 6 of table 3. Towns with more total open land, all things equal, zone significantly less open land. This empirical result has been surprisingly robust in recent housing supply studies.[33] However, towns whose residential areas are more densely built out seem to protect a significantly *higher* proportion of open land, ignoring the fact that fewer individual benefits are accrued. Although this result would be consistent with high-density urban towns that are nearly built out, a regression excluding the near-Boston suburbs has the same effect.[34] The effect of increasing open land per capita is only significant if protected land is constrained to that which is municipally owned, as would be expected since residents will not bear as much of the costs for open space owned privately or by a state, county, or federal government. Therefore, these results support Evenson and Wheaton's theory fairly well.[35]

Commercial Zoning Results

Erickson and Wasylenko suggest that wealthier towns have a pattern of zoning out industrial and commercial development.[36] We first test whether the ratio $C_i/(C_i+R_i)$, or the proportion of commercial and industrial land, has a negative income elasticity. In other words, we should expect to see less commercial and industrial land currently in use in wealthier towns. To begin with, we find that the proportion of commercial and industrial land is negatively and significantly correlated with income, with a correlation coefficient of $-.30$. A simple regression specified in logs yields an estimated elasticity of $-.83$, which is significant. However, income explains just less than 9 percent of the variation in the proportion of commercial and industrial land, and this estimate is sure to suffer from omitted variable bias.

The multivariate regression results in table 3 continue to show that wealthier towns zone significantly less of their open land for commercial

33. Evenson (2002).

34. The coefficient has a value of 0.02 and is significant if protected land is unrestricted. It has a value of 0.04 and is significant if protected land is restricted to that municipally owned.

35. Evenson and Wheaton are able to use these same data with different sample selection criteria, which are better aligned with the theoretical assumptions, to find significant support for their theory.

36. Erickson and Wasylenko (1980).

and industrial use. This is true for both the full sample of towns and the Boston CMSA towns. Towns whose per capita income was $1,000 higher in 1999 will zone approximately 0.2 percentage point less of their land for future commercial and industrial purposes. This means that the average town, starting with a little less that 9 percent of its open land zoned for future commercial or industrial development, would decrease that proportion by 2 percent.[37] In addition, wealthier towns significantly increase the amount of open land that is protected in both samples.

These results are consistent with Fischel's argument that less wealthy towns have an incentive to allow commercial and industrial building because these types of land use generate relatively large tax revenues and use relatively few resources.[38] In other words, fiscally constrained towns have an incentive to try to attract commercial and industrial tenants to help alleviate their budget constraints, but as residents become wealthier, commercial and industrial tenants are considered inferior goods in the sense that the negative environmental costs associated with such uses outweigh the benefits.

General Income Effects

We report the correlation of income with the proportion of protected land, with the expectation that protected open space is a normal good, so wealthier towns will have more. As expected, the coefficient is positive and significant in both the full sample and in the Boston CMSA sample.[39]

Surprisingly, wealthier towns do not seem to require less dense building of either residences or commercial and industrial buildings in any of the samples. This result, that income does not affect zoned density, is puzzling yet robust.[40] In effect, the very common conventional wisdom that small wealthy towns make themselves more exclusive is not sup-

37. For comparison, the average town in Massachusetts has 14,740.6 acres, which would imply a 29.5 acre decrease in commercial and industrial land for every $1,000 extra in per capita income.

38. Fischel (1975).

39. Interestingly, towns with more open land that is not zoned for future use do not seem to protect less of their open land, suggesting that residents view protected land and unzoned open land differently ($r = -.05$, insignificant).

40. We tried several specifications to test the robustness of this result, including but not limited to adding nonlinear terms, splitting the sample, and changing equation specification.

ported by the data at all. This result has significant implications for theoretical studies: the assumption made in exclusionary MLS zoning that wealthy towns get a bigger tax transfer from excluding relatively poor residents through zoning regulation has not stood up to independent scrutiny of detailed zoning data.

The conventional wisdom pervades the literature, yet the data suggest that the income elasticity may be an endogenous result. Specifically, a town's income per capita and the current residential density are codetermined, with current residential density being a much better predictor of future residential density.[41] Clearly then, more basic research on land use regulation would be a very useful addition to the future literature.

The results that open land and open land per capita both lead to increases in the density of open land zoned for future housing are contrary to the conventional wisdom. Towns with more open land per capita, holding total open land and residential density constant, have a smaller population living in a smaller area. Therefore, this result suggests that towns in which the cost of open space preservation is imposed on fewer people will zone for more dense future building (up-zone).

By the same token, towns with a greater total amount of open land, holding open land per capita and residential density constant, have a greater population. Although this result suggests that larger towns zone future building more densely, as expected from the conventional wisdom, this effect is outweighed by the former effect for residential building. For allowed future commercial and industrial density, neither effect is significant, which again does not match the conventional wisdom that smaller exclusive towns would zone less dense commercial and industrial land, when they allow commercial or industrial building at all.

Other Regression Results

As stated earlier, we also controlled for distance from Boston in the regressions and find that towns further from Boston tend to zone less of their open land for commercial and industrial uses. The result is consistent with a monocentric city model, in which residents commute from suburban communities to relatively clustered jobs. The density gradient

---

41. This raises several interesting questions about the timing of land use determination and the extent to which zoning regulations vary over time, which are beyond the scope of this paper.

implied by our results implies that towns that are, on average, ten miles further from Boston have about 0.5 percentage point less open land zoned commercial and industrial. The decrease in allowable commercial or industrial uses is not associated with a significant increase in residential land; but towns that are further from Boston protect a significantly higher proportion of their land. Towns that are, on average, ten miles further from Boston have about 1 percentage point more protected land.

These results are exactly reversed in the Boston CMSA sample. However, this is an artifact of the effect of the near-Boston suburbs, which tend to zone a relatively high proportion of land for commercial-industrial and protected uses.

Towns that are further from Boston also allow significantly less dense building (both residential and commercial-industrial), which was expected. The only exception is that the coefficient in the commercial and industrial density regression is not significant in the Boston CMSA sample, implying that towns further from Boston do not necessarily zone their future commercial-industrial land less densely than in the sample of "close" towns.

The implied density gradient is: for every ten-mile increase in distance, residential density decreases by 0.1 (full sample) to 0.7 (Boston CMSA sample) units an acre. This is borne out in the raw data, which shows cities like Cambridge zoning more than ten single family units an acre in some areas, versus, for example cities like Newburyport zoning about a third of a unit an acre in some areas. The commercial-industrial density results are slightly more consistent (although the significance is lost), with an implied density gradient that for every ten-mile increase in distance, commercial-industrial FAR density decreases by 0.16 (full sample) to 0.24 (Boston CMSA sample).

Summary and Conclusion

The body of empirical land use literature is relatively small due to a lack of good data with which to study the regulatory issues. We use a unique data set on Massachusetts land use, land use regulation, and buildout to examine the determinants of land use regulation. We are guided by theoretical studies on regulation, as well as the heretofore untested conventional wisdom that currently constitutes much of our knowledge about housing supply. This paper is unique in that we are able to directly analyze multiple forms of land use regulation across a significant geographic area.

Overall, the evidence supports both the current theoretical land use studies and the conventional wisdom, although the results are not always significant. We find some evidence of down-zoning by the communities, although it is not as strong as we had expected despite the conventional wisdom that extensive down-zoning is considered unethical. We also find evidence that current and future building are highly correlated, as was expected. Fischel's theory on fiscal zoning holds up especially well in the data. Wealthier towns tend to devote less land to commercial and industrial purposes in terms of both current and future land use. We also find evidence supporting Evenson and Wheaton's studies in 2002. In particular, we add to the empirical evidence suggesting that smaller towns have a greater incentive to impose land use regulation. We also find evidence that protected land is a normal good. Finally, we calculate implied density gradients such as those used in the monocentric city model of urban economics, using Boston as the center.

The most surprising nonresult is the total lack of evidence for fiscal zoning. We find no significant wealth effect among the determinants of either residential or commercial-industrial density. The conventional wisdom that minimum lot sizes are used to zone out relatively poor households is not borne out in the data. This may be due to a correlation between existing density and wealth, with the latter having determined both existing and future lot sizes.

An obvious further use of this data set would be to relate land use regulation to house prices, as is the focus of many current empirical studies (albeit at the metropolitan-area level). However, our results show that zoning regulations governing future building are highly correlated with current densities, town size, and other variables that will simultaneously and independently affect house prices. For example, towns with stricter land use regulations are likely to have both less commercial and industrial building and higher house prices. This endogeneity has likely led to omitted variable bias in this literature on top of the problems inherently created by the typical need to aggregate regulation into a single metropolitan-area-level summary statistic. The very distinct and time-dependent patterns of land use regulation shown here imply that a regression of house prices on regulation needs to use an instrumental variables approach to get a good measure of the true effect.

Although these data are very detailed and distinctive, there are still many questions the data cannot answer. For example, our evidence on how binding the regulations in our data are is still very weak. There is still very little evidence on the extent to which jurisdictions grant variances, which is an important issue in planning. Although these data are supposed to represent the *maximum* possible future building, the code or the interpretation of it may change, or unforeseen building possibilities may arise that cannot be accounted for in this analysis.

In addition, a more in-depth analysis of each of these land use topics and the theoretical arguments surrounding their previously "black-box" relationships would be very useful. For example, we have not explored the extent to which Tiebout sorting is confounded by land use regulation, nor have we examined the implications of these regulations on the often used practice of measuring Tiebout sorting by determining the level of income sorting.

Comments

Joseph Gyourko: The first important point to make about Evenson and Wheaton's paper is that it deals with an extremely useful topic, because how we organize ourselves spatially has important socioeconomic implications for many aspects of our personal lives and for the communities in which we live. While the analysis of land use regulation in general and zoning in particular has a lengthy pedigree in economics, the fact is that theoretical models are far better developed than empirical analyses.[42] Evenson and Wheaton set out to alleviate the primary reason for this—the lack of good data on land use controls.

Important new data based on a 1999 satellite-based survey of all open land in Massachusetts are matched with information on zoning ordinances in a large number of local towns and cities. A few other studies have amassed data on a specific type of land use control, but this is the first of which I am aware that allows one to observe multiple forms of land use controls simultaneously and do so over an area as extended as a state.

The goals of the paper are threefold: to document a new database, to report stylized facts about how towns actually do zone and regulate land use, and to produce results on certain key issues relating to how land use regulation varies with factors such as income. The paper is most successful in achieving the first two goals. Many of the empirical results are interesting in their own right, but more structure and even better data probably are needed to convince reasonable skeptics who propose alter-

---

42. For analysis of land use regulations, see, in particular, Fischel (1975); Hamilton (1978).

native explanations for the findings. Even so, the work points the way to much future research for those interested in this issue and provides a valuable new data source with which researchers can try to satisfy their curiosity.

The paper includes a useful discussion of the existing studies on minimum lot size (and exclusionary zoning), on the provision of open space, on the economics of allowing commercial development, and on the impacts of land use controls on housing prices. I would be interested in seeing the discussion and analysis extended to the issue of race. We know that there is substantial racial segregation in virtually all major metropolitan areas in the United States. The extent to which this might be correlated with how communities zone seems a potentially useful line of inquiry.

The data themselves are the best that urban scholars have ever had. As noted above, the key underlying source is a 1999 satellite survey of Massachusetts. The output for this survey is then merged into a variety of current land use files that allow the authors to know existing land use patterns as well as zoned land use patterns (that is, what the current law would allow for the future). The survey includes thirty-six detailed categories that range from residential lots of at least one-half acre to two types of bogs. These data are collapsed into four categories (residential, commercial, open space, and other) for the purposes of this paper.[43] I see no reason to require a more detailed breakdown for this initial foray with the data, but future work certainly should investigate the utility of using finer breakdowns. The zoning data themselves are current as of 1996 in virtually all cases (and are even more recent in most cases), so one can be reasonably confident that current land usage is matched with current zoning conditions.[44]

A fairly complex set of calculations and mappings of one data set to another is employed to compute the amount of buildout permitted under existing land use regulations. I was convinced from the authors' presentation that the results were accurate because they could pin down the correct status of various detailed parcels (for example, Boston Common). However, this fact is not entirely clear from the text, and the paper would benefit from an expanded discussion, possibly with examples from a few

---

43. For current land use data and collapsing procedure, see www.state.ma.us/mgis/lus.
44. For zoning data categories and collapsing procedure, see www.state.ma.us/mgis/zn.htm.

places, so that readers are convinced of the reliability of the buildout figures.

Readers would also benefit from a more detailed presentation and discussion of the data themselves. Tables 1 and 2 document the extensive heterogeneity in actual land use and prospective density. The density regulation data reported in table 2 indicate that the current mean of 2.5 residences an acre exceeds the 2.2 residences an acre that zoning for the future implies. The range across localities is huge, but most of the data are fairly tightly clustered around the mean. Some discussion of the outliers would be useful, given how extreme they are. In addition, a simple correlation table would be informative given the new and unique data involved. There are partial correlation coefficients in some later regressions, but summarizing the simple correlations in a convenient matrix up front would help.

The fiscal zoning results in table 3 show clearly that future density follows current density. This is evident from both the simple and partial correlations. While the qualitative results themselves are interesting, better exposition of the quantitative results is needed. At present, one sees only statistical significance, when we want to know about economic significance, too. Thus, standardized marginal effects with the results translated into the implications for the change in number of units (or square footage when relevant) would be very informative.[45]

The key finding from table 4 indicates that, near-in Boston suburbs excepted, current regulation effectively allows future residential building at no more than 60 percent of current density. In addition, higher current residential density is associated with higher allowable future commercial buildout.[46] Finally, no meaningful relation between income and zoned density is found in the data. This is a very interesting finding, but caution regarding its interpretation is appropriate. The authors rely on a single cross-section for identification, and that is asking a lot of any data. The result could be made more convincing by providing more structure to the model or by creating a panel data set. Since either task would likely be prohibitively burdensome for the authors, a reasonable alternative might be to expand the set of right-hand regressors to include a variety of other

---

45. The units the data are measured in are not clearly labeled in the tables.

46. The same comment made earlier regarding standardized marginal effects applies here.

socioeconomic and political variables that economists, political scientists, or urban sociologists probably would consider useful in explaining current and future land use patterns. This path recognizes the reduced-form nature of the specification while including more correlates of interest to a variety of readers.

Given that a number of people in the audience clearly believed that existing regulations are meant to be negotiated or surmounted or both, it would be interesting to see if certain demographic, economic, and political factors influenced the spatial pattern of regulation. This strategy also seems natural to apply to the results regarding open land. The authors emphasize that their finding that open land and open land per capita both are associated with increases in the density of open land zoned for future housing contradicts the conventional wisdom in the industry. Given the somewhat counterintuitive result, it would be useful to see if it stands up when other demographic, economic, and political variables are included in the estimation.

In sum, Evenson and Wheaton are to be (loudly) applauded for amassing a unique database on multiple land use patterns. Its utility should be obvious to all, as it holds great promise for a host of future research endeavors that will help us better understand how and why we organize ourselves and our businesses spatially within and across communities. I look forward to an even more detailed presentation of the data and results that provide insights into the role of additional socioeconomic and political forces that might be able to explain the variation in land usage across towns.

John M. Quigley: The Evenson-Wheaton paper is a tentative description of land use facts and land use rules from a single state. The interest in the paper derives at least as much from the tools employed in data gathering and information assembly as from the new results presented.

The paper begins with a review of the sketchy economics literature on community zoning of land uses. The authors review the theoretical and empirical studies on minimum lot size (MLS) rules for new development, the provision of open space, the regulation of commercial development, and the linkage between regulation of land and housing markets.

Economists have done the most thinking about MLS rules, arguing that with property tax financing these regulations could, in principle at least, convert an ad valorem property tax into a benefits tax. Even when this is not possible, the practice of requiring the marginal house to consume more land than the average house can improve the fiscal surplus of current residents.

Regulations requiring open space can surely benefit existing properties by providing the externalities of a local public good to residents and their residences. When landowners, collectively or through their local government, acquire this land at market prices, they face the appropriate incentives for public goods provision. When they acquire this land through condemnation, whether through wetland protection or rules about preservation, existing landlords can extract a surplus from owners of undeveloped land.

The limited literature on regulation of commercial and industrial zoning follows the analytics of MLS zoning in residential land—towns regulate commercial activities to maximize their fiscal gain, trading off tax revenues to preclude crowding and so forth.The positive effects of these rules on house prices have been subject to a variety of tests, noted and criticized by Evenson and Wheaton. In some part, the deficiencies of these empirical tests arise because land use regulations are themselves imperfectly measured.

The contribution of the Evenson-Wheaton paper is in the development of systematic positive measures of land use and zoning. Both arise painstakingly from complicated empirical research. First, on the matter of land use, aerial photographs taken from some 15,000 feet by the state of Massachusetts permit each parcel to be allocated into one of thirty-seven categories. The nuts and bolts of the taxonomy are described in general.[47] Joseph Gyourko notes that the categories are fine and include a category for cranberry bogs. I note that two different cranberry bogs are distinguished: those located in woods and in cleared areas. The authors sensibly aggregate parcels to the level of town and land use to four types: residential, commercial-industrial, open space, and unusable. Open space is further divided into that protected from building and that available for building.

I should note that these highly original data sources, aerial photographs, are beginning to be generally used in economic analyses of space. The Evenson-Wheaton effort is the tip of the iceberg. Satellite

---

47. For detail on current land use data categories and collapsing procedure see www.state.ma.us/mgis/lus.

photographs are now available for many of the world's urbanized areas. They can be bought from NASA for $500 to $1,000 each. They are fully digitalized, so the location of each pixel can be mapped to a location, and the shading of the pixel can be related to the intensity of land use. So it is now possible to follow land use changes, especially in the developing world, through systems like this.

The Evenson-Wheaton analysis takes the building block of land uses in each town and relates it to the detailed regulations governing usage. This is done by relying on digitized maps of open space and its regulation by the ordinances of each town. Finally, town-level data on land use and its regulation were matched to information on the maximum potential development that could take place under current law. Apparently the big advantage of this exercise was the idea of "potential development," given that these rules were consistently measured across the state. So, Evenson and Wheaton have a data set of remarkable detail about land uses, the rules governing them, and permissible future development—all gathered at roughly the same time in a consistent way.

The authors present some simple summaries of the data, noting for example that 43 percent of land in Massachusetts is open space without protection from development. Interestingly, the cities in Massachusetts allow only 2.2 residences an acre to be built on unprotected vacant land, while there are 2.5 residences an acre on land already developed for residential purposes. These regulations seem like attempts to generate fiscal surpluses for existing homeowners.

The analytical part of the paper is a sequence of regressions and figures relating the regulation of open land and the current regulation of future land uses to current land use types and incomes. In table 3 the authors show that the distribution of currently built-up land predicts the zoning of undeveloped land. Towns with higher residential densities permit a *smaller* portion of open land for housing. Towns with more commercial activity today permit a *larger* portion of open land for commercial activity. These results are true for the state and also for the Boston metro area. Income and the amount of vacant land seem irrelevant. Analogous results are presented for the determinants of the extent of development permitted. Outside of the very dense suburbs surrounding Boston, cities in Massachusetts permit future residential building at almost 60 percent of current density. Higher current residential densities are associated with higher permitted growth in commercial activity.

The statistical results about the insignificance of income in current zoning or current permission for future development puzzle the authors. I am less puzzled. To the extent that the *current* residential densities are determined by incomes—that is to the extent that Tiebout sorting already operates in Massachusetts—this is, already reflected in the statistical results. Towns with high residential densities protect more of their open space from development. This seems sensible, yet the authors find it counterintuitive.

There are three things that would improve the usefulness of this extremely interesting excursion into the difficulties of data collection on land use and zoning rules. Two of them can be done easily. First, the paper would benefit from some explication of the fiscal federal structure of Massachusetts. Many of the studies noted by the authors derive from the fiscal incentives faced by median voters. How does this play out in Massachusetts? For example, what are the rules for sales tax distribution and how does this affect the incentives for zoning in or zoning out commercial structures? What is the link between property tax rules for residences—Proposition 2½ and so forth—and the fiscal choices? For those who do not know these details about Massachusetts, many of these incentives are unclear.

Second, the paper would benefit from more description. There is a fair amount of description of the data collection exercise. That is perhaps understandable, given the difficulties of data assembly. But much of the interest centers on the spatial distribution of rules and the availability of space for development. Much of the motivation for these rules, which are chosen independently, is to affect the distribution of firms and households in a local housing and labor market. Cities are involved in a strategic game, choosing rules to attract some households and to repel others and rules to attract some kinds of nonresidential activity. Some clever maps and tables of local markets (Boston, Worcester) would be very helpful. What is the distribution of rules between markets relative to the distribution of rules operating within a housing or labor market?

Third, this paper would be more useful if there were some consideration of the meaning of these land use rules so carefully constructed. In California, for example, the published zoning ordinances are not really rules at all—they are invitations to deal in a complicated game in which developers petition to obtain a permit and a variance in return for some exaction. These games are complicated, and the ordinances signal *some-*

thing. Variations in the ordinances are differences in the first move in some N-player game among jurisdictions in a regional market. But the published rules have almost no relation to what can be built where. Anthony Downs has suggested that this phenomenon is widespread and this limits the economic value of the data collection supervised by Evenson and Wheaton. But I hope the next version of this paper considers the link between the rules and the reality of development.

In closing, I should note the potential value of data description for the regulations and impacts of land use rules. About a dozen years ago Anita Summers and her ten closest friends in Philadelphia undertook a large survey of existing land use rules. These data were then used in a couple of books by the data gatherers and in a series of papers by people completely divorced from the original data-gathering effort. Steve Malpezzi succeeded in building models to predict the values of restrictiveness across other jurisdictions, and this gave more "legs" to the Summers indexes.

We should hope that this analysis by Evenson and Wheaton will lead to a second generation of land use rules. Developing some measures of the stringency of regulation, and the determinants of regulations, based on the kind of data Evenson and Wheaton are collecting, can have a large social payoff.

References

Bates, Laurie J., and Rexford E. Santerre. 1994. "The Determinants of Restrictive Residential Zoning: Some Empirical Findings." *Journal of Regional Science* 34 (2): 253–63.

———. 2001. "The Public Demand for Open Space: The Case of Connecticut Communities." *Journal of Urban Economics* 50 (1): 97–112.

Brueckner, Jan K. 1996. "Modeling Urban Growth Controls." Working Paper 123. University of Illinois at Urbana-Champaign, College of Commerce and Business Administration.

———. 1998. "Testing for Strategic Interaction among Local Governments." *Journal of Urban Economics* 44 (November): 468–93.

Coase, Ronald. 1960. "The Problem of Social Cost." *Journal of Law and Economics* (October): 1–44.

Dale-Johnson, David, and Hyang Yim. 1990. "Coastal Development Moratoria and Housing Prices." *Journal of Real Estate Finance and Economics* 3 (June): 165–84.

Erickson, Rodney A., and Michael J. Wasylenko. 1980a. "Firm relocation and Site Selection in Suburban Municipalities." *Journal of Urban Economics* (July): 69–85.

———. 1980b. "Evidence on Fiscal Differentials and Intrametropolitan Firm Relocation." *Land Economics* (August): 339–49.

Evenson, Bengte. 2002. "Understanding House Price Volatility: Measuring and Explaining the Supply Side of Metropolitan Area Housing Markets." MIT Department of Economics.

Evenson, Bengte, and William Wheaton. 2002. "Why Local Governments Enact Land Use Controls." MIT Department of Economics (August).

Fischel, William. 1975. "Fiscal and Environmental Considerations in the Location of Firms." In *Fiscal Zoning and Land Use Controls,* edited by Edwin S. Mills and Wallace E. Oates, 119–73. Lexington Books.

Glaeser, Edward L., and Joseph Gyourko. 2002. "The Impact of Zoning on Housing Affordability." Discussion Paper 1948. Harvard Institute of Economic Research.

Haar, Charles, and Jerold Kayden. 1989. *Zoning and the American Dream: Promises Still to Keep.* Planners Press, American Planning Association.

Hamilton, Bruce W. 1978. "Zoning and the Exercise of Monopoly Power." *Journal of Urban Economics* 5 (January): 116–30.

Ladd, Helen F. 1975. "Local Education Expenditures, Fiscal Capacity and the Composition of the Property Tax Base." *National Tax Journal* 28 (June): 145–58.

Mayer, Christopher J., and C. Tsuriel Somerville. 2000. "Land Use Regulation and New Construction." *Regional Science and Urban Economics* 30 (6): 639–62.

Mills, Edwin S., and Wallace E. Oates. 1975. "The Theory of Local Public Services and Finance: Its Relevance to Urban Fiscal and Zoning Behavior." In

Fiscal Zoning and Land Use Controls, edited by Edwin S. Mills and Wallace E. Oates. Lexington Books.

Ozanne, Larry, and Thomas Thibodeau. 1983. "Explaining Metropolitan Housing Price Differences." *Journal of Urban Economics* 39 (May): 434–41.

Speyrer, Janet. 1989. "The Effect of Land Use Restrictions on Market Values of Single Family Homes in Houston." *Journal of Real Estate Finance and Economics* 2 (April): 117–30.

Thorsnes, Paul. 2000. "Internalizing Neighborhood Externalities: the Effect of Subdivision Size and Zoning on Residential Lot Prices." *Journal of Urban Economics* 48 (3): 397–419.

Tiebout, Charles M. 1956. "A Pure Theory of Local Expenditures." *Journal of Political Economy* 64 (October): 416–26.

Wheaton, William. 1993. "Land Capitalization, Tiebout Mobility and the Role of Zoning Regulations." *Journal of Urban Economics* 34 (2): 102–17.

White, Michelle J. 1975. "Fiscal Zoning in Fragmented Metropolitan Areas." In *Fiscal Zoning and Land Use Controls*, edited by Edwin S. Mills and Wallace E. Oates, 175–201. Lexington Books.